The Dynamics of International Strategy

The Dynamics of International Strategy

Susan Segal-Horn and David Faulkner

INTERNATIONAL THOMSON BUSINESS PRESS
I(T)P An International Thomson Publishing Company

London • Bonn • Johannesburg • Madrid • Melbourne • Mexico City • New York • Paris
Singapore • Tokyo • Toronto • Albany, NY • Belmont,CA • Cincinnati, OH • Detroit, MI

The Dynamics of International Strategy

A division of International Thomson Publishing
The ITP logo is a trademark under licence

British Library Cataloguing-in-Publication Data
A catalogue record for this book is available from the British Library

First edition published 1999 by International Thomson Business Press

Typeset by Saxon Graphics Ltd, Derby
Printed in the UK by TJ International, Padstow, Cornwall

ISBN 1-86152-015-8

International Thomson Business Press
Berkshire House
168–173 High Holborn
London WC1V 7AA
UK

http://www.itbp.com

Contents

List of Figures *ix*

List of Tables *xi*

1 Introduction **1**
'International' strategy is different 2
The management of international trade 3
Traditional and modern factors of production: mobile vs immobile 5
Types of international strategy 9
The roles of governments and the limits to regulation 10
MNC strategy as a war game 11
Types of competitive approaches to international expansion 15
Flexibility, risk and ethics 16
Objectives and overview of this book 23
Key themes 25

PART 1 THE NATURE OF INTERNATIONAL STRATEGY **27**

2 The context and economics of international strategy **29**
The rise of the MNC 30
Comparative vs competitive advantage for MNCs 33
Industry structure 35
Industry clusters: the 'diamond' framework 39
Economic paradigms 41
Summary 47

3 Regional strategy **49**
'The Triad' 49
The build-up of regional trading blocs: political and economic impact 51
Regionalization vs globalization 55
Developments in regional strategy 56
Cultural homogenization and the emergence of global markets 59
The standardization/adaptation debate 60
The advantages of complex global operations 62
The globalization of brands 64
Regional or global? 65
Summary 67

4 The dynamics of international competition **69**
Deregulation: the dynamic of nations and firms 69
International industry dynamics 70
Industry dynamics in the European food industry 76
Change over time in the European food-processing industry 77
Strategic groups and industry dynamics 82
Strategic space and industry dynamics 86
MNC's ability to compete 87
Summary 88

5 The role of culture in international strategy **89**
National culture and organizational culture 89
Why culture is relevant to international strategy 92
Cultural barriers in international strategy 93
Problems with culture in international strategy 97
Benefiting from cultural differences 98
Managing cultural diversity within international strategy 99
Achieving cultural fit 102
Summary 105

PART 2 ISSUES OF CO-ORDINATION **107**

6 The international corporate structure model **109**
The stage models of internationalization 111
Studies of the link between strategy and structure in MNCs 112
Recent organizational models of MNCs 113
Strategic issues affecting the four approaches 114
The international corporate structure model 120
Transitional pathways of development 128
Summary 129

7 The multidomestic form **131**
The pure multidomestic form 132
The modern multidomestic 137
Summary 143

8 The global and international exporter forms **144**
The global form 144
The traditional global corporation 148
The modern global corporation 150
The international exporter form 155
Summary 157

9 The transnational form **159**
Introducing the idea of the transnational 159
Being truly multinational 160
The central dilemma 163

The transnational 167
Building global flexibility and national responsiveness within the transnational 172
Comparing the M-form and the N-form 178
Summary 179

PART 3 NEW PATHWAYS **181**

10 International strategy in services **183**
Growth in international services 183
Managing 'intangibles' across borders 185
Scale and scope in services 188
The application of Chandler's model to services 191
The changed international potential of services 194
The potential for scale and scope economies in different types of service businesses 196
Rethinking services 201
The future for international services 202
Summary 203

11 Co-operation in international strategy **205**
Types of co-operative strategy 206
Why an alliance? 209
External stimuli 212
Types of internal stimuli 214
Partner selection 216
Choice of alliance form 218
Summary 220

12 The management of international strategic alliances **222**
The nature of general management 224
Alliance management success factors 231
Summary 235

13 International strategy and learning **237**
The nature of organizational learning 237
Categories of learning 238
Forms of organizational learning 240
Learning and organizational form 242
Requirements for learning 243
Barriers to organizational learning 248
The management of organizational learning 250
Summary 255

14 Conclusion: Looking forward **256**
Living with industry dynamics 256
The comparative advantage of nations and the competitive advantage of firms 257
Knowledge competition in MNCs 260

Knowledge myopias 262
What works over time: the sustainability of strategies 266
Summary 267

References **269**

Index **279**

List of Figures

Figure 1.1	Types of competitive approaches to international expansion	15
Figure 1.2	Exposure to political, regulatory and ethical risk	19
Figure 2.1	The decision tree	32
Figure 2.2	The competitive arena	36
Figure 2.3	An adapted Porter 'diamond'	40
Figure 3.1	'The Triad'	50
Figure 3.2	Regional trading blocs	53
Figure 3.3	Growth in intra-regional trade in Mercosur, 1990–95	54
Figure 3.4	Degree of Mercosur trade integration with the other three as percentage of total trade, 1995	55
Figure 3.5	FTA percentage of total world trade in 1996	57
Figure 3.6	Sales channels for mutual funds in Europe	58
Figure 3.7	The Benetton strategy	60
Figure 4.1	A 'map' of strategic groups in the European food-processing industry in the 1980s	84
Figure 4.2	Strategic space analysis	86
Figure 5.1	Management of cultural diversity in MNCs: four options	100
Figure 6.1	Configuration/co-ordination matrix	110
Figure 6.2	The Stopford and Wells matrix: pathways for international development	112
Figure 6.3	An 'integration-responsiveness' grid	114
Figure 6.4	The international corporate structure model	122
Figure 6.5	Common form transitions	128
Figure 7.1	Multidomestic communication and decision-making	133
Figure 7.2	The standardization-differentiation spectrum	135
Figure 8.1	The global form	147
Figure 8.2	Different degrees of global integration for different functions	151

Figure 8.3 The international exporter form 155
Figure 9.1 A transnational network organization 168
Figure 10.1 GDP in OECD countries, by sector, per cent, 1994 184
Figure 10.2 The service triangle 186
Figure 10.3 Standardization or customization of services 190
Figure 10.4 The dynamic of MNC growth, Phase 1 194
Figure 10.5 A historical view of scale and scope economies in various service industries 197
Figure 10.6 The dynamic of MNC growth, Phase 2 199
Figure 11.1 Levels of co-operation 207
Figure 11.2 Co-operative strategies fall into two distinct types 208
Figure 11.3 Alliances involve both co-operation and competition 208
Figure 11.4 The make/acquire/ally matrix 210
Figure 11.5 Partner selection 217
Figure 14.1 Stages in the transformation of knowledge into competitive advantage 263
Figure 14.2 The changed international strategy agenda 268

List of Tables

Table 1.1	Four approaches to being international	10
Table 2.1	Reciprocity index of intra-industry trade in the EU	42
Table 2.2	Market structures – three different models	43
Table 2.3	Sources of scope economies	45
Table 4.1	Phases of industry evolution in the European food-processing industry	78
Table 4.2	Possible sources of mobility barriers	83
Table 6.1	Global strategy, an organizing framework	116
Table 9.1	A geographic matrix structure	165
Table 9.2	Roles and tasks of management: the transnational	171
Table 10.1	Some sources of economies of scale and scope in services	192
Table 12.1	General manager roles in strategic alliances	227
Table 13.1	Types of learning in different MNC forms	243

1

Introduction

International strategy affects us all. It affects not only the planning departments of large multinational companies, or governments trying to attract the investment of such companies to create jobs for their citizens, it also affects the managers of small or medium-size firms and of neighbourhood stores, trying to retain the business of their local customers. Whether they know it or not, they are competing in an international marketplace for goods and services. Every initiative taken by an international firm has an impact on a local market and on the market share of local organizations and their ability to satisfy their customers. This has relevance for all organizations including national and local government, small and medium-sized enterprises, and even when they themselves have no activities outside their domestic market nor any plans to develop any in the future.

Many business decisions are taken in an international context and frequently involve managing across borders. This book should help you understand the development of international trade, the role of multinationals in international trade and how to structure and develop multinational corporations (MNCs) to meet changes in the international competitive environment. We will use the term 'MNC' throughout the book as a generic term covering all forms of international organization, although different authors have used different terminology. We will discuss what drives international strategy and both the advantages and the problems involved in implementing strategy internationally. We will explain the strategic alternatives open to an organization when it extends its activities across borders. For both products and services, international strategy may be seen as an outcome of the interrelationship of industry characteristics, strategic flexibility and organizational capability. Your organization may carry out no international activities whatsoever and yet be strongly affected by international trade and the strategies of MNCs. Whether we are aware of it or not, international strategy has an influence on us all.

The terms and conditions of trade for local providers of goods and services in their national/local markets (assuming no protective legislation) are affected by the most efficient potential providers of each product or service, whatever the sector. Larger providers are likely to have available to them resources and capabilities (financial, human, technical) of greater sophistication and usually (although not always) of greater efficiency. Whilst no such alternative provider exists in a domestic market, local providers can survive and prosper. As soon as national and then international concentration and restructuring begin (whether in aircraft manufacturing, media, coal or other energy sources, utilities, insurance services, health care, clothes or children's toys) local providers have to be able to provide a similar product or service at similar cost to the other providers or be able to offer additional added-value to justify higher local prices to the consumer. We are all familiar with such examples as local 'mom-and-pop stores' trying to stay in business against the greater product choice and cheaper prices of the local supermarket competitors by staying open for longer and longer hours. It is for this reason that their basis for competing has given rise to the label 'convenience store'.

All types of examples may be cited of industry change wiping out entire national industries or of shifts to niche markets to survive. The world textile and clothing industry has changed dramatically over the last century so that the locus of efficient mass production has moved away from Europe to Asia as both quality and price of raw materials and labour costs have made broad market competition impossible by the developed economies. They are still viable competitors in the higher value-added segments of the market where price competition does not dominate. When a new retail concept such the US-based retail chain 'Toys'R'Us' enters other international markets, it has the effect of transforming the sustainable bases of competition for children's toys, games and clothing, in the marketplace it has just entered. If the market for illegal drugs such as heroine, cocaine and crack is an international one, whilst the law enforcement agencies trying to combat them are national/local only, the relative scale of resources, and the scope of information and experience brought to bear, are incompatible. It is not surprising therefore that pressure builds up for the formation of international cross-border links to manage international drug-fighting or international terrorism more effectively.

'International' strategy is different

When an organization first decides to expand outside its domestic market, it faces a step change in the complexity attached to every business decision. For all businesses, operating internationally is much more challenging than operating solely within their domestic market. In every facet of managerial decision-making it creates greater risks and problems. For example, geographic market selection for international expansion is far more complex than expansion within an organization's domestic market. Although domestic expansion certainly requires careful judgement of relative market attractiveness, potential competition, adaptation to local market conditions and coping with problems of managing the business over the larger geographic area, wider challenges of a different order arise with selection of markets for international expansion.

International markets often contain barriers to trade, both tariff and non-tariff such as import quotas, or foreign ownership rules. Other obvious but daunting challenges include different laws, different planning regulations, different transportation infrastructure and distribution systems, different languages, different currencies and exchange rates, different consumer preferences and any number of varieties of differences in individual and social behaviour, political systems and religious or ethnic norms. As a result, operating internationally involves decisions about how, and to what extent, to adapt products, managers and investment plans to take account of these national and cultural differences. All of this means fine judgements about degrees of political risk, financial risk and commercial risk in every international business decision, which do not arise within the domestic home market.

Whilst all strategic thinking occurs in a dynamic context, developing robust strategies deliverable across international borders is the most dynamic and complex context of all. In the next section we will introduce for the first time a number of key concepts and themes that will be returned to and developed further in later chapters: modern factors of production; the theory of comparative advantage and its interaction with competitive advantage; how the MNC delivers advantage just because of what it is; some different types of international trade and some different types of international strategy; the role of government in international strategy; and the role of risk in international strategy. We hope to convey why local organizations find it difficult to cope with international competition and the repercussions that international trade and MNC activity have in the medium and long term on the opportunities for local organizations in their local markets.

The management of international trade

Until the last century, international trade was dominated by trading companies or investment houses. Within the last century, international trade has increasingly become dominated by multinational companies. The difference between the former and the latter is that the activities of multinationals are based on foreign direct investment (FDI) locating part of their activities such as design, manufacturing, assembly, sales, distribution or R&D, in other countries. Further, that these investments were actively managed as a single operational entity in unified corporations. This has in itself influenced the nature of international trade, since much of it is now internal to these international corporations, carried out between their own business units and operating divisions, either importing goods produced in their overseas subsidiaries, or exporting products to be sold by these subsidiaries. Multinationals are therefore responsible for overseeing immense resources and many have assets that exceed those of all but the richest national governments. This combination of factors means that such firms play an important role not only within their domestic economies, but also in the economies of the many host nations in which they have a presence. It is also the source of their impact on the conditions of local competition for the small and medium-sized firms within these various national markets. The quality of management in multinational corporations is therefore an issue which has implications far beyond the corporations themselves.

Over time, the task of international managers has changed. The early emphasis was on managing large-scale technologies of production and distribution for maximum benefit from scale efficiencies of output. This drove companies to international expansion beyond the domestic market, mainly to develop markets of sufficient size to absorb the new high levels of output and to provide continuity of supply. Chandler (1962) described these developments in detail and we will return to his analysis in later chapters. However, gradually overseas subsidiaries became more autonomous, often in response to protectionist barriers erected by national governments against foreign exports. The task of managers became the planning, control and administration of large independent overseas operations. From the 1960s onwards, another set of trends began a new pattern of convergence. Gradual economic integration via international trade agreements, the development of international communication and transportation systems and technological advances in the miniaturization of products and components, transformed the cost structures of many industries and necessitated a complete rethink of the basic economic assumptions of supply and demand on which they were based. It became possible to deconstruct the whole chain of activities of production and supply and redesign them from first principles. This rebuilding usually included much broader options and choices of where to locate business activities worldwide, in order to maximize both efficiency seeking by the firm and responsiveness to shifting patterns of demand in all its markets.

Clearly the management skills in this latest phase of international business are for high levels of integration and co-ordination across borders. That is the capability being emphasized in much current corporate advertising. The Swedish/Swiss engineering company ABB (Asea Brown Boveri) in its 1990s advertising campaigns featured captions such as 'The art of being local worldwide'. This is a rhetoric implying local presence, local roots and local services combined with international reach and resources, which can be brought to bear for the benefit of local customers. Such resources do not have to be directly owned by the company but may be available through an alliance or partnership with another firm. The rapid growth of co-operative ventures as a common feature of international business means that international managers at most levels must have the ability to adapt and learn from collaboration, as well as from competition, to be effective in the changing world arena.

Traditional and modern factors of production: mobile vs immobile

In international trade it is important to understand why the greatest economic welfare is not necessarily served by local firms serving their local populations. Adam Smith's (1776) theory of international trade was based upon the simple idea that an overall welfare gain was made if countries produced the goods in which they had an absolute cost advantage and traded them with other countries for goods in which those countries had *absolute cost advantages*.

David Ricardo (1817) increased the sophistication of this theory by developing it into the theory of *comparative advantage*, which is less intuitively obvious. Under this theory a welfare gain is possible so long as the internal cost ratios between the production of two or more goods in one country are different from the internal cost ratios from producing those goods in another country. Thus, Country A may produce all its goods at a lower cost than Country B but it will still benefit from trade with Country B so long as its costs are comparatively different in producing one good rather than another from those in Country B. The terms of trade will ensure that the goods are traded at prices advantageous to each country. Comparative advantage can be expressed as international differences in the opportunity costs of goods, i.e. the quantity of other goods sacrificed to make one more unit of that good in one country as compared to another country. Thus if, in a closed economy with finite resources, it is assumed that either cheese or cars can be made, the opportunity cost of cheese is the quantity of car output that has to be sacrificed by using resources to make cheese rather than make cars. Even when Country A produces both goods at a lower cost than does Country B, trade will still be beneficial to both since it is clearly most efficient in terms of resource usage for a country to use as many as possible of its resources on producing the goods it is best endowed to produce in cost terms, rather than those it is less well endowed to produce. Where economies of scale exist, the advantage of specializing in producing goods in which one has comparative advantage is even greater.

This law of comparative costs initially underpinned the development of all international trade, which was mainly in non-branded goods. In the Ricardo model, countries develop different costs in producing various goods because they are differentially endowed with the three traditional factors of production: land, labour and capital. Exchange between countries will generally be possible to the advantage of all and will lead to potential welfare gains. From this it follows that impediments to trade such as quotas, tariffs, and other forms of protectionist policy reduce overall welfare, although of course there may be temporary justification for them in specific circumstances, e.g. to protect infant industries so that they can reach maturity and achieve international competitiveness (Grindley, 1995).

This traditional economic theory of international trade based on immobile factors of production and companies without proprietary distinguishing features, culture, management styles or strategies is now too simplistic. Indeed Porter (1990) contends that classical factors no longer generally lead to comparative advantage. He stresses that a modern theory of international strategic management must take account of 'advanced factors' of production, which we will discuss further in Chapter 2. As a brief indication at this point, some typical 'advanced factors' might include *human resources*: in particular managerial and technological skills; *physical resources*: such as the quality and accessibility of a country's climate, natural resources or location; *knowledge resources*: educational and research infrastructure; *capital resources*: financial infrastructure such as the availability of start-up and other risk capital (indeed the developmental problems facing Russia's new conglomerates in 1990's post-'glasnost' Russia show the effects of the lack of such financial infrastructure); *infrastructure*: the transportation system, the communication system, the quality of life in the country and its health care facilities may all constitute advanced factors liable to give companies comparative advantage in some countries rather than others. Technological developments may provide the opportunity for rapid shifts in infrastructure advantage. Consider for example the spread of mobile telecommunications (telephones) in developing economies such as China or eastern Europe which replace the requirement for expensive investment in cable.

Almost all economies contain some potential sources of comparative advantage, which may be utilized by industries or organizations within it to generate potential competitive advantage, at least for short periods of time. Any specific comparative advantage is rarely permanent. Consider one of the most commonly cited sources of comparative advantage: labour costs. Low labour costs attract investment from MNCs wishing to sustain low production costs. Gradually, such investment changes the structure of wage levels in the local labour market and creates increased consumer demand from increased levels of pay in a more competitive labour market. Economic growth drives up labour costs and diminishes comparative advantage based on low labour costs.

The sources of potential comparative advantage in any given economy are extremely varied. Just to give one or two examples for explanatory purposes we might think of the advantages of climate in a given country and the specific opportunities to which that gives rise such as the wine industries historically clustered in the warmer southern countries of Europe and their growth more recently in the equally kind 'new world' climates of Australia, New Zealand, South America and West Coast USA. One may further consider climate and its effect on world leisure industries – whether sun-seeking or snow-seeking for ski-ing and so on. Strategic assets (Amit and Schoemaker, 1993) such as the pyramids and temples of Egypt, or the canals, churches and artworks of Venice, may be considered sources of comparative advantage in a similar way.

Where tariff barriers have been largely removed between countries, the gains from trade arise less from the exploitation of different factor endowments than from comparative cost advantages arising through specialization and reduction in comparative unit costs through the economies of scale and scope that a larger international market allows. Indeed the search for scale and (increasingly) scope economies form an important element of international strategy-making. To define and illustrate the importance of economies of scope for MNCs read the brief account in Box 1.1 of the acquisition by Gillette in 1996 of the battery manufacturer Duracell for $7 billion. Our definition of an economy of scope is: 'using a resource acquired for one purpose for additional purposes at little or no extra cost'. It can be a powerful tool in international strategy.

Box 1.1 Economies of Scope in International Strategy

'Gillette snaps up Duracell' was the headline in the UK newspaper the *The Sunday Times* Business News on 15 September 1996 to describe the successful bid by the US consumer products company Gillette for Duracell, the world's top alkaline battery maker.

The deal cost Gillette $7 billion (£4.5 billion) and its strategic objective was to achieve bigger sales of Duracell's batteries through Gillette's existing huge global distribution network, which was described by Al Zeien, Gillette's Chairman, as including "... every kiosk up the Amazon river....". Gillette had achieved remarkable growth in the 1990s, and this surprise acquisition was seen as a brilliant strategic move to sustain its recent growth momentum. The deal should result in higher earnings from Duracell's business as Gillette starts selling batteries through its global distribution network.

••▶

cont.

Shares in both Gillette and Duracell rose after the deal was announced. The move is Gillette's most recent step in its diversification from razors and blades. It is already the world's top dental-care products producer, having bought Oral-B in 1984, and the largest writing products supplier, owning Parker Pen (acquired in 1993), Waterman and Papermate. It is also a big toiletries supplier and owns Braun, a leading manufacturer of coffee makers, shavers and other small appliances.

Gillette's new product push began with the successful introduction of the Sensor razor in 1989 under the previous Chairman, Colman Mockler. Since becoming Chairman in 1991, Zeien has been spending 50 per cent of operating profits on research and development, capital spending and advertising, and launching more than 20 new products a year. He has also expanded overseas and 70 per cent of sales now come from outside the US; Gillette has four joint ventures in China and two in Russia (one with the Sputnik razor company). New markets, such as Turkey, India, Poland and Hungary, have helped it lift razor-blade sales by 2 billion a year since 1992.

Zeien's problem has been to find ways to keep profits growing. To match the growth rate from 1989 to 1996, Gillette has to pump out new products and persuade customers to switch to more expensive lines. Zeien believes in short product cycles, and makes big investments in innovative products that he hopes will command premium prices. Recently, analysts had begun to wonder how Gillette could sustain its tremendous growth and profit record. The deal with Duracell, which in 1996 had sales of $2.3 billion (up 11 per cent from 1994) and net income of $254.6m (up 9 per cent), will make batteries Gillette's top product after razors and blades, and reduce the revenue from blades from 39 per cent to less than 30 per cent of the total. Duracell is America's top battery maker but heavy investments in new overseas plants and poor market conditions in Europe have depressed Duracell's profitability since the early 1990's.

The logic of this acquisition should now be immediately obvious, since it is based on a very strong logic indeed: achieving increased efficiency from scope economies. Gillette will sell Duracell's batteries through its existing global distribution network; batteries and razors are similar types of purchases and the definition of an economy of scope is: 'using a resource (Gillette's global distribution network for razors) acquired for one purpose for additional purposes (selling Duracell batteries) at little or no extra cost'.

Source: Adapted by authors from press articles. ■

Types of international strategy

The body of knowledge encompassed by the field of international strategy is very wide. It includes a whole range of subject areas such as theories of international trade, exchange rate theory, theory of the multinational enterprise, the structure of international investment and a whole set of conceptual approaches governing the evolutionary stages of internationalization (Stopford and Wells, 1972; Melin, 1992). In addition, each separate management function, R&D, production, information systems, finance, marketing and human resource management and strategic management, are all elements which must be made to serve an effective international strategy.

It is important to recognize that there are many different ways of being international. Different approaches to international strategy suit different companies in different industries at different times. Indeed, a company may pass through many stages in its own approach to being international. It may simultaneously pursue strategies that are widely different in the different countries in which it has a presence around the world. These differences may weaken the company by loading it with a bloated cost structure, riddled with unnecessary duplication, inconsistent and poorly controlled quality, a confused image to its customers and poor bargaining power with its suppliers worldwide. Or, by contrast, it may be that the duplication of dedicated overhead and the variegated positioning in each of the national markets in which it operates is precisely the reason for the success of the company in those sectors and markets in which it competes. Both these strategies are viable. What is important, of course, is that they are each viable in a different context, for specific products, in a specific market, at a specific point in time. Therefore international strategy must, above all, be understood as contingency management theory par excellence.

The four main approaches to being international which firms have most frequently adopted are summarized in Table 1.1. It distinguishes between *Multidomestic* firms which treat each country market as independent and best serviced by a subsidiary dedicated to meet its local needs and conditions, and *Global* firms which emphasize worldwide strategies to benefit from operational scale. They are heavily centralized, with direction and control emanating mainly from central headquarters. The third type, *International exporters*, may achieve lower levels of efficiency than the global firm and also lower levels of responsiveness to local conditions than the multidomestic, but it limits its direct presence in overseas markets to sales and marketing. The fourth type, the *Transnational*, is attempting to build and benefit from interdependent networks worldwide, which both develop and share specific knowledge and expertise held at dispersed international locations. In later chapters each of these four types will be explored in greater detail.

There is a rich and confusing terminology in international strategy. What we have called the 'multidomestic' corporation (Porter, 1986) in Table 1.1, Bartlett

Table 1.1 Four approaches to being international

Organizational characteristics	Configuration of assets and capabilities	Role of overseas operations	Development and diffusion of knowledge
Multidomestic	Decentralized self-sufficient and nationally autonomous	Sensing and exploiting local opportunities	Knowledge developed and retained within each unit
Global	Centralized and globally scaled	Implementing parent company strategies	Knowledge developed at and diffused from centre
International exporter	Core abilities centralized	Purely sales	Knowledge developed and retained at centre
Transnational	Dispersed specialized inter-dependencies	Integrated worldwide operations and differentiated country contributions	Shared centre/ periphery knowledge development and shared learning worldwide

Source: Adapted from Bartlett and Ghoshal (1989)

and Ghoshal (1989) call the 'multinational'. It means an organization which competes internationally by building a strong local presence through sensitivity and responsiveness to national differences (usually to take account of specific local trading conditions or differences in consumer preferences from domestic market to domestic market). 'Global' organizations build cost advantage through integration of centralized scale operations. 'Transnational' organizations exploit parent company knowledge and capabilities through worldwide diffusion and adaptation. We will be using these terms and discussing the suitability of the international strategies and structures that they represent throughout the rest of this book. Before exploring these different approaches in more detail, we need to develop a perspective on the broad objectives of international strategy.

The role of governments and the limits to regulation

International strategy is not a zero-sum game, unlike domestic market strategy. To paraphrase Henderson (1989), to enlarge the scope of your international advantage, need not 'only happen at someone else's expense'. The mere fact that low labour-cost economies do not remain cheap permanently, makes the point that economic growth through trade creates substantial changes over time in the standard of living within those countries.

Japan, Malaysia, Singapore and South Korea are all examples of cheap labour economies, which have rapidly become rich and developed and hence expensive, as general expectations of standards of living have risen, leading to displacement of labour-intensive jobs elsewhere (e.g. Vietnam, China). Governments have to cope with the internal political tensions this creates as MNCs shift production elsewhere. Only higher value-added jobs are likely to be retained long term within developed economies. In international strategy terms it is cheaper for Germany's BMW and Mercedes-Benz car companies to build new plants in the USA than in Germany or to invest in Poland or the Czech Republic, and if they do not do so, the comparative disadvantage of their high-cost German plants will render their necessary price differential unsustainable against (perceived) equally good Japanese models like the Toyota 'Lexus'. Such MNC production-shifting raises ethical issues, which will be returned to later in this chapter. Governments (national or regional) meanwhile must provide public welfare (e.g. through education) and protection (e.g. labour law, consumer protection, pollution policy). However, Grindley (1995) insists that the role of governments in exerting regulatory authority is 'to provide the conditions for the market to work and if necessary correct potential excesses', but not to act as a backdoor way of supporting national industries or firms or of implementing national or international industrial policies. Since these approaches most often result in less robust industries or firms, in the longer term neither industries, firms nor consumers benefit.

In spite of the short-term nature of comparative advantage, there are examples of the benefits arising in the short to medium term from government intervention in industrial or competition policy. A well-known example is the intervention of Japan's Ministry of International Trade and Investment (MITI) which for decades has acted to provide local Japanese firms and industries with an invaluable period of protection from foreign competitor entry into the Japanese domestic market, until they are strong enough to compete themselves. It must be stressed, however, that greatest benefit from protection is gained for short-term specific objectives rather than long-term general ones.

MNC strategy as a war game

Whittington (1993) pointed out that the interaction of oligopolistic international competition may be likened to the Cold War between the USA and the

USSR between 1949 and 1989. They followed a doctrine of 'mutually assured destruction' (MAD) which was seen as essential to maintaining peace between these two superpowers. However, during the 1970s, the USSR began to question the USA's (and indeed, the West's) will to launch an all-out nuclear war. Since the stability of MAD depended upon the underlying assumption that each superpower was willing to launch its nuclear weapons at the other if necessary, this perception of a possible loss of such will in the USA led to greater instability, e.g. the Afghan War. It was only when the West 'toughened' its stance once more by deploying tactical nuclear weapons that stable state was restored. Whittington (1993) described this situation as follows:

> To preserve stability in the game, therefore, all participants must maintain both sufficient parity to punish potential transgressors, and the reputation for being willing to take the risks of retaliation. Equilibrium would be jeopardized either if any participant became powerful enough and secure enough to launch an all-out war which it could actually win or if one of the participants looked like being soft on aggression. (p.104)

This military metaphor of MAD may be usefully applied to MNC competition. Procter & Gamble (USA)and Unilever (UK), giants of the fast-moving consumer goods (FMCG) industry worldwide, have competed ruthlessly against each other for decades in all the markets of the world and in all product sectors in which they have a presence. In 1994 Unilever launched a new brand of their market-leading washing powder: 'Persil Power'. It was aggressively marketed as using an innovativc technology, which delivered substantial washing superiority. They hoped to gain considerable market share from their rival. Procter & Gamble responded fiercely to this new launch by actively campaigning to undermine the credibility of Unilever's new product. They claimed that Persil Power actually rotted clothes. Such aggressive action can often result in destruction of profits for the whole sector and for all rival competitors involved. A similar pattern of events occurred in the equally oligopolistic cigarette market when Philip Morris (USA manufacturer of 'Marlboro' and other well-known brands) suddenly in 1993 launched a price war by drastically slashing the price of its leading cigarette brands. Philip Morris had hoped to attract customers away from rival brands and 'own-label' generic supermarket products. Instead their move triggered instability in the industry and led to dramatic reductions in prices and profitability for all competitors in their sector, including a spectacular plunge ('Black Friday') in the share price of Philip Morris itself, as well as emotional debates about the 'death' of brands.

OPEC's (Organization of Petroleum Exporting Countries) change in oil extraction and production quotas in 1986 was another well-known example of aggressive action generating instability and destroying oligopolistic profits, which had flourished in the previously stable situation. Between 1979 and 1986, the OPEC cartel enjoyed such great market power that they were able to raise international crude oil prices to levels three times higher than the historic average. Given that crude oil was a commodity product this was a significant demonstration of market power by OPEC cartel members restricting and withholding supply. However, over the time period in question, OPEC members gradually broke ranks and began cheating on their individual agreed production quotas, assuming that Saudi Arabia would always adjust its own production to support the price. Saudi Arabia unexpectedly boosted its own production levels in 1986, with the result that the crude oil price dropped spectacularly from $26 to $8 per barrel in under two weeks, as supply dramatically increased. Prices have never subsequently returned to the OPEC-highs, since the assumptions underlying its credibility and oligopoly power are demonstrably no longer either sustainable or enforceable.

Obviously there are many possible outcomes of an oligopolistic international war game, but they do all assume that the competitors will act rationally and understand the criticality of stability and equilibrium for general profit maximization, except where one competitor (e.g. Unilever, Philip Morris or OPEC) believes that they can win greater market share or greater market power by launching a unilateral offensive. Box 1.2 provides one such example described by Hamel and Prahalad (1985).

Box 1.2 What Drives Global Competition

... It begins with a sequence of competitive action and reaction:

An aggressive competitor decides to use the flow generated in its home market to subsidize an attack on markets of domestically oriented foreign competitors. The defensive competitor then retaliates – not in its home market where the attack was staged – but in foreign markets where the aggressor company is most vulnerable.

As an example, consider the contest between Goodyear and Michelin. By today's definitions, the tyre industry is not global. Most tyre companies manufacture and distribute for local markets. Yet Michelin, Goodyear and Firestone are now locked in a fiercely competitive – and very global – battle. In the early 1970s, Michelin used its strong European profit base to attack Goodyear's American home market. Goodyear could fight back in the United States by reducing prices, increasing advertising or offering dealers better margins. But because Michelin would expose only small amounts of its worldwide business in the United States, it had little to lose and much to gain.

●●▶

cont.

Goodyear, on the other hand, would sacrifice margins in its largest market. Goodyear ultimately struck back in Europe, throwing a wrench in Michelin's money machine.

Source: Hamel and Prahalad (1985) p.140) ■

Similarly Hamel and Prahalad describe events in the USA television market in the 1970s. Japanese consumer electronics companies such as Sony and Matsushita competed internationally, whilst the US companies such as Zenith, GE and RCA remained domestic USA competitors only. Thus, when companies such as Matsushita of Japan began their entry into the US domestic market, the local US producers fought Japanese competitors' penetration of their US domestic market with price cuts in their own domestic market. Since they had no other competitive venue, price reduction at home meant that the US companies put their own margins under pressure on 100 per cent of their (100 per cent US domestic) sales volume. Meanwhile its Japanese attackers were not similarly exposed since their US trade was merely a fraction of their total trade and their Japanese domestic market was unaffected.

In this approach to international competition, the more competitive venues the better. More locations offer more choices and locations for possible aggressive or defensive strategies. This type of war game theory suggests that competitors should only launch a market share offensive if they are sure they can achieve domination. Otherwise market leaders normally provide a price umbrella from which they and others benefit. Even where a market is not itself global (e.g. the tyre market), international competitors still need 'global strategic co-ordination' (Prahalad and Doz, 1987). This is a view of international strategy based on battles by MNCs for market share of international *cash* flows rather than international *product* flows. Thus, cash flows from one market can be used to subsidize market share battles in other markets. This approach to international strategy based on military war games therefore dictates that retaliatory or aggressive action must be taken in those markets where a competitor is most vulnerable to a 'cash flow siege'. This is the basis for effective international strategies being aggressive in style rather than purely defensive.

Much of Prahalad and Hamel's analysis is derived from study of the international strategies pursued by many Japanese MNCs in the 1970s and 1980s. Notions of 'aggressive' and 'defensive' moves do capture well the nature of these international strategies and the battles that resulted from them. Some of these aggressive and defensive strategy objectives, and the choices underpinning them, are captured in the 'map' given in Figure 1.1.

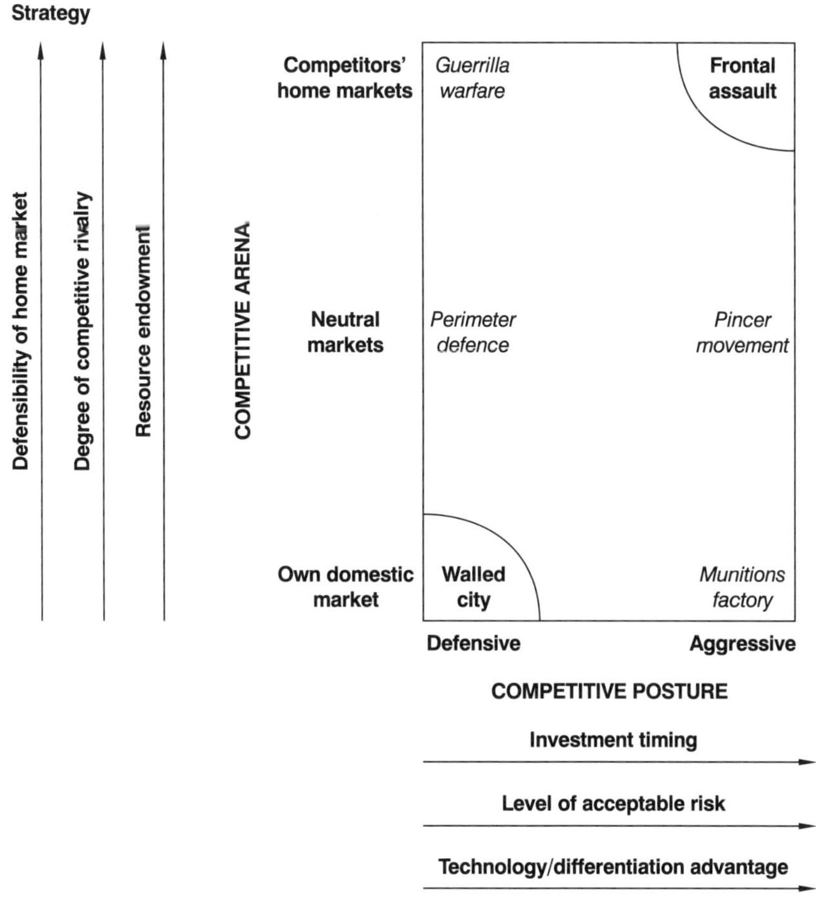

Figure 1.1 Types of competitive approaches to international expansion. *Source:* Adapted from Hamel and Prahalad (1985)

Types of competitive approaches to international expansion

Following Hamel and Prahalad's work described earlier, the 'map' in Figure 1.1 suggests that choice of competitive arena (and therefore location of a battleground) is dependent upon*: the defensibility of the home market*, so that the more protected a company feels in its own domestic market, the more it feels safe in attacking competitors' home markets; the *degree of competitive rivalry,* so that the fiercer the competition, the greater the likelihood that a company will carry the battle outside its domestic market and especially into its competitors domestic markets; the *resource endowment of the firm,* so that the stronger a company's own resource base (financial, physical, human. technological), the more likely it is to exploit those resources in a variety of markets.

Similarly, aggressive or defensive strategy will be dependent upon: *investment timing,* which must take account of managers' judgements about windows of opportunity and the potential benefits of 'first-mover advantage' or 'second strike' strategies; *level of acceptable risk,* since all investment decisions are dependent upon the nature of the company's risk profile and that of its senior management and aggressive strategies require a higher risk profile than defensive strategies – although in the longer term the aggressive strategy (certainly in the international arena) may be the less risky, since attack may indeed be the best form of defence; *technology/differentiation advantage,* means that lack of differentiation and ease of imitability tend to encourage defensive rather than offensive strategies. The reverse is also often the case.

Figure 1.1 captures a range of different strategic possibilities arising from the variables described. The same company may choose any or several of these strategies at different times and in different markets, according to their perceptions of their own and their competitors' strengths and weaknesses. Some of the characteristics of the potential strategies suggested by the 'map' are as follows:

- The 'walled city' strategy is about heavily defending a home market. This is rarely successful in the longer term on its own, as was described earlier of the US TV firms RCA and Zenith in their home market. If your domestic market is 100 per cent of your total market, then 100 per cent of your total market is vulnerable to attack.
- 'Frontal assault' strategies are the most risky. They are aggressive strategies and they depend for success on careful timing, together with confidence that the home market can be successfully defended against retaliatory action of the sort that Goodyear used against Michelin.
- 'Pincer' strategies are also aggressive, but more subtle than 'frontal assault'. This is because they take place in a neutral or less important market, in order to attract less attention and less chance of immediate retaliatory action. This gives the intruder time to establish a firm foothold before retaliation is likely to occur. Hamel and Prahalad (1985) describe Komatsu, the Japanese earth-moving equipment manufacturer, using this strategy to encroach gradually on the dominant world position of their American rival Caterpillar. It was so successful that by the 1980s Komatsu could shift to 'frontal assault' on Caterpillar in their US home market.

Flexibility, risk and ethics

It may be appropriate at this point to make some simple statements about international strategy and the role of MNCs. They are complex organizations;

difficult to manage; often castigated in the press and public opinion; and frequently caught out degenerating into bloated and dysfunctional bureaucracies, inflexible and unresponsive or slow to change. What then is the point of them?

The main strategic benefit in being an MNC is that it gives you flexibility and options. As with life in general, so with international competition; options allow you to choose between ways of doing things. For domestic firms, their domestic market is 100 per cent of their potential market. Much domestic market strategy is defensive, trying to defend and protect existing positions while more and more volume of world trade is cross-border. MNCs have available to them a wider range of strategies arising simply from the fact of being international and operating across borders.

Governments and supra-national organizations erect regulatory, institutional and tariff barriers to trade, whilst MNCs attempt to configure their international operations to exploit those barriers that are favourable to them (such as international agreements about routes and prices in the airline industry) and avoid those that are not. Such trade barriers include: high tariffs; import quota systems; refusal to sanction licences; nationalistic purchasing and ownership policies; centralized 'command' economies; and excessively chauvinistic domestic demand.

Governments tax immobile assets and national-based consumption and try to set corporation taxes at levels which will provide them with useful sources of tax revenue to spend on services without forcing the corporations to shift their investments in jobs, buildings, research or technology elsewhere. It is for this reason that governments try to attract quality inward investment by MNCs into their countries by offering capital grants, regional grants (especially in employment 'blackspots'), tax-free zones, etc.

Small is not often beautiful in terms of international competition. Large organizations have available to them an array of advantages. Kogut (1985) summarizes these as: production shifting; tax minimization; financial markets; information arbitrage; global co-ordination; and political risk.

An example of *production shifting* might be the announcement by Ford of Europe in January 1997 that it intended shifting European car production from one of its British factories (Halewood at Merseyside) to its factories in Spain and Germany. The company argued that the move was to rationalize production of certain models at its most efficient plants, having lost $472m in Europe in the third quarter of 1996 alone and against a competitive picture of fierce price-cutting by all car manufacturers alongside increased output and general overcapacity. Employees and trade unions were outraged that their acknowledged huge improvements in productivity and relatively low wage rates appeared to have made no difference. This example may also contain an instance of *tax minimization* since the Ford UK workers claimed that they were being chosen for closure instead of their counterparts in Spain or Germany because of the lower redundancy payments, which Ford would incur in the UK. In more general tax terms, MNCs are able to minimize their tax burden as far as possible by moving their internal and external transactions to the most advantageous national tax location.

Governments often create *financial markets* and financial arbitrage opportunities for MNCs via their policies to attract inward investment (such as export credit, guaranteed loans). MNCs can also create innovative financial products to benefit from financial flexibility. It is perhaps also an obvious point to make but an important one that large organizations tend to have better credit ratings than smaller organizations and therefore benefit from cheaper cost of capital (Choi and Rajan, 1997). MNCs also organize themselves to benefit from *information arbitrage* including such things as transfer of knowledge about products and markets and the transfer of product or process developments from one location to another.

These have so far all represented what Kogut (1985) calls 'arbitrage opportunities', where the MNC seeks to benefit from the exploitation of differences. These differences may be in the price of an asset, a product or an activity between different marketplaces. These last two he calls 'leverage opportunities', by which he means 'the creation of market or bargaining power because of the global position of the firm'. *Global co-ordination* may cover such possibilities as differential pricing/price co-ordination to consolidate or build market position, or building coalitions for competitive leverage. Since MNCs can usually decide where they carry out particular parts of their operations, the management of *political risk* is both a problem and an opportunity. The point about leverage opportunities is that they capture the bargaining power arising from having dispersed operations. The key to this power is the leverage that different links of the international value chain exercise on operations in national markets.

Judgements about the levels of risk and reward attached to each potential investment opportunity must be evaluated. For example, relatively high political risk of investments in China or India must be weighed against the attractions of each of those markets in terms of overall size and long-term development potential. Figure 1.2 shows a matrix of types of exposure to political, regulatory and ethical risk to provide a summary of such contingencies and their potential effects on MNCs.

Figure 1.2 refers to 'the actions of legitimate government authorities' and 'events caused by actors outside the control of government'. Despite the fact that individuals and nations differ in the values or beliefs they hold and the experiences that shape those values and beliefs, Hosmer (1994) suggests that there are indeed some fundamental ethical principles that do transcend cultures, time and economic conditions. Whether or not this proposition is tenable, ethical values are an important part of the formal policies and therefore culture of many organizations. Ethics and values affect both the decisions that companies make and their ability to implement those decisions in accordance

	Source of Risk	
	The 'actions' of legitimate government authorities	Events caused by actors outside the control of government
Types of Impact		
The voluntary loss of control over specific assets without adequate compensation	■ Total or partial expropriation ■ Forced divestiture ■ Confiscation ■ Cancellation or unfair calling of performance bonds ■ Withdrawal of licences or ownership of property	■ War ■ Revolution ■ Terrorism ■ Strikes ■ Extortion
A reduction in the value of a stream of benefits expected from the foreign controlled affiliate	■ Non applicability of 'national treatment' ■ Restriction in access to financial, labour or material markets ■ Controls on prices, outputs or activities ■ Currency and remittance restrictions ■ Value-added and export performance requirements ■ Sudden cancellation or change in agreed terms of a contract ■ Bureaucratic blockages	■ Nationalistic buyers or suppliers ■ Threats and disruption to operations by hostile groups ■ Externally induced financial constraints ■ Externally imposed limits on imports or exports ■ Corruption/nepotism and 'cronyism' ■ Ethical or pressure-group driven investment policies

Figure 1.2 Exposure to political, regulatory and ethical risk. *Source:* Adapted from De la Torre and Neckar (1988)

with, or in conflict with, governments or non-governmental forces. Changes in perceived 'ethical' behaviour also affect standards as to what is good or bad in managerial or organizational conduct and hence changes the degrees of risk attached to international decision-making.

Do organizations which act unethically achieve some superior advantage? Hosmer (1994) encapsulates this position when he points out in discussing ethics and strategy:

> I do not claim that all equitable acts lead to strategic and financial success. I do not claim that all inequitable acts lead to strategic and financial disaster. I do however, claim that a pattern of equitable acts over

> time does indeed lead to trust and that trust to commitment, and that a committed effort, which is both co-operative and innovative on the part of everyone, does eventually lead to success. That success may be slow, but it is certain enough to warrant the attention of management scholars.

Some examples of the conflicts and complexities involved in the interplay between MNC strategic flexibility, business ethics and international strategy are considered in Box 1.3.

Box 1.3 MNCs, Risk and Ethics

Throughout the decade of the 1990s, MNCs have been increasingly attracting protests against their activities in developing countries. In 1996 American protesters demonstrated at Unocal petrol stations across the USA to complain about the oil firm's involvement (together with France's Total) in an off-shore gas field development in Myanmar (previously known as Burma). The protesters claimed that the project will help to prop up an unpleasant, undemocratic regime. At the same time two European brewers, Carlsberg and Heineken, pulled out of investments in Myanmar. In Malaysia, a $5.5 billion hydroelectric dam to be built by a consortium including ABB Asea Brown Boveri, the Swiss-based multinational, was attacked by local people and Western environmental groups for destroying rainforest. Royal Dutch/Shell, the (Dutch/UK oil giant) suffered massive public outcry in 1996 over its aborted plans to dump the Brent Spar (a very large, deep-water oil exploration platform) at sea and again, in 1997, on its relations with the military regime in Nigeria, which provoked an international outcry when Nigeria executed nine dissidents. It was seen as part of the responsibility of an MNC to exert economic influence on the political regimes of the countries in which they invest and from which they usually derive profit.

These ethical issues have become high profile and high risk because external stakeholders such as consumer groups or environmental pressure groups have successfully influenced public opinion, affecting both consumer buying patterns (including occasional consumer boycotts)and internal staff morale (many Shell employees opposed the sinking of the Brent Spar). Government sanctions may sometimes also be imposed. For example, in the USA, the state of Massachusetts recently banned contracts with firms doing business in Myanmar.

●●▶

cont.

Some MNCs have been in the forefront of campaigning for higher ethical standards, drawing up ethics statements and appointing ethics officers. To some extent this 'ethical' strategy has paid dividends. Multinationals have shaken off their old sinister image. The United Nations, which used to try to control them, now regards them as agents of modernization and good practice. The developing world, having once feared them, now competes to attract their factories. But they are also now being judged against the high ethical standards which they themselves have helped to promulgate. Many of the poor nations that nationalized mines and oilfields in the 1960s and 1970s are now welcoming multinationals back. However, at the same time, the multinationals' fiercest critics, environmental and human-rights lobbyists, have become more organized.

Greenpeace, for example, is no longer an amateurish affair of beards and T-shirts but a professional, global organization with offices in 33 countries, including Latin America and eastern Europe, and which is in many ways similar to the multinationals it shadows. In South-East Asia, groups representing local people co-ordinate their campaigns using e-mail. In Asia and Latin America tribes have put old enmities to one side and joined forces to exert pressure on multinationals and governments; such groups have formed alliances with the rich world's green campaigners.

The difficulty for companies attempting to avoid trouble is that they may forfeit the best growth opportunities. Much of the world's raw material wealth is located in countries with dubious political regimes and unstable environments. Many MNCs therefore have chosen to combine continued pursuit of their overseas investment strategies with a closer liaison with the campaigners and paying more attention to indigenous groups. Keen to avoid repeating the mistakes it made in Nigeria, Shell met local tribespeople before signing a recent deal to develop a gas field in Peru. It has launched a Brent Spar site on the Internet to encourage people to debate the issue of decommissioning, and the company also holds consultations and workshops with anyone interested in the subject.

Local political or environmental problems, which were once seen solely as the concern of governments, are now seen as the responsibility of the MNC too. This rising concern of consumers in the richer developed economies with where and how their goods and services are produced often raise complex moral dilemmas which are also about commercial necessities and which have serious unintended as

●● ▶

cont.

well as intended consequences. Consider the issue of child labour. Even here there are many views and a range of difficult consequences as to the long-term or short-term benefits and trade-offs between the developed and the developing economies. For example, where does 'protection' for children end and 'protectionism' of Western markets and rich economy jobs begin? Consumers in the West are increasingly choosy about the origin of the goods they buy, but the codes of conduct agreed by companies, such as Reebok and Nike, cut little ice in the developing world. Faced by sharp cuts in overseas aid and the need to export to pay off their debts, they see the offer of cheap and compliant labour as their source of comparative advantage – the bait for footloose global corporations.

The globalization of the world economy is more than simply a question of cheap imports from the developing world. The Brussels-based International Confederation of Free Trade Unions is at the forefront of a battle raging with the World Trade Organization as to whether countries that fail to abide by five core labour standards should be given unrestricted access to the world's markets. The unions, backed by most of the developed Western nations, say there should be a universal right to organize and to freedom of association. Child and forced labour should be outlawed, as should all forms of discrimination at work. Countries refusing to abide by these standards should face being deprived of access to the West's lucrative markets. Most of the developing world, together with Britain and Germany, argue that this is merely backdoor protectionism, a subtle attempt by the rich countries to respond to high unemployment by pricing low-cost goods out of their markets. Consumer groups also oppose bringing labour standards into the trade arena. They argue that it will inevitably lead to protectionism, raising the cost of goods for consumers, particularly those on low incomes who buy Bangladeshi T-shirts and dresses from Hong Kong.

Source: Compiled by authors from various press articles. ■

We have no simple answers to these complex questions. We wish merely to indicate some of the complexity involved. Thus, ethical values are in part shaped by culture and are part of culture. They are part of the values that we as individuals bring into organizations. In some cases our values might clash with those of the organizations we work for, so that our interests as employees or managers may not be congruent with our preferences as consumers, parents, voters, tourists or environmentally concerned individuals.

Objectives and overview of this book

Our aims in writing this book include:

1. Extending the conceptual and analytical tools of strategic management to the formulation and implementation of international strategy.
2. Developing greater understanding of some of the major problems facing managers of international organizations, especially those working within multinational corporations, as well as those organizations competing or doing business with MNCs within national markets.
3. Building awareness of the greater complexity, including both increased opportunities and increased risks, that accompanies international operations.
4. Exploring alternative patterns of strategy, structure and operations, appropriate in different international contexts and changing international market conditions.

In reviewing theories of international trade and the changing pattern of international competition, this book draws not only on strategic management research, but also on the fields of organizational behaviour, economics and marketing. As an extended Introduction Chapter 1 has provided a brief overview of international trade theory in order to explain the theory of comparative advantage and its role in international strategy. This Introduction has explained the sources of advantage available to multinational corporations (MNCs) and the complex relationship between MNCs and governments. Initial definitions of some different types of international strategy have been given. We have stressed that what drives international strategy is strategic flexibility: the creation of a broader set of strategic options and choices.

Part 1 sets out the economics, the geography and the structural, cultural and competitive movement over time that are the essential determinants of the context in which managers have to create viable international strategies. Chapter 2 takes an economic perspective on international strategy. It deals with advanced factors of production and comparative advantage within the national 'diamond'. It explains the assumptions of three dominant economic paradigms and their relevance to, and impact on, international strategy. Chapter 3 deals with the formation of regional trading groups, the impact of regionalization and the relationship between regionalization and globalization. It debates the degree of cultural homogeneity that exists across world markets and the current relevance to strategic thinking of issues of standardization and adaptation across and within international markets. Chapter 4 illustrates the dynamic nature of international competition and its impact on the strategies of firms through the extended example of the European food industry. Chapter 5 examines the role of culture, both national culture and organizational culture, in international strategy. It offers an analysis of the impact of culture on the implementation of international strategies, seeing it both as a barrier and an opportunity. Some approaches to managing cultural diversity in MNCs are discussed.

Part 2 emphasizes that whether markets are local, regional or global changes the nature of the co-ordination that the MNC must try to achieve. Often MNCs have to have the capability of being effective on all three levels simultaneously. A model of types of international strategy is developed in Chapter 6, which will form the basis of the analysis of the different approaches to international strategy covered in the succeeding three chapters, discussing sources of advantage from global, local or 'glocal' strategies. It considers these different types of international strategies and structures in more detail. Chapters 7, 8 and 9 cover multidomestic, global, international exporter and transnational strategy and organization respectively. These discussions include an overview of the drivers of globalization and their consequences and the 'configuration' and 'co-ordination' of geographically dispersed international value chains appropriate for different industry structures and placing differing organizational demands on MNCs. Each chapter presents organizational structures for complex international strategies, including global, multidomestic and transnational organizations and their role in different types of international strategies.

Part 3 highlights international strategy issues that have grown greatly in importance in the last decade. This section begins with a consideration in Chapter 10 of the problems of service organizations in managing intangible services across borders. In Chapters 11 and 12 we will examine different modes of international strategy development – the popularity of strategic alliances and the traditional route of mergers and acquisitions. Both provide a means of acquiring instant market share, adding capabilities or resources. Any objective for an alliance may equally well be a reason for a merger or acquisition. They are simply different means to the same ends. However, since the indirect (non-financial) costs of an alliance may be very high, these chapters focus on the managerial and operational issues in making alliances work effectively. Strategic alliances have become an enormously popular approach within international strategy. Despite their popularity, they are problematic to manage successfully and are prone to high levels of failure. We provide reasons for these failures and recommendations for enabling alliances to work more constructively. Finally, in Chapter 13 we discuss the role of organizational learning in MNC strategy. This term emphasizes that organizations as well as individuals can acquire new knowledge and skills, to sustain their existing strengths and to help to build new ones. The capability of MNCs to transform individual knowledge into organizational learning is at the heart of their ability to survive the future.

Chapter 14 is intended to be more than a conclusion. It is a revisiting of some of the themes from the book which we feel are of greatest importance for the future competitiveness of MNCs.

Key themes

This book will use well-known basic strategy frameworks such as five-forces industry analysis or the value chain, as well as introducing you to new concepts to help you make sense of the dynamics of international competition and international strategy. More importantly, we seek to approach the subject of international strategy in an eclectic way, choosing to designate particular themes, ideas and understandings as critical.

We take the view that flexibility of thought and approach is an essential attribute for devising robust international strategies and coping with those of rival organizations from either existing or new industries. International strategy operates in a context of complexity, mess and hyperactivity. International industry dynamics and international organizational dynamics are givens. MNCs have also to deal not only with the dynamic of industry and firm, but also the dynamics of nations and firms: a perpetual search for firm-specific advantages within a cluster of potential national sources of advantage. Another dynamic element is the structures of the international firms themselves, and, further still, the relationships of co-operation as well as competition between firms within and across industries. This is what we refer to as flexibility in the internal boundaries of the firm (what 'transnationals' and the variety of federal structures of MNCs are struggling to develop) and in the external boundaries of the firm (as exemplified by types of joint ventures or alliances).

The key themes of flexibility; industry dynamics; co-operation and competition; firm-specific advantage and national advantage; the increasingly federal structures of MNCs; and the changing external and internal boundaries of the firm in the search for international advantage – these are the themes which will be repeated within each chapter.

Above all, we seek to explore frameworks, not to generate 'recipes'. International strategy is contingent, dynamic and aggressive. Defensive strategies are not robust strategies in the international frame. We are developing a particular perspective about the means and ends of international strategy. It is about interaction and positioning across the globe. What drives international strategy is the creation of a broader set of strategic options and choices. The key management issue is the organizational structure, capabilities and flexibility with which to realize them.

Part 1

The nature of international strategy

2

The context and economics of international strategy

In this chapter our purpose is to show the relevance of economic theory to international strategy. Whilst some traditional economic theory is of limited relevance, other more recent economic thinking gives insight into the appropriateness of different types of international competitive strategies in different contexts. The roots of the structural analysis of industries within strategic management (Porter, 1980, 1985, 1990), both nationally and internationally, lie within economics. This gives such analysis both its strengths and its weaknesses. Understanding the respective roles of nations and firms within international strategy, and the economic rationale for much international activity, should give meaning to the discussion of particular MNC international strategies and organizational structures in later chapters.

International trade has a history going back at least to the Phoenicians (*circa* 500 BC and perhaps even earlier). Many of the great expeditions and celebrated explorers in the history books as well as many wars and colonial conquests, were about discovering, or usurping control of, new trading routes or sources of wealth to be traded. The world has generally been dominated by the strongest trading states or nations in each era. Their political power rested largely on their economic power derived from trade, such as that of the Republic of Venice in the late fifteenth and sixteenth centuries in Europe. Throughout the seventeenth, eighteenth and nincteenth centuries, the European 'powers' of France, Britain, Holland, Belgium, Spain and Portugal expanded into Africa and Asia, South and North America. Imperialism and colonial aggrandizement often followed swiftly on the heels of trading exploits.

However, until modern times international trade was dominated by trading companies like the East India Company (India), Hudson Bay Company (North America) or Inchcape Plc (Asia) who took products manufactured in the home and the trading countries and made money on the exchange. In the twentieth century, however, international trade has increasingly come to be dominated by multinational corporations (MNCs) who engage in foreign direct investment (FDI) and are organized as unified hierarchical corporations; or more recently, by competition from more loosely organized coalitions of companies and networks led by flagship firms (Rugman, 1997).

This has in itself influenced the nature of international trade, since much international activity is in the nature of transfers within these MNCs, between their business units and operating divisions, either importing goods produced in their overseas subsidiaries or exporting products to be sold by these subsidiaries. The largest MNCs have grown to be more important economically than all but the richest of national economies. Such firms play an important role not only in their domestic economies, but also in the economies of the many overseas territories in which they have a presence. How then is this possible if international trade is firmly based on the principle of comparative costs?

The rise of the MNC

The classical theory of comparative costs would suggest at first sight that local companies would be likely to have inherent advantages in their own countries compared with multinational corporations. Local companies would have lower transport costs, a better understanding of local tastes, better local networks and lower need for the overheads that come with international co-ordination. Yet branded goods sold through MNCs generally dominate most consumer goods markets. By 1970, of the 100 largest economic entities in the world, nations ranked by GNP accounted for 39 positions whilst multinationals (MNCs) accounted for 60. Some of these MNCs have existed longer and are more stable than many countries. Why is this?

MNCs are large companies that produce in more than their home country and operate in international markets. In MNCs comparative costs determine where a particular activity is carried out. Raw materials may be mined in one country, converted into product in another and marketed and sold in a third. Comparative costs will play a large part in determining which activities are carried out in which countries, but all may then be bundled together and sold through the agency of and under the brand name of a multinational corporation (Krugman, 1995). Dunning's eclectic theory provides a framework for explaining why MNCs exist and are able to achieve competitive advantage in competition both with local firms and firms who restrict their international activities just to exporting. Dunning's (1998) 'eclectic paradigm' has three 'OLI' factors attached to it:

- Ownership
- Localization
- Internalization

Ownership (O) factors imply that the company owns certain key resources or capabilities giving advantage in certain markets, e.g. strong brand names, specific and unique technologies or particular and relevant know-how. These factors give the MNC potential advantage over a local company. Such advantages, combined with high sales volume, contribute to lower unit costs through economies of scale.

Localization (L) means that the multinational finds it an advantage to locate an activity to benefit from some comparative advantage such as low cost or highly experienced labour, or to avoid national or regional tariff barriers.

Internalization (I) suggests that there are advantages to carrying out certain activities (such as R&D or marketing) internally within the MNC because not to do so would generate a high risk of losing proprietary knowledge to potential competitors. Outsourcing, quasi-integration with suppliers, or setting up a joint venture or strategic alliance for these critical functions may be ill-advised, since they contain the risk of loss of proprietary information or loss of sources of innovation.

Thus in Dunning's (1998) OLI paradigm for the development of MNC activity, it is the second factor, localization (L), that is critical for international activity.

Consider the four main types of international trade:

- Exporting
- Foreign direct investment (FDI)
- Licensing
- Strategic alliances

If the conditions governing the ownership (O) or internalization (I) factors are reduced or removed then the opportunity for strategic alliances arises. The theory of foreign direct investment, and of alternative organizational forms to develop business across frontiers, is set out effectively by Rugman *et al.* (1985), who develop a rational decision tree for choosing between the various alternatives. This decision tree is given in Figure 2.1.

Thus, exporting is best in conditions where trade barriers are absent since unit costs can be reduced to a very low level from large-scale production. If trade barriers exist, however, players need to set up manufacturing in foreign countries to get underneath them (i.e. become an MNC), and they will do this under tight ownership conditions if they fear losing competitive advantage as a result of the loss of proprietary knowledge. If this is not a major concern, a strategic alliance or joint venture may be the appropriate move.

Dunning's paradigm is called 'eclectic' because the actual circumstances which make becoming a multinational the appropriate solution, are many, varied and particular to a set of circumstances. However, in Dunning's view the decision about whether the MNC route to internationalization is the

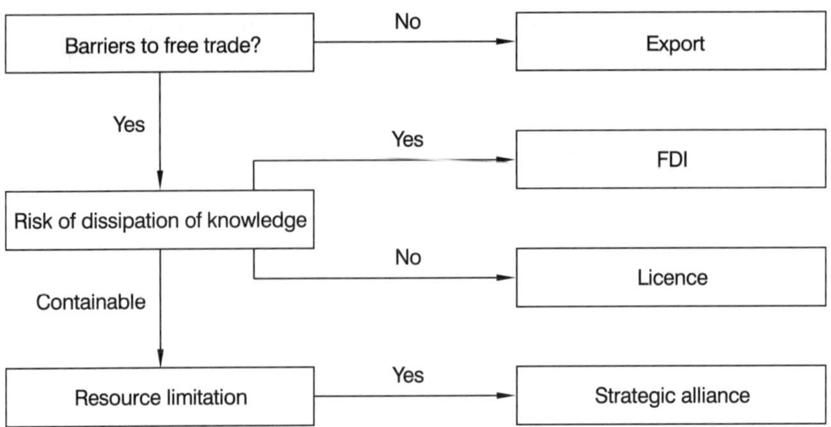

Figure 2.1 The decision tree. *Source:* Adapted from Rugman, Lecraw and Booth (1985)

appropriate one or another route would be more effective given the conditions, will always need to be made with regard to the three OLI characteristics: ownership, location and internalization. With only ownership (O) factors the company could export to a licensee, and subcontract virtually any of its activities. With only internalization (I) it could operate from a home base and found all its international activities on export trade as international traders did generally prior to the nineteenth century. With ownership and internalization, it is committed to carrying out itself certain key activities, lest it lose control of those advantages to a competitor. And with all three–ownership, localization and internalization – it is committed to setting up abroad in some form to meet the criteria. In other words, it has to become a multinational corporation.

The acronym OLI explains how MNCs prosper through 'Ownership' advantages, e.g. brand names; 'Locational' advantages where there is for example cheap labour; and 'Internalization' needs which protect their proprietary knowledge and information. The way for a firm without OLI advantages to succeed in international trade is to configure and co-ordinate a joint value chain with a partner, a possibility that will be returned to later in the book.

Multinational corporations are, in Kogut's (1985) view, able to win against most domestic operations because they can access both the comparative advantage of nations in which they carry out foreign direct investment and can achieve competitive advantage by investing in their value-added chains in appropriate activities. The value-added chain enables one to identify sources of comparative (country) and competitive (firm) advantage. Where to carry out activities involves comparative advantage; where in the value chain to invest is a question of competitive advantage.

Comparative vs competitive advantage for MNCs

The Caterpillar/Komatsu minicase, in Box 2.1, is intended to illustrate the difference between comparative advantage and competitive advantage. It shows how companies may be able to turn comparative advantages into sources of competitive advantage; at least for limited periods of time.

Box 2.1 Caterpillar and Komatsu – Comparative Advantage and Competitive Advantage

In strategy terms it must be stressed that although an understanding of comparative advantage is critical to understanding and formulating international strategies, one must never lose sight of the important difference between *comparative* advantage and potential *competitive* advantage. A well-known example is that of the global competition battle for domination of the world earth-moving equipment industry between Caterpillar (US) and its initially tiny rival Komatsu (Japan). Throughout the 1950s, 1960s and 1970s Komatsu skilfully built up its position against an unwary Caterpillar which then dominated over 50 per cent of world market share in that industry. By exploiting significantly lower comparative costs in raw materials (steel – 30 per cent cheaper than US prices) and labour (60 per cent cheaper than US prices), it gradually undermined the classic differentiation strategy pursued by Caterpillar, i.e. premium pricing for perceived high levels of quality, reliability and service. These latter (reliability and service) rather than price, were the key purchasing criteria for customers for earth-moving equipment. In an industry where one large piece of equipment could cost $1 million, it was the threat of lost 'downtime' and the possible disruption of scheduling on major construction projects that was the overwhelming anxiety for managers. No wonder customers were prepared to pay high prices for reliability – and Caterpillar was very successful.

The situation gradually changed as Komatsu used a time window in the 1960s, provided for it by MITI (the Japanese Ministry for International Trade and Investment) which had refused permission for Caterpillar to begin production in the Japanese domestic market and had instead licensed a Japanese joint venture between International Harvester (IH – a US rival) and Komatsu for the production of earth-moving equipment (EME) in Japan. Komatsu used this opportunity to embark on a series of dramatic quality improvement programmes,

••▶

cont.

beginning with its lowliest product – the backhoe. It learned rapidly from IH's technology. Eventually it bought out IH's technology licences very cheap when that company was strapped for cash in the early 1970s. However, its greatest success lay in its programme of continuous internal improvement which turned it from a domestic supplier of such poor quality that Japanese domestic firms would not buy from it, into a rival which could match and occasionally exceed Caterpillar quality, but at much reduced prices. This had the effect of destroying Caterpillar's sources of competitive advantage, since it could no longer justify its 20 per cent price premium on the basis of significantly higher quality. As worldwide customers gradually grew to trust Komatsu's quality, Caterpillar was required to reduce prices to match Komatsu. It was unable to do this easily or quickly, since not only had the seemingly effortless dominance of its market persisted for 30 years, rendering the company relatively inefficient in its internal operations, it was also suffering from comparative cost disadvantage in labour and raw material costs compared to Komatsu. This had not mattered while Komatsu was a poor supplier of unreliable products but became very problematic indeed when Komatsu was able to match both Caterpillar's quality and product range.

Another aspect of international competition exemplified in this case was the role of government intervention. Not only did Komatsu benefit from MITI's support in blocking Caterpillar entering Japan at a critical time, but this should be contrasted with the bad luck experienced by Caterpillar in the 1980s when the then American President Ronald Reagan banned all USA firms from involvement in the Alaskan pipeline project – the biggest construction project in the world at that time. That intervention gave Komatsu a golden opportunity for a prestigious shop-window to demonstrate the reliability of its products under difficult geographic conditions, at the end of which all remaining industry doubts had been removed.

Of course, the situation did not remain static and Caterpillar fought back vigorously. It had received a tremendous cultural shock in experiencing five consecutive years in deficit in the late 1980s/early 1990s. It embarked on a draconian series of worldwide plant evaluations resulting in some closures while only those evaluated as most efficient were retained and provided with considerable further investment and upgrading of technology and systems. It has continued to have persistent labour relations problems and difficulties in implementing flexible working practices against US trade

••▶

cont.

union opposition – practices which would have matched similar working practices that Komatsu had been benefiting from for decades. So the issue of relative labour costs for the two companies was not just one of absolute levels of wages but also working practices affecting the relative productivity of that labour, a much more fundamental issue since absolute levels of wages tend to be only a transitional cost advantage because wages rapidly rise with economic development in any industrializing economy. The same point may be made regarding fluctuations in exchange rate differentials. The situation in the late 1990s sees the two companies still dominating the world market for earth-moving equipment. Caterpillar has regained a proportion of its lost market share and become a much more efficient company as a result of Komatsu's efforts. Komatsu has consolidated its position as the industry's world number two, with a consistent annual world market share of over 25 per cent.

Source: Compiled by authors from various press articles. ■

Komatsu certainly benefited from significantly lower comparative costs in raw materials (steel 30 per cent cheaper than US prices) and labour (60 per cent cheaper than US prices). However, it is important to draw lessons from this example about the difference between comparative advantage and potential competitive advantage in international strategy. There is no doubt that Komatsu had comparative cost advantages over Caterpillar in terms of steel and labour, but these in themselves were not the source of Komatsu's changed competitive position or the source of Caterpillar's difficulties. These arose from Komatsu's strategic intent (Hamel and Prahalad, 1989) in the formulation and implementation of a viable long-term strategy to establish itself in world markets. It was this which enabled existing sources of comparative advantage to support international competitive advantage.

Industry structure

Although the theory of comparative costs still underlies some current trade as it did in classical times, a modern theory of international strategic management must account for the changes that have taken place in the pattern of international business since the eighteenth century. Industry structure in most areas bears little resemblance to the perfect competition paradigm implicitly underlying the theory of comparative costs.

The model of industry structure given in Figure 2.2 demonstrates the amount of variation industries face in the forces influencing them. The model (adapted from Porter's (1980) five forces framework) indicates that an attractive industry, to an incumbent firm, is one in which the five forces are all low in power. An unattractive industry is one where they are high in power. For example, in developed countries, the mini-cab industry is relatively unattractive in most urban areas for the following reasons. Competition is very strong as there are many other mini-cars touring cities only able to charge the going rate and with no differentiating ability. The existence of substitutes is high in the form of official taxi services (such as black cabs in London; yellow cabs in New York), trains, bicycles, private cars and walking. There are few barriers to entry so if profits became high, any reasonably enterprising person could enter the market and undercut rates. Only supplier and customer powers are relatively low, which enables the cab drivers to at least make a living.

At the other end of the scale, the pharmaceutical industry is very attractive to a company with a patented cure for cancer, or any other major disease. Substitutes are limited and entry barriers are very high, for example from high research and development (R&D) costs, so the threat of new entrants is relatively low, although there is increasing competition from generic drugs and the potential for substitutes from the emergent biotechnology sector, and some modest growth in market share for 'alternative' therapies such as

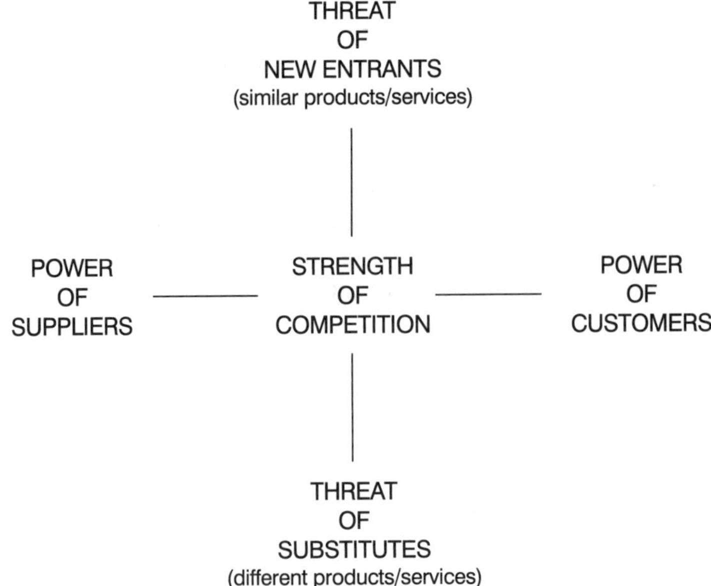

Figure 2.2 The competitive arena. *Source:* Adapted from Porter (1980)

acupuncture or Chinese medicines. There are strong international competitors and concentration in the industry is continuing, with ever-larger mergers (Smith Kline Beecham, Glaxo Wellcome, etc.) often between international firms. Competition is, however, constrained within particular clusters of diseases such as bronchial or viral, and supplier power and customer power are mostly low. Customer power is increasing somewhat as governments in advanced economies struggle to contain spiralling healthcare costs and as hospitals, medical practitioners and insurance companies become gradually more vertically integrated to enlarge their bargaining power, as in the American system of Health Management Organizations (HMOs). Nevertheless, despite such industry developments, pharmaceutical companies can still expect to make extremely good profits in the developed economies.

The attractiveness of an industry to an incumbent firm will be dependent upon the power of each of the five industry forces in Figure 2.2 and the strength of a company's position in relation to them internationally, just as it is in a national context. In an international context, in addition to the distortions provided by governments, e.g. through tariffs and other forms of protection, there are also additional factors of production to complicate the picture still further. These 'advanced factors' are more relevant than the classical basic factors in determining international competitive advantage. Typical advanced factors are human resources, physical resources, knowledge resources, capital resources and infrastructure, as referred to briefly in Chapter 1. We will now discuss these advanced factors in more detail.

In later work focusing on sources of national competitiveness, Porter (1990, 1998) outlines those particular 'advanced' factors that need to be stressed in the international context. The keys to international competitiveness have become more than the traditional factors of production. As we shall see, these 'advanced factors' have a claim to greater importance in the modern world than the traditional factors and it is these which are of greater relevance to international strategy. The overall effect of these advanced factors is to explain why the 'perfect market' model of an economy does not work in practice.

Internationally mobile factors of production

Land may still be immobile but its ownership may shift from that of the nation in which it exists to a multinational corporation owned and run offshore. Labour is becoming increasingly mobile in a globalizing world. Well-qualified professionals from India or eastern Europe migrate to wealthier countries for employment in pursuit of a higher standard of living or simply a different lifestyle. Similarly, the 'brain drain' of doctors, scientists and academics from the UK in the 1970s and to a lesser extent in the 1990s, illustrates the increasing willingness of individuals with scarce skills to seek better career opportunities, better working environments or resources, or to escape high taxation areas for lower taxed ones. Recent developments have emphasized that improving communications, homogenizing lifestyles, the growth of the English-speaking world and the rise of multinational companies employing international executives equally at home in any of the Triad regions, i.e. USA, Europe or Japan (Ohmae, 1985) have made the immobility of labour, at least at executive level, a thing of the past. Declining capital barriers between nations has also led major companies to be able to trawl the world to raise capital at the best rates.

Specific and fast changing technology

Technologies are fast changing and very specific in the modern world. In many industries, such as electronics, telecommunications or software, no sooner does a technology become widely adopted than another one appears on the horizon to challenge it. It is also impossible to protect technologies despite the use of patents and copyright. These give only temporary protection while imitators catch up and attempt to improve the technology still further or use the information published in the patent registration to create marginally redesigned alternatives. Largely for these reasons, an equilibrium condition is rarely reached in any widely traded industries.

Monopoly power

Monopoly power is the ability to fix prices above marginal costs and to maintain them successfully at that level. The traditional international trade model does not allow for monopoly power in the hands of MNCs. In a market where monopoly power exists, which means all advanced economies to some extent, each product has something of a market of its own and is only imperfectly substitutable for a competitor product. As a result, the producer has some discretion in setting his price and is not in the position of having to accept the externally determined price, as might be the case with commodity products such as oil or wheat, which have no distinctive brand characteristics. The consequence of this is a distortion of international trade to the advantage of the monopolist. Of course in global markets, monopoly power is likely to survive for less time than in more restricted markets, due to the larger number of potential suppliers.

Mobility barriers

These may take the form of entry barriers, exit barriers or any barriers that inhibit the movement of companies from one strategic group to another. McGee and Thomas (1986, 1989) define a strategic group as a cluster of firms within an industry following similar generic strategies and having similar market positioning. Such mobility barriers are amongst the 'five forces' identified by Porter

(1980) as determining the intensity of competition in an industry. The most powerful mobility barriers are those that are difficult or impossible to imitate, for example know-how, market leader brand names or strategic assets such as the art and palaces of Venice (for a discussion of strategic assets see Amit and Schoemaker, 1993; Kay 1993). Other barriers that inhibit new entrants, and that exist in most industries, are such factors as access to distribution, learning curve, scale and scope advantages, government regulation, and so forth.

Branded products

The classical trade theory does not allow for the effects of brand names. Brands become powerful because customers lack the skills to judge between competing products on the basis of their perceived qualities. They therefore choose a brand that they know and respect, since they believe that the company owning that brand will stand behind the product in the event of its failure, and furthermore that the company in question is unlikely to field an unreliable product. By definition, customers trust successful brands. This leads to a market distortion as customers develop an over-commitment to a particular branded product or service, rather than to its similar rivals. The effect of this is similar to the creation of monopoly power.

These 'advanced' factors of production therefore provide sources of comparative advantage in global markets for companies operating in countries which may be deficient in the classical basic factors of production. Such an analysis goes some way towards explaining how countries such as Japan or Korea are able to compete very successfully in world markets against countries like the USA, which are far better endowed in classical terms.

Industry clusters: the 'diamond' framework

Porter (1990) has incorporated his five-forces framework into an additional framework for the analysis of international industry competitiveness. This takes the form of a 'diamond', as shown in Figure 2.3. This model blends the five forces with the advanced factors of production already identified, and which Porter sees as largely responsible for the comparative advantage of a nation, or more accurately, of any strong industry clusters within that nation.

What he means by an industry cluster is: 'geographic concentrations of interconnected companies and institutions in a particular field. Clusters encompass an array of linked industries and other entities important to competition.' (Porter, 1998, p.78).

He gives examples such as the California wine cluster or the Italian leather fashion cluster. The Porter diamond can be illustrated by considering the example of Benetton in Box 2.2.

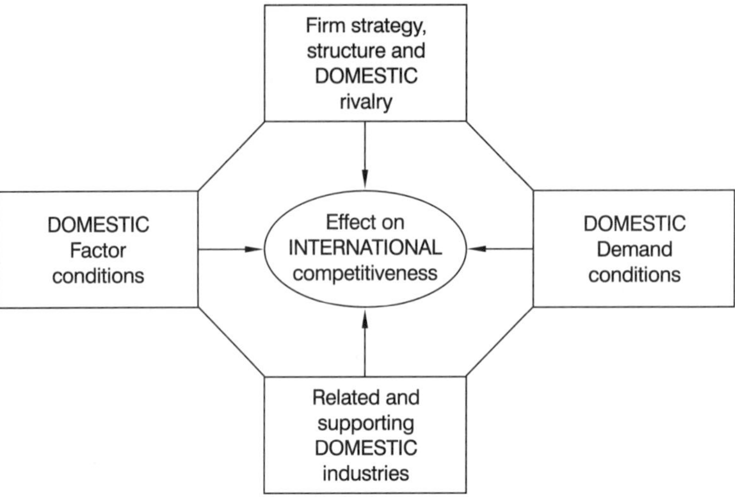

Figure 2.3 An adapted Porter 'diamond'

Box 2.2 The Benetton Diamond

Domestic factor conditions

The textile industry is a historic industry in Italy with hundreds of years of specialized skill and experience to draw on. Benetton is not just able to use cheap labour in a poor part of Italy, but also highly skilled and experienced cheap labour.

Domestic demand conditions

The Italians as a nation are amongst the most sophisticated customers in the world of fashion. As such they provide a demanding and critical marketplace for Benetton's designs. If you can survive as a fashion retailer in Italy you are likely to have a product that will survive in other international markets.

Related and supporting domestic industries

Italy has a national cluster of very strong industries both in the fashion industry itself, with its numerous designer labels, fashion houses and high priests of the Milan fashion shows, but also in many related industries such as leather goods, shoes, handbags, belts, luggage and furniture. All these industries share common factors such as high design skills and knowledge of materials. There is

••▶

cont.

also a strong network of largely family-owned intermediate supporting industries to provide an efficient infrastructure for the fashion industry.

Firm strategy, structure and domestic rivalry

Items for consideration in this part of the diamond are the five forces industry analysis issues. Here the point Porter wishes to make is that firms located in very competitive industries with high levels of national rivalry are the ones most likely to do well in international markets. Those with few or no national rivals are unlikely to be as efficient or as responsive to customer requirements. They may, nevertheless, survive and prosper within a relatively protected domestic marketplace, but are unlikely to perform strongly internationally. Benetton is located in an overcrowded domestic fashion market, from whose competitive rigours it will benefit as an international firm.

Source: Authors. ■

The Porter diamond is therefore seen as a tool for analyzing the potential of a company, within a given industry, for achieving international success. Porter (1990, 1998) suggests that internationally successful firms are most likely to be those that operate in strong domestic diamonds.

Rugman and D'Cruz (1993) extend the Porter diamond to demonstrate, by means of their concept of the 'double diamond', that successful MNCs do not need to operate solely from strong national diamonds. They can access other countries' diamonds, particularly those in Triad countries and thereby configure their productive assets to give themselves comparative advantage even if their home country lacks it. The authors point out that this is how successful companies operating from Canada succeed. They leverage their productive capacity off the strong US diamond.

Economic paradigms

The economic model of international trade developed between the world wars provides a variant of the traditional comparative cost Ricardo model described in Chapter 1. It tells us that trade reflects an interaction between the characteristics of countries and of the production technologies of different goods. Countries will therefore export goods whose production is intensive in the factors with which they are abundantly endowed, e.g. countries with a high capital:labour ratio will export capital intensive goods. Such a theory would suggest that countries with abundant factors relevant to industrial goods would normally export to less developed agriculturally based economies and import food products from them. This seems theoretically plausible.

Despite such theoretical plausibility, this is not how the pattern of international trade has evolved. In general, the main trading partners of industrially developed economies are other rather similar industrially developed countries. Table 2.1 shows such trade inter-dependency for the countries of the EU. Part of the reason for this must be that only developed countries have the wealth to import expensive capital and consumer goods; but that is not the only reason.

The table records an index ranging from 0.00 where one country exports a product and only imports other products, to 1.00 where there is complete two-way trade in the product range. Generally the more products are undifferentiated the more comparative cost theory operates effectively, so that the country with the resource abundance does the exporting and hence has a low index in the table. For branded products, as we have already explained, comparative advantage may lose some of its importance as customers buy brands for a variety of reasons not all of which are to do with externally testable value. Thus intra-industry trade becomes more significant.

Often nowadays, tariffs have been largely removed between geographically closely related countries such as the EU. Where this is the case, the gains from trade arise less from the exploitation of different factor endowments, than from the advantages arising from brand name specialization and resultant brand marketing, with the consequent reduction in comparative unit costs through the economies of scale and scope that a larger international market allows.

In present day international trade, brand marketing is one of the key factors for success. With the close communication that radio, television and travel provides, a brand developed successfully in one country may instantly have the key to entering a new market and achieving immediate market share in relation to domestic rivals. Coca-Cola or Gillette, for example, are brands known worldwide and are instantly recognized and powerful brands in any new country they may wish to enter.

Table 2.1 Reciprocity index of intra-industry trade in the EU

Primary commodities	0.58
All manufactures	0.80
– Road vehicles	0.70
– Household appliances	0.80
– Textiles	0.91
– Other consumer goods	0.80

Source: GATT International trade cited in Begg, Fischer and Dornbush (1994)

Table 2.2 Market structures – three different models

	Perfect competition	Monopolistic competition	Oligopoly
Assumptions	Complete information Homogeneous products Commodities Constant and rising costs	Incomplete information Proprietary products Differentiation Scale/Scope economies	Interdependence Collusion opportunities Differentiation Scale/Scope economies Few large rivals
Key characteristics	Price taking Comparative costs are key Brands unimportant	Price discretion Advanced factors are key Branded goods Limited substitutability	Price strategy interdependent Advanced factors are key Branded goods High advertising Game theory
Examples	Wheat Steel Minerals	Travel services Electronic goods Consumer goods Automobiles	Aircraft manufacture Major machine tools Defence manufacturers National newspapers

Our purpose in this chapter is to explain the relevance of economic theory to international strategy. Economic theory does have within it models which are able to explain modern international trade: however, three models are required rather than one. The characteristics of these three different models are given in Table 2.2. This is important since so much of international trade is based not on the comparative costs of a perfect market, but on the monopolistic competition power of MNCs and the strength of brand marketing to differentiate products that might otherwise be sold purely on the basis of their costs.

Perfect competition

The classical theory of international trade has underlying it sometimes implicit assumptions of perfect competition. This abstract and idealized form of economic model assumes perfect rationality, complete information, homogeneous products, profit maximization, and that firms cannot fix prices, but have to accept the 'market price'. Such a model is useful in the analysis of food and other agricultural commodities, e.g. rice, potatoes or wheat, or indeed any other commodity product that defies branding. These products will sell on a world market based on their comparative costs. Their price will only in reality be distorted by transport costs and by the intervention of governments aiming to prop up prices to support their farming industry. The Common Agricultural Policy (CAP) of the EU is a current example of the way in which governments can distort agricultural prices that would otherwise be governed by the laws of supply and demand in close to perfectly competitive conditions.

Monopolistic competition

A monopoly is a market in which only one company is able to do business. This may be because the government gives that company and none other a licence to trade in particular goods, e.g. a television franchise; or it may be that only one company has access to a particular good, e.g. state-owned utility companies such as electricity, water or telephone services, which, unless privatized, are mostly monopolists within their geographical areas. In world trade however, monopolies are difficult to sustain due to the existence of a large number of governments and a wide variety of at least imperfectly substitutable resources.

In addition, much international trade takes place in industrial branded goods for which the perfect competition paradigm is not only useless, but positively dangerous. It must not therefore be used as a basis for strategy formulation. Internationally traded industrial goods and consumer goods generally take place in conditions of at least monopolistic competition. Let us consider the implications of this.

Monopolistic competition (Chamberlain, 1939) is the name given by economists to that form of imperfect competition that takes place between branded goods produced by competitive companies supplying similar needs, but which are regarded by consumers as substitutes only to a limited extent. A case in point might be the keen devotee to Coca-Cola who would only reluctantly accept Pepsi as an adequate substitute if very thirsty, despite their obvious similarities.

Under monopolistic competition perfect knowledge is not assumed, so advertising can affect the strength of demand. Consumers are still assumed to be rational in their choices, but with the seducing effects of advertising it is possible to act rationally by buying a product in response to its perceived qualities, rather than any actual superior qualities of that good. This gives firms the power to determine the price of their goods within a range limited by the acceptability in the market of their nearest competitive good (e.g. margarine or butter). They have then a market niche in which they have power by virtue of their committed customers. They can choose prices then to some extent, and are not therefore governed by the 'market price'. They are therefore able to develop the size of their production units beyond that possible in a commodity market by developing brands, which give them a specialized market. It may be said that they control 100 per cent of the market share for their brand and are only vulnerable to the extent that the market is willing to accept other products as substitutes for theirs. Thus, they are able to reduce their unit costs through economies of scale, and if they are multi-product companies often economies of scope as well.

Scale economies arise through a number of technological factors that make it cheaper in unit cost terms to produce a large amount rather than a small amount of a product. Scope economies come about because once one product has been produced and marketed, some of the factors needed for its production and marketing, such as its brand name, can be used at relatively little additional cost for a second product. A third factor, namely the experience curve, aids this cost reduction process even further. Under the influence of this process, costs reduce with cumulative production of a product as producers develop better and better ways of producing a product of a given quality. Table 2.3 illustrates some of the possible varieties of scope economies and of the sources from which they may be derived. We have deliberately used as examples in Table 2.3 some of the companies that we will be discussing in various chapters of this book. The scope economies arising from the use of common distribution channels by Gillette has already been discussed in Chapter 1; and the advantages of flexible production of multiple products in relation to Komatsu in Chapter 2.

Economies of scale and scope and the experience curve thus enter into the competitive picture and enable unit costs to fall as output increases, either in volume terms or in respect to product range. This may act as a countervailing force to comparative cost theory, if the less well endowed countries are able to achieve sufficiently high levels of sales. It could enable countries poorly endowed with appropriate factors of production to match, or even improve upon, unit cost levels of better endowed countries.

We have therefore explained how scale, scope and experience effects can and do enable large companies to succeed internationally even when they operate

Table 2.3 Sources of scope economies

	Product range	Market spread
Shared physical assets	Factory automation with flexibility to produce multiple products (Caterpillar, Komatsu)	Global brand name (American Express, Philips)
Shared downstream activities	Using common distribution channel for multiple products (Matsushita, Gillette)	Servicing multinational customers worldwide (Citibank, Hewlett-Packard)
Shared learning	Sharing R&D in computer and communications business (ISS)	Pooling knowledge developed in different markets (Cap Gemini Sogeti)

Source: Adapted from Ghoshal (1987)

within an economy not well endowed on a comparative cost basis. One of the effects of the increased globalization of world markets is that the bigger the market, the bigger the opportunity for the company. Firms have contributed to this process by seeking increased market size. Under these circumstances, market share opportunities are limited only by market size and not by costs. That is what Teece, Pisano and Shuen (1997) mean by the dynamic capabilities of firms within a dynamic marketplace. There is no 'natural' equilibrium in a modern world market. The only limit is the total size of the potential market, as for example when every possible business and home user of a computer has bought Microsoft's Windows 97 or its later versions. Conceptually, there is no definite limit to potential economies of scale for firms, especially in knowledge-based products and services. In the modern world economy, ever faster technological change seems, in some markets, to lead to a situation in which marginal costs continue to decline with increasing output. With ever declining unit costs there can be no equilibrium, since such a state is only reached when the revenue from selling an extra good is no more than the extra cost of making it. and it is no longer profitable to attempt to sell one more unit. In a dynamic theory of monopolistic competition, continuously changing technology needs to be accepted as a realistic assumption, and therefore the existence of equilibrium in such markets becomes questionable. Turbulence is a more realistic basic assumption.

Products internationally traded under monopolistic competition conditions currently include automobiles or electronic goods. Indeed monopolistic competition applies in all areas where there are many sellers of branded products with only partially acceptable substitutes, such that each player has some, but only limited, power to set prices. Since advertising is also able to distort demand, it too is therefore a powerful weapon in such competition.

Oligopoly

Whilst monopolistic competition is limited by the size of the market, oligopolistic competition is limited by the actions of relevant rival firms. An oligopoly is a market where a small number of competitors feel themselves constrained more by the actions of their rivals than by those of their customers. It is monopolistic competition with a significantly reduced field of competitors. This third form of competition applies in international trade where there are so few global players that the predominant concerns of each are with the possible behaviour of its rivals, with the threat of new entrants and with the risk of substitutes emerging through new technology or change in consumer taste.

Under conditions of oligopoly neither the comparative cost requirements of generous factor endowments nor the power of scale, scope or experience curve economies to reduce costs, nor the power of advertising to increase demand, become the primary concern of international strategists. Although these latter two factors clearly will still have a place in these strategic calculations, the primary concern becomes being able to second-guess rivals.

Aircraft manufacture is a good example of such an oligopoly where Airbus Industrie, Boeing/McDonnell Douglas need to keep a keen eye on each other's actions if they are to prosper. An effective understanding of the principles of game theory therefore becomes a critical skill of the strategist under oligopoly. They need to guess correctly what a rival's response to a price change will be, to understand when a new entrant should be accommodated rather than driven out and when a rival should be colluded with, either implicitly or explicitly, rather than fought in cut-throat fashion. Oligopoly is seen to have emerged out of monopolistic competition when competitors in a global market have become so few that their primary concerns become each other's actual and potential actions, rather than solely the changes in the market.

Summary

Clearly then international trade and its changing nature has played a critically important role in the economic development of the world, and in the power relationships between nations. It is important to understand therefore how it came about in the first place, and why the greatest economic benefit does not inevitably derive from independent local firms serving their local populations, without MNCs being able to find a source of competitive and comparative advantage in relation to them. We do not live in a world of small firms producing according to their comparative advantage in factor cost, exporting their surplus production and importing products that they are less well endowed to produce. Rather we live in a world of MNCs, which we have defined as single corporate entities selling on a global scale, with activities in many parts of the world, and operating generally in monopolistic competition conditions. MNCs carry out global strategies which involve either producing standardized products with minor variations and marketing them in a similar fashion around the world, or, where appropriate, adjusting these products or services to local needs, tastes and cultures. MNCs source assets and activities on an optimal cost basis, only selling in countries where at least break-even can be achieved and employing contestability[1] principles to this end wherever possible. Modern MNCs that

[1] A contestable market is one in which a firm can enter and exit at will costlessly (Baumol *et al.*, 1982). Such markets may well be more common than is normally allowed if one considers MNCs with existing products deciding whether or not to operate in an $n+1$ country when n is already a large number. If so, prices in that potentially contestable country will be influenced not by existing players, but by the price necessary to prevent newly entering MNCs.

carry out such global strategies differ from those of earlier times in that, as will be described in Chapters 5, 6, 7 and 8, they work with a shared knowledge base, a common set of values, and an agreed set of priorities and performance measures. Given these conditions, they may be organized into a relatively decentralized network of companies.

3

Regional strategy

This chapter will explore issues concerning the formation of regional trading blocs, together with an appreciation of the impact of regionalization on the formulation and implementation of international strategies. Regionalization may have its roots in political and economic factors, but it has major consequences on the dynamic evolution of both industries and firms. Discussion will include the 'triad' and also the potential for not three, but five, six or seven massive world trading blocs in the near future: an emerging 'hub-and-spoke' structure for international trade. Regionalization may be viewed as a stepping-stone on the way to full globalization, or as an entirely different construction of resources and trading partners and patterns. It is possible to make a case for globalization as the obsolete concept with regionalization emerging as the dominant form, rather than the other way round. It is equally possible for regional trading blocs to be viewed as problematic barriers to the further evolution of world trade.

'The Triad'

Regional strategies are of increasing significance for multinational firms planning their international strategies. Any discussion about regional strategy is initially based on observations of the gradual evolution of trading blocs in the world's most economically developed regions: Europe, Asia and North America. These three regions have become known as 'the Triad', a term popularized by Kenichi Ohmae (1985) and illustrated in Figure 3.1. Most discussions about world trade and regional trade accept the existence of the Triad as a fact and many aspects of the internal management practices of MNCs reflect this. For example, MNCs employ international executives who are expected to relocate between, and feel equally at home operating within, any of the three major regional trading blocs of the Triad. Some MNCs, such as SKF, the Swedish world leader in bearings manufacture, conducts its internal financial reporting in three world currency zones reflecting the Triad trading zones, denominated in dollars, yen and German marks respectively.

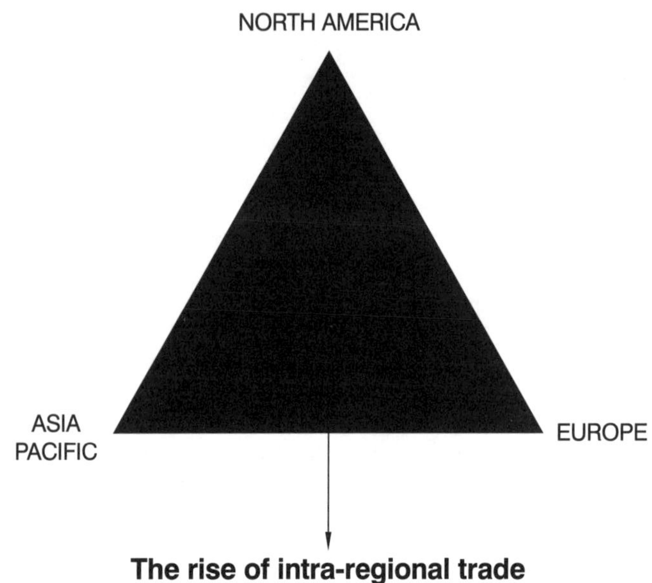

Figure 3.1 'The Triad'

Causes behind the formation of regional trading blocs have consisted of a mixture of social, economic and political factors. Several macro-environmental changes have had far-reaching implications for both consumers and producers of goods and services. Socio-demographic change, higher incomes, smaller households, concern for health and environment, preference for greater choice and control, are developments which have been taking place at varying rates across the world and are viewed by many writers (Ohmae, 1989) as a driving force behind the emergence of cross-market segments, providing opportunities for more international strategies. For example, Ohmae (1985) spoke of the 'Californianization' of the young within the Triad, forming a massive lifestyle-related international consumer segment identifiable as such in totally different parts of the world. Other such identifiable global customer segments might include the business traveller or possibly even babies (since nappies/diapers for babies are a universally understood product with a universal customer and universal usage pattern). These constitute specific customer segments towards whom companies can direct specific products or services worldwide. The business traveller segment has been the basis of successfully targeted global services by airlines, car hire companies, hotel chains and financial service companies. The youth market has been targeted in clothing, media, music and leisure.

The effect of technology upon transparency of electronic information, global media and communications, has been instrumental in creating some discernible similarities between consumer tastes across geographical boundaries. Such influences on consumption patterns include art, films, clothing, television programmes, the Internet, ethnic foods, travel and popular music. Such developments are not confined to Organization for Economic Cooperation and Development (OECD) countries. In India, for example, the market for consumer durables, once confined to a very small number of wealthy families, has grown at an unprecedented rate, reflecting the rise of a large middle class, now estimated to stand at approximately 20 per cent of a total population of over 900 million. This means that a possible market of up to 200 million in India could afford to buy relatively sophisticated and expensive products such as consumer durables. Demand for international brands in India now makes it an attractive market for companies which already trade on a global basis. The relaxation of many of India's barriers to foreign trade and investment since 1992, has created a rapid expansion of multinational activity in the subcontinent.

The build-up of regional trading blocs: political and economic impact

Much recent management practice in international strategy has been aimed at restructuring and rationalization at a regional rather than a global level. This has reflected the build-up of regional trading blocs in the three major trading regions worldwide: NAFTA, the North American Free Trade Association; ASEAN and APEC in Asia-Pacific; and the European Union (EU).

Advantages accruing from international trading agreements include overall growth in international trade and political stability, policed by the World Trade Organization (WTO) – the successor to the General Agreement on Tariffs and Trade (GATT)). Moves towards the liberalization of international trade have gone hand-in-hand with this formation into larger and larger, and more and more, regional trading blocs. These two issues of overall growth in international trade and increased political stability will be discussed further.

The EU has expanded from its original six members after the end of World War Two, to reach 14 member countries by 1998, and has another 15 applications for membership outstanding for consideration from the countries of northern and eastern Europe, of whom a 'first tier' for early membership of six had been agreed by 1998. Much debate within the European Union has focused throughout the 1990s on the issue of what is called 'broadening versus deepening' of the EU. This is about the issues raised by a potential rapid doubling of membership ('broadening') and whether the EU ought not instead to concentrate first on internal issues for current members ('deepening'), such as making a success of its new currency the 'Euro'. Many of these potential new members, such as those from eastern Europe (e.g. Hungary,

Poland, the Czech Republic) represent a potential significant drain on the EU's social and welfare funds, away from claims of existing members, as well as creating economic and policy difficulties between EU members in such industries as agriculture. Nevertheless 'broadening' is to go ahead and is seen as one way of contributing to the stable adjustment and development of the post-USSR, post-Soviet bloc economies and hence the overall long-term stability of Europe as a whole.

An enlarged NAFTA (currently the USA, Mexico and Canada) may well gradually extend to include much of Central and South America. Already there are many trading agreements in place in South America, such as the Andean pact between Venezuela, Colombia and Bolivia, or the Mercosur Free Trade Association (FTA) between Brazil, Argentina, Uruguay and Paraguay. Since 1987, the USA has signed 16 'framework' agreements with Latin American countries. The groundwork exists for a Pan-American trading bloc embracing all the Americas: North America, South America and Central America. A Free Trade Area of the Americas (FTAA) has outline agreement between 34 countries in North and South America. Such a grouping would certainly contribute greatly to political stability across that geographic zone, which in itself would be likely to encourage a follow-on increase in investment and levels of trade. Indeed, by comparison with the 1970s when South America was mainly ruled by military dictatorships and its national economies suffered from hyperinflation, instability and debt, Mercosur is now the world's fourth largest integrated market and a child of the democratic governments now in place in its member countries. It has attracted steady inward investment from corporate and private investors with high but acceptable levels of risk. Mercosur has a (mostly) internal tariff-free zone between members and is some way to creating an integrated external customs union for 'outsiders'.

Evidence is mixed for the existence of a 'yen' bloc in Asia, centred around Japan, although the yen is used as a regional currency. Intra-regional trade between Japan, Hong Kong, South Korea, the five ASEAN countries (the Association of South-East Asian nations: Singapore, Malaysia, Indonesia, Philippines and Thailand), Australia and New Zealand, has grown to 43 per cent of the region's total exports reflecting Asia's high economic growth rates and trading opportunities of the 1980s until the mid-1990s. It also once again reflects a trend towards the growth of intra-regional trade. All of these growth rates for the Asia-Pacific region were severely damaged by turmoil in the capital markets and financial systems throughout South-East Asia in the late 1990s and in countries such as Thailand and Indonesia (previously regarded as 'tiger' economies) and even in Japan, the region's 'lead' economy, growth rates are expected to be tiny or even negative into the next century. This serves to illustrate some of the power of 'regionalization' and the interdependence of modern economies in development and trading terms. These groupings are captured in Figure 3. 2.

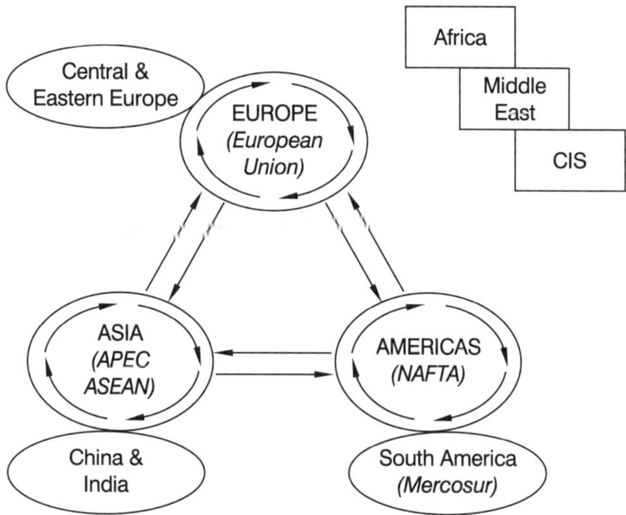

Figure 3.2 Regional trading blocs

Recipients of foreign direct investment (FDI) tend to be dominated by a Triad member in the same region e.g. Latin America by the USA, eastern Europe by the European Community (EU), Asia by Japan. Developing countries are thus under pressure to strengthen regional links or risk losing their place in the investment pecking order.

Figure 3.1 (given earlier) refers to 'the rise of intra-regional trade'. International trade and international investment are both exhibiting faster intra-regional than inter-regional growth. Consider, for example, Figure 3.3 which gives some data on the growth in intra-regional trade in Mercosur, the larger of the two South American trading blocs (the other is the Andean pact). As can be seen, intra-Mercosur trade has soared. From $4 billion in 1990, trade among the four members of Mercosur had more than tripled to $14.5 billion in 1995. The bulk of this has been accounted for by Mercosur's two largest members, Brazil and Argentina, who seem to have overcome historic mutual resentment and recognized their proximity and interests as natural trading partners. Between them they account for 97 per cent of Mercosur's GDP. Obviously, the currency and world stock markets turmoil in the last part of the 1990s and centring particularly on Brazil's ability to withstand massive deflationary pressures brought such growth to a halt, as elsewhere in the world, for a period.

Also worth noting, as Figure 3.4 demonstrates, this increase in intra-regional trade has led to a high level of trade dependency amongst Mercosur's members, particularly Uruguay and Paraguay.

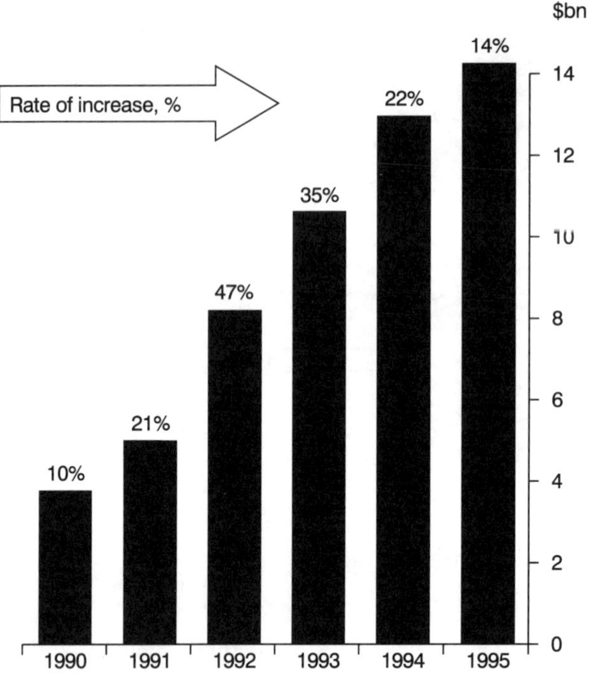

Figure 3.3 Growth in intra-regional trade in Mercosur 1990-95. *Source:* IMF, quoted in *The Economist*, 27 September 1996

This discussion of regional trading blocs has centred mainly on the three largest and best-established Triad blocs (NAFTA, EU and Asia-Pacific) with some attention to developments in South America. However, there are still many 'sleeping giants' that we have not yet discussed. They were all hinted at earlier in Figure 3.2. In terms of sheer size and potential, China and India both may in the near future constitute regional trading blocs of their own. Each market has the potential to dominate world trade in the next century. It makes little sense to consider a future China as a member of the Asian regional groupings. There is little to encourage such a development historically and anyway it would totally swamp the combined economies of all the other 'partners'.

Neither have we yet discussed Africa. In that context we may find it useful to reflect on the fact that each of the Triad blocs features a 'lead' economy: for NAFTA, the USA; for the EU, Germany; for Asia-Pacific, Japan. When Nelson Mandela took over as President of South Africa, managing an unexpectedly peaceful transition from white minority to black majority rule, there was a surge of optimism that Africa may have also found its 'lead' economy. South Africa was home to almost all of Africa's indigenous MNCs and

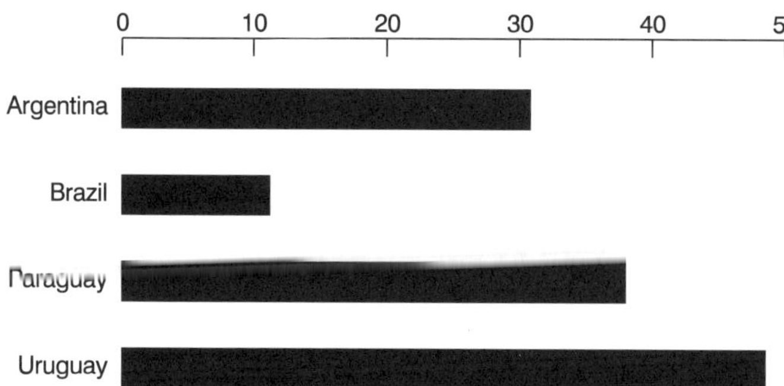

Figure 3.4 Degree of Mercosur trade integration with the other three as percentage of total trade, 1995. *Source:* IMF, quoted in *The Economist*, 27 September 1996

possessed a sophisticated financial infrastructure, despite severe damage inflicted by world economic sanctions during the apartheid era. Several years on, the optimism has faded, since most of Africa is again either embroiled in internal warfare or plagued by political instability, or both. Potential inward investors have once again been scared away by unacceptably high levels of risk, associated with unreliable government and political instability. The relationship between political stability and economic growth is thus demonstrated.

Regionalization vs globalization

> Proliferating Free Trade Areas have become a pox on the world trading system. (Jagdish Bhagwati, quoted in *The Economist* 18 October 1997)

Bhagwati, the economic policy adviser to GATT from 1991–93, argues that FTAs are not the same as free trade since free trade areas are, by definition, discriminatory rather than multilateral. The argument is that FTAs deny trading opportunities to 'outsiders' and, in addition to this, may cause 'trade diversion'. That means that instead of importing goods from countries that can supply most cheaply, members of FTAs are encouraged to buy from fellow members. Thus, rather than creating trade where there was none before, FTAs may divert it from efficient sources to inefficient ones. This distinction between trade creation and trade diversion is at the heart of thinking whether regional trading blocs enhance or reduce economic benefits. Even more important is the question of whether a world with a multitude of FTAs has overall achieved lower trade barriers and hence is moving towards a global freeing of trade. There is no doubt that the development ('proliferation') of regional trading blocs is not the same as unilateral non-discriminatory trade liberalization as achieved by successive GATT rounds of world trade negotiations in the past. It remains to be seen whether its successor (the WTO) may follow multilateralism in the future, possibly in a 'millennium' round of talks between all the 132 members of WTO (see Figure 3.5). This might achieve a broader approach and the necessary agreements about trade-offs between WTO members wearing their 'regional' rather than their 'global' hats.

Developments in regional strategy

Examples of developments in regional strategy include PepsiCo of the USA – a major operator of restaurants and provider of beverages and snacks internationally. It had given local divisional managers autonomy in managing their national businesses, to grow the local markets. In September 1994, the company announced that it was centralizing purchasing across all its various European businesses. By so doing, PepsiCo expected to save $100 million per annum, which represented 5 per cent of its annual operating costs of $2 billion. PepsiCo and other divisions, Pizza Hut and KFC, were identified as having many items in common, such as the large volumes of cardboard which Pizza Hut uses for its cartons and PepsiCo for its soft drinks trays. Volume savings are expected from sugar, cooking oil, flour, packaging materials and even advertising costs. If successful, these regional policies will be copied for North and South America and Asia-Pacific.

VISA International considers global TV advertisements to be inappropriate for their local markets worldwide. It does, however, utilize some 'regional' advertisements in the EMEA (Europe, Middle East and Africa) region. This consists of a basic 25-second commercial to which a VISA member company (such as a local bank) adds on a 5-second ending which promotes the individual bank within the overall VISA brand.

Nike is a US sports shoe and clothing manufacturing company which markets its products worldwide. In Europe it had traditionally utilized local national warehousing to supply retailers. In its very competitive industry sector Nike is now seeking to replace more than 20 national warehouses with one single European distribution centre located in Belgium. Developing a single European distribution hub follows the company's successful centralization of its American operations at a single hub in Memphis. Such regional concentration of warehousing and distribution are intended to help Nike reduce inventory, avoid duplication, stock a wider range of its products centrally, so reducing costs whilst improving availability to stores and customers.

The European insurance market has historically been highly fragmented. This has enabled large price differentials to flourish between national markets and has protected national providers. For example, a similar policy could cost three times in Portugal what it cost in France. Since 1994, the European

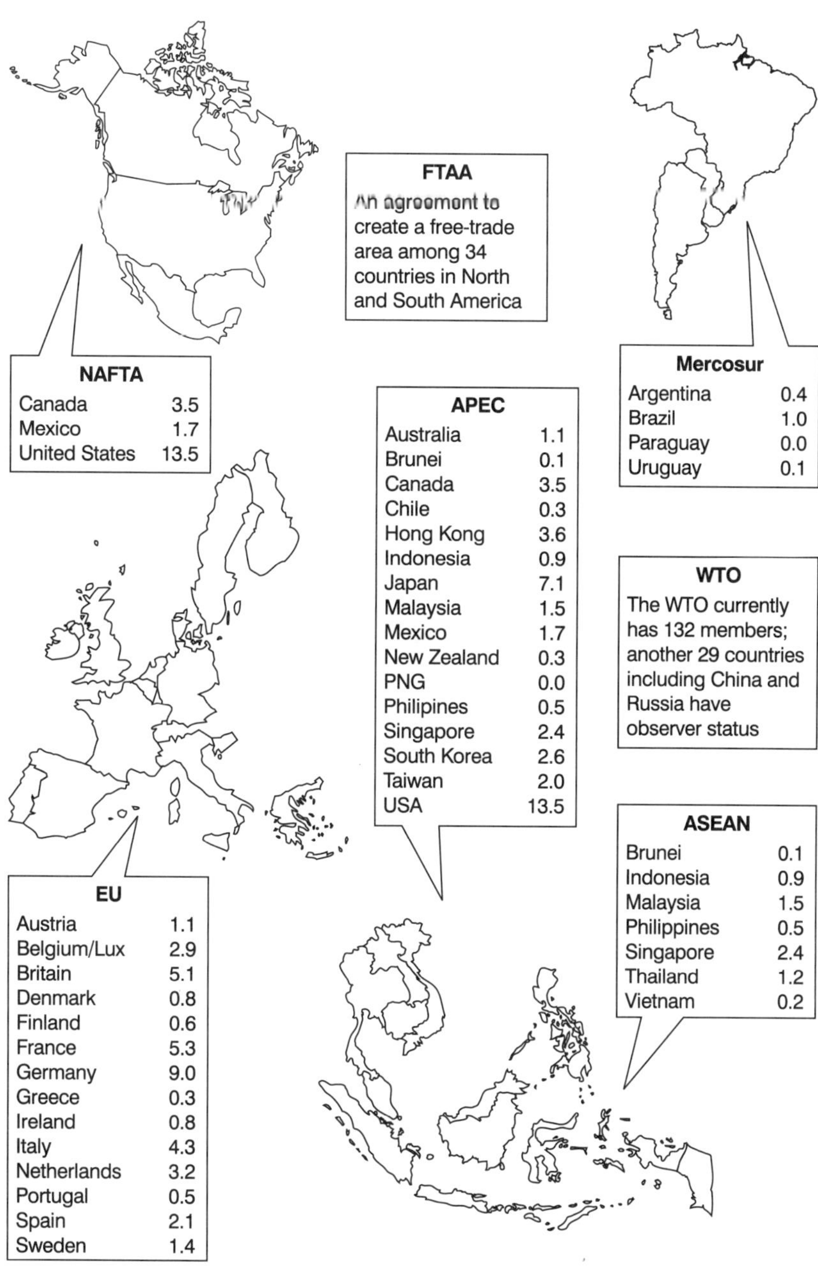

Figure 3.5 FTA percentage of total world trade in 1996. *Source:* IMF, quoted in *The Economist*, 12 October 1996

Union has developed a series of 'framework directives' which have gradually opened up the European markets to cross-border competition. These directives have brought about two basic changes: first, they allow companies to sell policies anywhere in Europe based on the regulations in their domestic market; second, they remove the need to submit cross-border policies to local offices for approval. The long-term impact of these changes is expected to be increased industry-wide competition undermining the hitherto protected position and profitability of some national champions.

Cross-border market penetration using lower-cost channels such as direct telephone sales has already begun. However, market differences such as local tax regimes, cultural preferences for different types of insurance products, legal factors and incidence of different types of claims will ensure that cross-border entrants will still have to meet country-specific requirements for the foreseeable future. Figure 3.6 shows some of these local market differences in the types and structure of distribution channels for financial services within Europe in the late 1990s. However, these types of remaining differences are not stopping some of the giants in European financial services such as Germany's Alliance and Italy's Generali from carefully exploring other European markets.

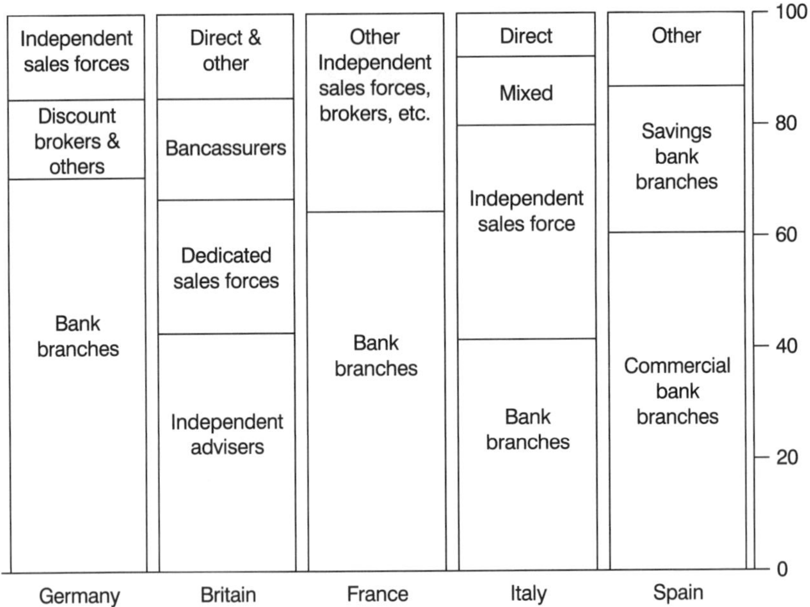

Figure 3.6 Sales channels for mutual funds in Europe. *Source:* Boston Consulting Group, 1997

Cultural homogenization and the emergence of global markets

There has been a long-standing and vigorous debate surrounding the validity of the argument that an increasing similarity exists between certain groups of consumers within global markets. The debate centres around the question of the desirability of standardization of products or services for broadly defined international market segments. The belief in consumer homogeneity is controversial. It coexists with the view that fragmentation rather than homogenization may more appropriately describe international consumer trends. Much discussion has taken place over the opportunities for, and barriers to, such standardization (Alden, 1987; Douglas and Wind, 1987; Kotler, 1985; Quelch and Hoff, 1986). It was triggered by Levitt (1983) and predicated on the convergence of markets, as a result of the types of economic and socio-cultural interdependencies across countries and markets discussed above. He argued that the new communications technologies are a key influence in the growing homogenization of markets, reducing social, economic and cultural differences, including old-established differences in national tastes or preferences. This process has meant that companies need to examine any growing similarities between consumer preferences.

Market segmentation based on lifestyle has been around for a long time (Sheth, 1983). However, the argument for global markets does not necessarily mean the end of market segments. It can mean instead that they expand to worldwide proportions. The retail chain Benetton has built its whole strategy on precisely these assumptions, as shown in Figure 3.7. Certainly there is some adaptation of such things as colour choice for different domestic markets, but such adaptation occurs around the standardized core of Benetton's 'one united product' for its target market segment worldwide. It sells 'active leisurewear' globally to 15- to 24-year-olds.

Globalization offers the advantage of economies of scale for a segmented marketing strategy. Considerable standardization of international marketing has occurred for some time. This does not necessarily mean providing the same product in all countries, but offering local adaptations around a standardized core. Just as Benetton balances standardization with some local adaptation, for example of its colours, so Pizza Hut protects the core elements of its brand by copyrighting its individual product brand names (such as Perfect Pizza). It also ensures standardization across markets by operating a strict specification of product ingredients. However, the Pizza Hut concept is adapted to suit local needs in differing ways. Some elements of the menu (such as desserts) will vary, as will store design, and even the way in which products are served to the customer. This illustrates the point made by Quelch and Hoff (1986) that the relevant issue in international marketing 'is not whether to go global but how to tailor the global marketing concept to fit each business'. Alden (1987) quotes the example of the American firm Johnson Wax and its early attempts to sell its

The Benetton Strategy

Rationale behind globalization

- European domestic markets are relatively small and a successful concept can reach saturation coverage fairly quickly.
- The development of 'lifestyle' based on clear segmentation of the target market is the perfect platform for global marketing.
- The success of 'lifestyle' retailing is indicative of similar international market segments.
- International IT systems provide the channel for fast response to shifts in consumer demand and risk-free low inventory.

The strategy

- Putting fashion on an industrial level.
- To develop one product line of sufficient breadth to accommodate through similar stores the particular needs of world markets: 'one united product'.

Putting the strategy into operation

- The offering: 'paletted' good design and colours of universal appeal.
- Innovative merchandizing: making space and inventory more productive.
- Control over worldwide store design and location, to further control other elements in the service concept.
- Information systems linked to factories does away with the need for inventory.
- Inventory risk elimination: produce to firm customer orders.
- Financial risk elimination: agency 'franchising' for capital investment in stores while retaining strategic control.
- Logistics network: rapid access to information on demand.
- Innovatory manufacture to allow 'customized' batch production in response to demand.

Figure 3.7 The Benetton strategy. *Source:* Compiled by authors from press reports

Pledge furniture polish in Japan. They found it to be unpopular with older Japanese consumers. After further market research it was discovered that the lemon scent in the polish reminded them of the smell of the toilet disinfectant which had been widely used in Japan in the 1940s. After the scent was changed, sales rose considerably.

The standardization/adaptation debate

The creation of regional trading blocs and the extent of international consumer homogeneity are central issues affecting the economics of all industries and therefore the most viable strategies of firms competing within those industries. They affect potential economies to be derived by companies from the way they structure their activities in research and development, sourcing, design, manufacturing, distribution and many aspects of marketing, both within and across trading blocs. The range and complexity of the factors involved suggest not only the potential benefits, but also the difficulties and limitations of global, or indeed regional, strategies. These issues will be returned to in Chapter 6 when we discuss the configuration of international activities by MNCs. Whilst the concept of configuration is concerned with the supply-side issues of the global and regional strategies of firms (i.e. where do we locate our various value chain activities for optimal efficiency), in this section we are concerned with market segments – the demand side of the equation. Is there a global customer or a regional (pan-European, pan-Asian) customer for this product or service?

The core of the standardization / adaptation debate in international strategy is the question of how far, if at all, it is appropriate to design, market and deliver standard products and services across national market boundaries, or the extent to which adaptation to local market requirements is mandatory. The debate raises important assumptions concerning the conditions for successful global or regional strategies: that global market segments exist; that global economies of scale exist; and that a distribution infrastructure is available to realize these potential economies of scale worldwide.

Douglas and Wind (1987) were early critics of the argument for standardization, calling it 'naive and oversimplistic'. Since then there have been waves of research and practice supporting globalization, 'glocalization' ('think global, act local') and transnational management (Bartlett and Ghoshal, 1989). The arguments in favour of global standardization, as initially stated by Levitt (1983), contained three assumptions:

1. That consumers' needs and interests are becoming increasingly homogeneous worldwide.
2. That people around the world are willing to sacrifice preferences for such things as product features, functions, and design, for high quality at low prices.
3. That substantial economies of scale in production and marketing can be achieved through supplying global markets.

There are, however, a number of problems associated with these propositions. First, this belief in consumer homogeneity is controversial and probably overstated. There is a lack of evidence of homogenization. As has already been discussed, significant differences still exist between groups of consumers across national market boundaries and it has been argued by managers and academics alike (Alden, 1987; Douglas and Wind, 1987; Kotler, 1985; Makhija *et al.*, 1997) that the differences both within and across countries are far greater than any similarities. Second, there has been a growth of intra-country fragmentation, leading to increased segmentation of domestic markets. Third, developments in factory automation allowing flexible, lower cost, lower volume, high variety operations are challenging the standard assumptions of scale economy benefits by yielding variety at low cost.

The argument put forward here is that such an approach to global strategies is oversimplified, focused on the benefits of standardization when the emphasis internationally is more complex, often encompassing global, regional and local simultaneously.

The advantages of complex global operations

Spreading operations across a number of different national markets can provide some opportunities to standardize the way in which the product or service is marketed to the consumer. Companies as diverse as Sony and Matsushita (both Japanese) in consumer electronics, Burger King (UK) and Kentucky Fried Chicken (KFC) (USA) in fast food, or Benetton (Italy) and IKEA (Sweden) in retailing, have developed their products and services to have universal appeal across global markets, allowing for more standardized marketing and distribution strategies for their products and services.

Substantial cost savings may be available. In advertising costs, for example, PepsiCo's savings from not producing a separate film for individual national markets has been estimated at $10 million per year. This figure is increased when indirect costs are added, for instance the speed of implementing a campaign, fewer overseas marketing staff, and management time which can be utilized elsewhere.

The restructuring of international supply chains for transportation and distribution has created opportunities for rethinking international logistics operations. Cost reductions, shorter journey times and dramatic technological developments in transportation, have together created new international markets for products which previously had no shelf-life beyond local consumption. Container systems which use computer-controlled temperature, humidity and atmosphere levels have extended the geographic scope for such products as fresh fruit or flowers, just as surely as international information systems have created transparent 24-hour trading in financial products.

Global or regional standardization of activities is utilized by practitioners at whatever points in their value chain advantages can be derived, although often falling short of global operations across all functions. Benefits are possible from globalization in any or all of the following: design, purchasing, manufacturing operations, packaging, distribution, marketing, advertising, customer service or software development. Globalization makes possible standardized facilities, methodologies and procedures across locations.

Companies may be able to benefit even if they are able to reconfigure in only one or two of these areas.

Such a contingent approach has long been recommended for product and market standardization, to allow flexibility between the two extremes of full global standardization and complete local market responsiveness. Indeed, both approaches may be used simultaneously to achieve the advantages to be had from global structuring of part of the product/service offering, whilst adapting or fine-tuning other parts of the same offering to closely match the needs of a particular local market. This process of combining the advantages of both global and local operations has become known as 'glocalization'.

The experience of KFC, an American international fast food chain, may illustrate the point. After its initial entry into the Japanese market KFC rapidly realized that it was necessary to make three specific changes to its international strategy. First, the product was of the wrong shape and size, since the Japanese prefer morsel-sized food. Second, the locations of the outlets had to be moved into crowded city eating areas and away from independent sites. Third, contracts for supply of appropriate quality chickens had to be negotiated locally, although KFC provided all technical advice and standards. After these adaptations to the product and the site, KFC have been successful in Japan. Similarly, Pampers disposable nappies (made by Procter & Gamble of the USA) were only successful in Japan after adapting by sizing downwards to accommodate smaller Japanese baby bottoms. McDonald's hamburger restaurants now serve Teriyaki burgers in Tokyo and wine in Lyon. Each of these local market adaptations of the core offering was critical. Yet the global strategy remained unchanged in its essentials. It is debatable therefore to what extent these companies are pursuing 'global' or 'regional' strategies.

Companies are also in danger of forgoing the benefits of differentiation from recognizing and capitalizing on country-specific and regional opportunities. In pursuing a global strategy, managers should not ignore the existence of regional and country-specific differences. Many successful product or service innovations have been the result of ideas observed elsewhere. A presence in international markets creates antennae for gathering market intelligence, mentioned by many international companies as one of the most important benefits of a varied international presence and a factor which is leading to a rethinking of over-centralized global operations (as with Matsushita of Japan discussed in Chapter 4) into regional groupings.

One of the most significant advantages of global trading is associated with size and spread of operations. Economies of scope and scale allow for greater efficiency in current operations (Chandler, 1990b). Economies of scale provide not just lower unit costs, but also potentially greater bargaining power over all elements in the company's value chain. Economies of scope can allow for the sharing of resources across products, markets and businesses. Such resources may be both tangible, such as buildings, technology or salesforces, or intangible, such as expert knowledge, teamworking skills and brands.

The globalization of brands

Branding is a useful illustration of economies of scope available from global strategies and the close relationship between global and regional strategies pursued by MNCs. Philips, the European consumer electronics and white goods manufacturer, merged its white goods business with US domestic appliance manufacturer Whirlpool in 1989. Whirlpool dual-branded its products Philips Whirlpool until 1992, when the Philips name was dropped. This approach was adopted in order to give European consumers enough time to become aware of the Whirlpool brand in association with Philips strong brand reputation. By 1992, Whirlpool's internal figures showed that awareness of its brand across Europe had reached 97 per cent of the Philips level. This was deemed sufficient to move on to the next phase of the strategy to benefit from rationalization of the global brand.

An increasing number of multinationals are standardizing their brands to send a consistent worldwide message and to take greater advantage of media opportunities by promoting one brand, one packaging and uniform positioning across markets. Rather than a patchwork quilt of local brands in local markets, the owners of international brands increasingly want simplified international brand portfolios. Many of these local brands have been nurtured lovingly over the long term by high advertising spend and careful handling and are often held in great affection by their local population. Despite this, they are likely to be swept away. A typical example of this occurred in the UK banking sector (see Box 3.1).

Box 3.1 The Demise of Access

Access was the local brand for MasterCard, but was virtually unknown in the rest of the world. The Access brand name had been invested in heavily in the UK market over many years with high-profile television advertising campaigns and slogans such as 'your flexible friend'. In 1996 MasterCard negotiated with the four UK clearing banks which owned a stake in it, to regain control, and rebranded the card as MasterCard. While Access was a strong brand in a national market, MasterCard is a global company wishing to build its global brand; this meant that the pressure for replacing Access became overwhelming.

Source: Compiled by authors from press articles. ■

Companies increasingly feel that they have to unite behind key brands and rationalize products, brands and the advertising agencies handling their accounts. Focusing on fewer strong brands is seen as the best way of coping with fierce competition, from other brands and private-label products, as well as getting the best value from expensive investments in advertising.

Another way in which issues of global branding are being felt is in the branding of companies themselves. A trend is observable as companies become established as MNCs rather than just as domestic market champions. Names that are felt to be too parochial or nationalistic are made more universally acceptable. Obvious candidates for such treatment have been previously state-owned enterprises so that British Telecommunications became BT, British Petroleum became BP, and the Korean chaebol Lucky Goldstar became the internationally unexceptionable LG. Similarly, the name AXA was chosen to cloak the French origin of this insurance MNC and thereby make it more regionally and globally acceptable.

Regional or global?

Few companies or industries lend themselves to 'naive' global strategies. All require some degree of adaptation to regional and national conditions. The international strategy agenda has been over-emphasizing standardization at the expense of adaptation and complexity. STAR TV provides a useful illustration of the need for market responsiveness (see Box 3.2).

Box 3.2 Guiding STAR

Local Asian markets have caused difficulties for Rupert Murdoch's News Corporation empire which owns the STAR TV satellite network. STAR claims to broadcast to about 53.7 million households across Asia and to have a viewing audience estimated at about 220 million. News Corps' strategy, after taking control of the network in 1993, was to aim at the top 5 per cent of television viewers by providing English-language programmes. This strategy was soon abandoned in favour of supplying programmes broadcast in the local language. Its original global segmentation strategy was based on the assumption that a homogeneous television product could be sold across Asia both to advertisers and to an elite end-consumer. However, it quickly became evident that advertising depends on ratings and ratings depend on providing programmes that people in Asia

cont.

want to watch. It is this commercial logic that has driven STAR's transformation to local programming, in local languages and a regional management structure.

Source: Compiled by authors from press articles. ■

Managing successful market entry into the emergent Chinese market has been causing similar problems while firms become more familiar with local adaptation requirements. China is consuming more and more Western products: breakfast cereals, batteries and bubble gum sales are booming. Yet the emerging China market has presented a curious set of market research problems. For example, such standard procedures as setting up and tracking panels of shops or consumers, are rendered highly problematic by continuous sample change such as shops closing down and re-opening. In an area like Shanghai they are rebuilding a block a week. Areas are changing physically month by month. In addition to these market structure issues, it is difficult to judge the positioning for each product. For example, chewing gum is so popular because it is one of the few Western pleasures within the financial reach of Chinese parents. Packaging and distribution channels are also unique. For example, hair shampoos are sold predominantly in sachets rather than in bottles, because people are paid weekly and prefer to make smaller weekly expenditures. The most favoured distribution outlet for shampoo is barber shops rather than grocery stores, since going to the hairdresser in China is a social occasion.

Other common problems concern cultural differences, regulatory requirements and human resource issues like recruitment, retention and approach to decision-making. China is an extremely bureaucratic country. If a company wishes to operate in five different provinces, it needs to establish a company in each of the five provinces, each of which will require a great number of permits and approvals to proceed. Income tax returns must be submitted monthly in most provinces and the company's accounts usually must be approved by the government's accountants. Even company computer systems need approval by the authorities. High quality technical skills are readily available, but financial, business and managerial skills are not.

Similarly, McDonald's took 14 years to extend its chain to Russia, not only because negotiations with the Soviet authorities at the time were notoriously slow, and fundamentals, like legal ownership of outlets, difficult to establish, but also because no supply chain existed for sourcing of the raw materials for hamburgers and french fries. The company had to go to extraordinary lengths to create a reliable supply chain of appropriate quality ingredients for its product. These included not only agreements with farm co-operatives to grow the right strain of potato needed for McDonald's french fries, but even importing American bull sperm to ensure that Russian beef herds yielded the correct beef quality expected in the hamburgers. Even on opening, aspects of the offering were almost incomprehensible to the local customers, such as the menu itself, since the notions of choice and availability were not familiar to the Russian consumer at that time.

Inadequate understanding of the Canadian and French markets by Marks & Spencer, a UK multiple chain, led to several years of poor trading, and possible overpayment for its purchase of Brooks Brothers in the US. In 1990, the collapse of the UK speciality retailer Sock Shop due to inappropriate locations and massive debt incurred in funding a rapid expansion in the US, showed the dangers of attempting to rework a successful domestic concept internationally. One of the most important lessons learnt by retailers who operate internationally is that formats, merchandising, store design and store location have to be customized to local conditions to achieve success. Even Benetton, the Italian global leisurewear retailer, offers a larger range of colour combinations in its Asia-Pacific stores than in its European ones. And to respond to specific demands of each national market, McDonald's hamburger chain began to provide tea on the menu of its outlets in the UK and wine in France.

The learning to be derived from these company war stories of what standardization or adaptation meant for them in each situation is to understand the relationship between global, regional and local. It is not a matter of trade-offs, but of achieving the balance between interdependencies. Regional trading blocs and regional strategy are part of the current pattern of international trade. As such they are amongst the factors driving the emerging 'hub-and spoke' structure of MNCs to support their interweaving of global, regional and local into their international strategies.

Summary

One of the most dramatic developments in international trade in the last two decades has been the gradual build-up of regional trading blocs and the accompanying noticeable increase in intra-regional trade within those regional trading blocs. There is currently some concern as to whether these regional trading blocs are trade creating or trade diverting and what their overall effect on the liberalization of world trade may be in the future.

In many ways, the strength of regionalization denotes the limits of globalization. Many MNCs have had embarrassing experiences in local and regional markets. Such experiences made clear the necessity for adapting their products and services to regional market requirements, and often to local market requirements and structures. This need for adaptation may be interpreted as meaning that global standardization is ill-conceived and unworkable, or it may refer only to relatively trivial adjustments leaving the core of standardization intact. There is, however, no right solution to the choices open to MNCs between stronger global structures or cross-border regional integration (De Koning *et al.*, 1997). Indeed, sometimes such choices are influenced more by the interests of local divisional managers than by the MNC's strategic approach to international expansion (Forsgren *et al.*, 1995). Nevertheless there has undoubtedly been a degree of cultural homogenization in some segments of most world markets. This has created opportunities for MNCs to benefit from additional sources of scale economies and scope economies in their international operations. How this translates into viable international strategies will vary according to industry, product and market segment, and the internal processes of individual firms.

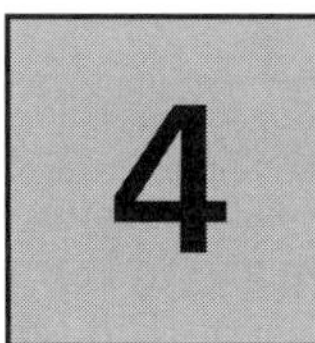

The dynamics of international competition

Whilst all strategic thinking occurs in a dynamic context, developing robust strategies deliverable across international borders is the most dynamic context of all. This contention and its consequences will be illustrated by looking at two industries: a brief comparison between two rival companies in the world consumer electronics industry and a more detailed discussion of the rapid evolution of the European food industry and its impact on the structure of international competition and the strategies of local and multinational corporations (MNCs) within that industry. The discussion of the European food-processing industry in the 1990s takes advantage of the circumstances surrounding the enactment of the European Single Market in 1992 to analyze the impact of environmental, political and regulatory change on competitive strategies within that industry. The extended industry analysis will show the gradual transformation of this industry from multidomestic (with strong domestic firms) to regional (strong international firms), with a few firms positioning for the possibility of future global strategies in some sectors. The trigger factors for these dramatic developments were predominantly regulatory change within European markets arising from 'harmonization' within the European Union (EU), combined with some important technological change affecting buyers, suppliers and distribution across the industry. These factors began to affect the balance of power between national firms and MNCs in this industry.

Deregulation: the dynamic of nations and firms

> Global strategies rest on the interplay of the competitive advantage of firms and the comparative advantage of countries. (Kogut, 1985)

Deregulation is a deliberate attempt to improve the efficiency of markets by opening them up to increased competition. It has been most visible in the world financial markets, where the removal by governments of fixed commissions and ceilings on foreign ownership has shifted competition from service to price and triggered a massive shakeout in the industry through either mergers or business failure. The same process occurred earlier in the 1970s in the USA when President Carter deregulated the US airlines in order to encourage competition. The short-term effect was to encourage many new entrants. The longer-term effect was a massive shakeout in the industry leaving a few internationally competitive 'supercarriers' and higher entry barriers. The same effect is likely in the European airline industry as the EU 'open skies' directives agreed in 1991 are implemented from 1999 onward.

Despite the social, cultural and technological changes behind the development of global market segments discussed in Chapter 3, there are additional economic and political pressures on governments to create barriers to this increasing transnational flow of goods and services. Protectionist policies such as quotas or tariff barriers create constraints on global competition. Such government protection is most likely to occur in industries that are 'salient', i.e. those that affect government policies regarding defence, regional development or employment. However, they may also occur as a response to severe imbalance in volume of international trade between nations (as between Japan and the USA, and Japan and the EU in the 1980s). The very need for artificial trade barriers is evidence of the strength of international demand by consumers for international goods and services. The two policies (deregulation and protectionism) exist in relation to each other. Fierce international competition and the changed economic structures of many industries may devastate many firms or indeed entire sectors in their home markets (Hamel and Prahalad, 1985), leading to political pressure for protection. Comparative cost, influenced by governments' economic policies and financial inducements, may influence the location of particular MNC activities, but not necessarily where the firm itself is located.

This continuing cycle of events explains why Ohmae (1985, 1989) suggests that global companies operate as what he calls 'true insiders', honorary citizens perceived as direct investors in each 'home' (i.e. national) market in which they operate.

International industry dynamics

Box 4.1 provides a brief description on the international competitive position of the Philips Group of Holland as it developed over many years. Whilst reading about this company, consider whether the difficulties Philips faced at different points in time occurred as a result of political or economic pressures or as a result of the strategy of the firm itself.

Box 4.1 The Dynamics of International Competition (1): The Philips Group of Holland

Philips is Holland's premier industrial company and the largest consumer electronics company in Europe. It is the last significant European competitor in an industry which has relentlessly been overwhelmed and dominated by large Japanese MNCs such as Sony Corporation, Hitachi, Sharp Electronics and Matsushita Electric (MEI). Philips reached its centenary in 1991. However, what should have been a cause for celebration was overshadowed by problems for the company and its future.

Problems at Philips

Early in May 1990, Dr Wisse Dekker, chairman of Philips supervisory board, suddenly had to cut short a visit to America to fly back to Philips home town of Eindhoven for an emergency meeting. Philips faced a crisis unprecedented for a major industrial company with some of the best known and most widely used brands in the world. Few European households were without a Philips television, shaver, light bulb or audio equipment or possibly records by artists such as Pavarotti on the Philips record label. The company was one of the bastions of European business with annual sales of almost £19 billion. However, by 1990 it had sunk to an unprecedented low. Profits in the first three months of 1990 were down to a dismal Fl 6 million (£1.9m) from Fl 223 million (almost £75m) in the same quarter a year before. Worse still, only three weeks earlier, Cornelius van der Klugt, Philips president, had told shareholders that Philips was on track to achieve its target earnings for 1990. A brief and very tense press conference was held on 15 May. As chairman of the supervisory board, Dekker appeared alone at the press conference to apologize for Philips financial and ethical failure.

Van der Klugt made a rapid and ignominious departure, together with the head of Philips disastrous computer division. By the end of 1990 and including heavy restructuring charges, Philips had a net loss of Fl 4.53 billion. It was the biggest loss in Dutch corporate history.

Causes of Philips decline

From the late 1980s onwards, Philips was under fierce assault from Japanese and Korean competitors and was struggling to restructure itself in order to meet the competitive threat. It was attempting to

●●▶

cont.

reshape its organization structure, management procedures, style and culture. In fact van der Klugt had succeeded Dekker as president in 1987 with a brief to carry out these transformations. What Philips was trying to do was to move from being a dispersed international corporation to a centralized global one. Its main problem was high costs and lack of sufficient central financial and managerial control. It had tremendous strengths as a company. As a technical innovator Philips was second-to-none. This was a critical strength in consumer electronics, which was an industry characterized by rapid new product development and continuously advancing technologies. Philips strengths in R&D and new product development were respected worldwide. Unfortunately, it was far less effective at ensuring it achieved the market share and financial return from its innovative product stream.

Philips problems thus had two main sources: its extraordinarily high domestic market labour costs, relative to those of its Japanese competitors; and an unwieldy decentralized, international corporate organization structure, based on a matrix system with nine product groups and 60 countries ('national organizations') with separate national managerial autonomy. Friction between the centre (Eindhoven) and periphery (the autonomous national subsidiaries) was frequent. It helped to explain the unfortunate gap between Philips superb product innovation and poor marketing.

By the end of the 1980s Philips still had only 10 per cent of its production in the Far East and 65 per cent in Europe; also the single world concept seemed no nearer. Efforts had been made to streamline the organization structure by reorganizing into four international product divisions: consumer electronics, lighting, professional products and components; and a new central management committee were formed. The reorganization was intended to shift from a focus on national geographic markets towards international product divisions.

Two of the deep problems that Philips never really got to grips with were: first, its heavy commitment to 'home-base' jobs and payroll in Holland; and second, the decentralized decision-making procedures which gave country subsidiaries and country general managers great autonomy in running their local national organizations. Philips payroll is a political issue in Holland. The company is Holland's largest single employer and is extremely socially responsible. Holland is a very high labour-cost country and the company still employed 65 000

●●▶

cont.

people there when van der Klugt departed in 1990. Also, decentralization had benefits in terms of local market knowledge.

The changing competitive map

The decentralized approach became a liability when Japanese competitors began to enter the European market with a much tighter cost-base and centralized control systems, R&D, marketing and distribution and very high quality products. Consumer electronics had become a global industry in which it was possible to develop and market highly standardized products and components across world markets. Philips still had a high local cost-base which only made sense if those costs were the necessary costs of local adaptation of products to suit the needs of different local marketplaces. Local adaptation of products like televisions and stereo systems was, however, minimal. Japanese competitors developed broadly homogeneous products for a world market. Philips was bearing local costs in a global market. In the three years between 1987 and 1990 Philips closed or merged 75 of its 346 plants spread over 50 countries. It also shed over 38 000 employees worldwide. However, that still left it with too many factories, over half of them in Europe where labour costs were high, compared to the lower production and labour costs of its main (Asian) rivals. It also had permanent problems with exchange rates since it had such a small percentage of sales (6 per cent) made in its domestic currency. A new chairman (Jan 'The Butcher' Timmer) was appointed in July 1990 as a change agent to centralize Philips product policy and streamline its planning process. Despite drastic job-cutting and transferring more power to the worldwide product divisions, Timmer was a disappointment and was replaced in 1996 by an 'outsider', the first in Philips' history – Cor Boonstra, recruited from America's Sara Lee. In 1996 and 1997 Philips was still reporting losses.

Source: Compiled by authors from various press articles. ■

Now compare the competitive issues facing one of Philips major rivals in consumer electronics, Japan's Matsushita. It has quite a different history and contrasting approaches to its `international expansion, international strategy, structure and culture. We have explained the rise of the MNC – single corporate entities selling on a global scale and with activities in many parts of the world. Philips does not fit the profile of MNCs carrying out global strategies which involve producing standard products with minor variations and marketing them in a similar fashion around the world, sourcing assets and activities on an optimal cost basis and adapting where necessary to local cultures and tastes. Matsushita, by contrast, did fit this profile of the global MNC very closely. However, by the late 1980s, that type of international strategy and organization structure no longer met its requirements for further development. It needed to move away from its centralized structure and give more autonomy to its national divisions. External market conditions and internal new product development needs have exerted pressure for the development of a relatively decentralized network of companies, which is what Matsushita is working towards (see Box 4.2).

Box 4.2 The Dynamics of International Competition (2): Matsushita (MEI) of Japan

Matsushita's global strategy

Matsushita was founded with $100 in a workshop in his own home in 1918 by a young entrepreneur (Konosuke Matsushita). By the early 1980s its overseas sales revenues were $1575 billion. It was run as a highly centralized company with no local autonomy. Its strategy was low-cost, but with a steady stream of new products to attract and keep market share. Its Japanese nickname was 'maneshita' – loosely translated as 'copycat'. It regarded itself as a technology 'follower' rather than a technology leader or innovator (like Philips). It has some of the world's most powerful consumer electronics brands including Panasonic and JVC. Matsushita operated a policy of 'hungry divisions'; one product/one division. This was a deliberate approach aimed at avoiding any tendency to organizational inertia arising from successful products and revenues. It set very tight financial targets monitored from the centre. In its international expansion, key positions were always given to internal Japanese expatriates who were regarded as custodians of Matsushita's very strong culture and 'spiritual precepts' of management. Its founder had declared himself as setting the terms of a strategy for 250 years, for which each managerial generation would be responsible for 25 years, starting with himself.

Matsushita's problems

The problems Matsushita faced in the late 1980s were different from those of Philips. They were: first, that the company needed a replacement product for the VCR, which was entering its mature phase; and

●● ▶

cont.

second, there were problems arising from successful centralization. The VCR provided the bulk of Matsushita's revenues. Over the seven-year period from 1977 to 1984, in response to rapid increases in demand, Matsushita had famously multiplied production of the successful VCR product line by 33 times capacity, showing it had excellent responsive capabilities in manufacturing and marketing. This enabled it to drop the price by one-third over the same period. By 1984 the VCR was generating 45 per cent of all its worldwide revenues. It was not obvious where a replacement product of similar magnitude could come from. By late 1980s all the signs were that the next generation of consumer electronics products were likely to spring from technology convergence, perhaps in multimedia. Such a development would require a different organizational structure from the centralized global hub suitable for controlling standardized global production and distribution. Therefore Matsushita wanted to become less of a centralized hub controlled from Japan and more 'truly international'.

Matsushita's localization ('glocal') strategy

Matsushita also faced macro-economic pressures including: rising protectionist sentiment in some of its main markets; a high yen making its products more expensive; a dearth of qualified software engineers in its domestic market; a need to understand technical capabilities abroad and share learning back home internally. So, just at the time that Philips was struggling to exert stronger central control, Matsushita was seeking to show more sensitivity to local markets. By late 1980s it had granted greater local autonomy to national subsidiaries in: hiring and promoting more local personnel; local sourcing and purchasing; modifying designs for local markets; adapting corporate processes and technologies; incorporating local components; becoming altogether more 'local'. The risks it faced in so doing were of diluting its strong internal culture and values; lower volume outputs and therefore reduced manufacturing economies of scale; and loss of processes which provided consistency of quality, product and process. In pursuit of synergies from the convergence of 'hardware' (TVs, videos, stereos) and 'software' (the programming contents – TV programmes, films, records) Matsushita bought MCA/Universal film studios in Hollywood in 1990 for $6.1 billion. It was subsequently divested in 1995. (A rival Japanese consumer electronics giant, Sony, bought Columbia/Tristar pictures in 1989 for similar reasons. By the late 1990s Sony had spent more than $8 billion on its purchase.)

●●▶

cont.

The currency and stockmarket turmoil in the late 1990s which should have benefited Matsushita by boosting exports as the yen fell dramatically in value, unfortunately coincided with a collapse in demand in many of its major markets, especially those of East Asia. By 1998, 'next-generation' product rivalry in consumer electronics was focused on recordable digital video discs (DVDs). Matsushita's Japanese arch-rival, Sony, had teamed up with Philips to promote a rival DVD system to the European standard-setting body in Geneva, Switzerland.

Source: Compiled by authors from various press articles ■

In many ways Philips already possesses what Matsushita is trying to create, since it has historically been the 'true insider' described by Ohmae (1989), perceived as a 'home' citizen wherever they have a market presence. Yet Philips achieves this insider status at too high a cost since it has been achieved by means of its multidomestic organization, which is both inappropriate and too expensive in a global industry. Matsushita, on the other hand, has been a global competitor and is now attempting to remake itself as a transnational.

By applying Porter's 'diamond' framework it is possible to make a further comparison between the two international consumer electronics rivals. Philips and Matsushita are both international competitors in the consumer electronics industry. Each faces entirely different conditions in their 'home-base' country (domestic market). On balance, Matsushita's national 'cluster' is far more advantageous than the one Philips has. Matsushita has a huge domestic market of sophisticated, discerning consumers; demand conditions are excellent. Factor conditions are fairly neutral, although there has been a recent shortage of software engineers. This may be contrasted with the negative factor conditions (expensive local labour) and tiny domestic market of Philips. Local competitive rivalry and supporting industry clusters once again favour the Japanese corporation rather than the Dutch one. Matsushita is surrounded by equally powerful rivals and therefore faces stiff competition in its domestic market in all the sectors in which it competes, whereas Philips dominates its domestic economy and bears a high degree of social cost within it.

Industry dynamics in the European food industry

Understanding how industries and firms change over time is much more difficult than understanding the structure of an industry or the strategy of a firm at a specific point in time. Chapter 3 discussed the evolution of industry structure arising from major changes in industries and markets, such as the globalization of markets, the development of regional trading blocs or technological development. There is thus a need in international strategy for models which can help understand longer-term industry dynamics, i.e. how industries may change and develop over time. Before suggesting a framework with which firms can begin to map their international strategies against the moving target of changing industry structures, we will describe some of the recent history of the European food-processing industry. This should provide enough information to understand the dynamic analysis of industries and organizations. It will also illustrate the concept of strategic groups *within* an industry and how some of the key competitive resources and capabilities of firms within those groups can wither away over time.

Structural change in an industry often also means changes in how the industry and its boundaries are defined. This will in turn challenge the relevance of the competitive strategies pursued by each firm in the industry and provide an opportunity to rethink them in the light of the changed industry conditions.

Change over time in the European food-processing industry

This industry contains all firms involved in the production of processed foods of all types beyond primary ingredients (i.e. canned, frozen, chilled, prepared, packaged, baked, etc.). Well-known names within the industry include Nestlé, Mars, Danone, Kellogg and Unilever. The recent history of this industry will now be summarized.

Industry background and recent developments

In its recent history the European food processing industry has passed through a number of distinct phases. Each of these phases has been dominated by different types of competitive strengths, reflecting particular resources, asset structures and market positioning and the relative power that these factors have bestowed upon existing firms. These stages of development have been broadly described (McGee and Segal-Horn, 1992; Segal-Horn, 1992) as follows:

1. Before the 1930s it was dominated by wholesalers who were the agents between the buyers (retailers) and suppliers (manufacturers).
2. Between 1930 and 1960 there was a rise in manufacturer power when companies such as Mars and Kellogg became household names (brands).
3. This was replaced by the power of the retailer from 1960–90 as the huge supermarket chains built up massive purchasing power (retailer buying

power) directed against the manufacturers who supplied them, with the wholesalers gradually squeezed out of the supply chain.

4. Post-1990s, we may be seeing the resurgence of manufacturer power to service the emerging pan-European consumer segments. However, the battle between manufacturers and retailers continues as the retailers too (Aldi, Netto, Carrefour, and Tesco) move across European borders and into each other's domestic marketplaces.

At each of these stages different combinations of resources were important and they were owned by different groups of competitors in the industry. These shifts in industry structure also meant that the relative balance of power accruing to competitors located in different parts of the supply chain varied at different times in the history of the industry. This process is illustrated in Table 4.1, which shows which resources and assets were relevant at different stages in the evolution of the industry and who controlled them – the manufacturer or the retailer.

Manufacturer power from 1930–60 was derived from economies of scale in production, which supported the build-up of manufacturers' brands. The food processing industry, as part of the consumer packaged goods industry, was

Table 4.1 Phases of industry evolution in the European food-processing industry

	Mobility barriers	**Phases of development**		
		(1) 1960–75 The scale economy brander	**(2) 1975–90 The rise of the retailer**	**(3) 1990s onward The Eurobrander**
1	National sales force and distribution	✓	×	×
2	Getting shelf space/access to distribution	✓	×	✓
3	Intensive media support at preferential rates	✓	×	✓
4	Superior product quality	✓	×	?
5	Low-cost processing	✓	×	✓
6	Sophisticated support services	✓	✓	✓
7	Volume discounts on purchasing	✓	×	✓

Source: Adapted from Segal-Horn (1992)

selling to a highly fragmented set of customers. At the retail distribution end of the industry shops were typically fairly small, consisting of thousands of small outlets ('mom and pop' stores). Economies of scale were available to the suppliers but not to the customers. Big manufacturers with proprietary technologies sold to small retail outlets. The food companies benefited from mass marketing via national sales forces, national advertising campaigns and sophisticated support services. Distribution too was controlled for the most part by the food manufacturing companies. Powerful manufacturers' brands were created which became household names. These manufacturers' brands were perceived by the customer as custodians of quality and reinforced the strength of the manufacturers. They became the most visible barrier to entry behind which many oligopolies flourished.

Between 1960 and 1990, as large chains replaced small independent shops at varying speeds in the different European national markets, the relative positions of the food manufacturers and the retailers began to be reversed. Many general factors contributed to this rise in retailer buying power. A decline in proprietary technology allowed the entry of efficient smaller food processors; and a virtual revolution in distribution and logistics gave rise to new concepts such as centralized warehousing controlled by the retailers not the manufacturers. The gradual rise of supermarkets, both as very large units of retail space and as concentrated chains of retail outlets, shifted the balance of power from the manufacturer to the retailer.

For example, let us take the first item from Table 4.1, 'national sales force and distribution'. This was a significant source of advantage when the retail end of the industry was highly fragmented, with manufacturers needing large numbers of sales representatives to visit thousands of small local stores. As the local stores withered away and were replaced by supermarkets or hypermarkets, these retail chains used centralized purchasing systems and expected key account managers to deal with their needs. The massive salesforces were redundant, rather than a source of advantage that was costly to set up and manage and that had therefore previously acted as a significant barrier to entry for the manufacturers.

Competition was now as often based on price as on quality. This was exacerbated by the rapid development of cheaper retailer 'private-label' brands, which removed some of the absolute control of quality from the manufacturers' brands. National retail accounts supported by centralized purchasing, warehousing and distribution, either directly controlled by the retailer or contracted-out, dramatically reduced the economies of scale of the manufacturers from distribution, and reduced their national salesforces to irrelevant overheads. It was now the retailer who controlled the allocation of supermarket shelf space in their stores and hence the availability of products to the consumer, rather than the manufacturer rationing his brands to small shopkeepers, as before (see item 2 in Table 4.1). Just as retailers began marketing to the consumer, so food companies had to cope with both trade and consumer marketing costs, as well as the rising costs of R&D and technology to support sophisticated new product development to fight off the inroads of retailers' private-label 'own brands'. Thus the efficiencies of the retailers undermined thc assets and strategies of the manufacturers.

Technological and market changes, together with the consequences of the formation of the European Single Market in 1992, created another new phase for the industry – the post-1990 resurgence of manufacturer power with the emergence of pan-European consumer segments. Historically the structure of the European food industry was extremely fragmented country by country. This was, first, because the patterns of consumer tastes and preferences had traditionally varied markedly from country to country. Second, the structural and regulatory conditions present in each market (including production systems and patterns of ownership) were highly varied, creating both tariff and non-tariff barriers to cross-border trade. The cumulative impact of these barriers was to protect potentially weak domestic companies, and inversely, to encourage strong companies to expand domestically rather than attempt cross-border expansion. These trade barriers had therefore reinforced the relative fragmentation of the EU food industry. Their removal after 1992 changed two key elements: cost and demand.

Impact of the changes

Traditional obstacles to cross-border trade have been steadily dismantled, at the same time as other factors which had always reinforced domestic market boundaries have also weakened. National markets have become more responsive to international food products and offerings. Greater access to channels and variety of advertising media encourage manufacturers to try to market similar products in several national markets, to offset the impact of shorter product lifecycles and higher development costs. National laws are less dominant. Distribution networks are being set up Europe-wide. Information systems allow centralized purchasing and distribution to be attempted across European markets. Also, operating across national boundaries gives manufacturers the opportunity to search for countervailing power against strong national retailers. Manufacturing economies of scale begin to seem feasible if market size is no longer purely nationally determined. Rationalization of production capacity is resulting in fewer more flexible plants, to service a wide product range, responsive to many market segments. This in turn creates greater opportunities for European-wide sourcing.

The structural characteristics of this industry have shifted for the first time towards a European-wide industry structure and away from domestic market focus. This is in complete contrast with the historical structure of the industry where everything from manufacturing to marketing was constructed and delivered on a local market basis. Strategies were formulated for specific domestic markets to ensure responsiveness to local consumer tastes and preferences and to take advantage of structural differences. Economies of scale across national market boundaries were hard to find.

Implications of the industry dynamics for the strategies of firms

Opportunities for significant lowering of the cost base for manufacturers include increased efficiencies from production, distribution and marketing, which have already encouraged restructuring and consolidation, with large reductions in the number of plants and the numbers of manufacturing companies (for example, production of Kellogg's breakfast cereals in Europe is now consolidated in just two manufacturing plants for Europe). Successive bouts of acquisitions within the food industry have been directed at acquiring companies with specific resources such as strong brand portfolios or distribution networks. A handful of giant food conglomerates appears to be emerging, such as Nestlé (Swiss), Unilever (Anglo-Dutch), Danone (previously BSN, French), and Philip Morris (USA). Cross-border acquisition is being used by companies as a route for making new strategic moves to establish new product/market positioning. Many small and medium-sized companies will be under pressure to exit as a more polarized industry forms. This polarization will be accompanied by more cost-based European strategies as powerful low-cost own-label competitors emerge.

Changes are also being driven by new patterns of demand. The greater the convergence of consumer demand across national boundaries, the greater the potential for new forms of competition based on pan-European market segments, pan-European brands rather than national brands, and new product lines. Already this has led to many 'swaps' between companies, as acquisitions are accompanied by divestments (e.g. selling snack foods such as peanuts or cakes and biscuits, while buying yoghurts to deepen existing coverage of the dairy segment). This rationalizes product portfolios whilst also filling out product lines within selected segments. These opportunities to pursue efficiencies whilst simultaneously developing strategies based on marketing and product innovation, has created a high level of disturbance of the existing industry structure, from which new patterns of competition and fewer, stronger, competitors are emerging.

The two main themes are 'cost-push' and 'demand-pull'. 'Cost-push' is towards scale economies and major changes in unit costs, in an industry historically distinguished by low levels of scale economies determined by national market boundaries. 'Demand-pull' is stretching those market boundaries to encompass emergent European-wide segments, with a corresponding European-wide positioning of firms and brands, and some standardization of products and marketing. This represents a radical agenda for an industry which, for structural, regulatory and market reasons, had been local and multidomestic for so long and for firms which have traditionally operated close to their national markets, within a fragmented industry structure.

Given the types of shifts described here, the establishment of integrated European strategies to replace national strategies now makes sense. Table 4.1 provides a summary of this discussion of the phases of evolution in the European food industry. It illustrates the drivers for change and the dynamics of this industry over time. It also demonstrates why pan-European (regional) rather than local/domestic strategies now make sense in this industry.

Changed conditions thus challenge the logic of existing strategies and also provide opportunities for redirecting strategies. This is particularly so in the international arena. Part of the challenge to existing strategies caused by changed conditions is the appropriateness of the investments in assets which the firm has made to support its existing strategy. The value of these investments may be eroded both by external changes (e.g. shifts in consumer preferences; legislative or regulatory change) or by internal changes within an industry or a firm (e.g. new product or service development; technology change affecting manufacturing, design, channels, etc.). Despite the fact that throughout the second half of this century, industries have been characterized by consistently high rates of change in both external and internal factors, the dynamic analysis of industries has not been much explored. To some extent that may be because dynamic analysis is much more complex than static analysis. Part of that complexity is the effect of industry dynamics on the patterns of resource accumulation and capability-building by firms. A useful way of understanding strategic change is to track how firms adjust their resources and capabilities over time to cope with external and internal shifts affecting their industry.

Strategic groups and industry dynamics

Our description of some of the recent history of the European food-processing industry will now be used to show how the 'strategic groups' in this industry are changing. The concept will be used to explore a dynamic analysis of markets, industries and competition. Such an analysis can help us to understand the future strategies of firms within a given industry and the implications of industry evolution for current resources and capabilities.

Firms can adopt very different competitive strategies within the same industry. The strategic group concept looks at groupings of firms *within* an industry. We used McGee and Thomas's (1986, 1989) definition of the term 'strategic group' in Chapter 2: 'a cluster of firms within an industry following similar generic strategies and having similar market positioning'. A 'strategic group' is therefore a way of making sense of different types of competitors and different competitive strategies within the *same* industry. Members of the same strategic group are not necessarily equally effective or efficient. Diversity of capability and of performance are therefore to be expected of firms within the same strategic group.

Membership of a strategic group rests upon configurations of resources common to group members. These configurations of resources act as 'mobility barriers'. Caves and Porter (1977) see mobility barriers as locking strategic group members into specific resources and thereby making it difficult for them to acquire different ones, or move from an existing group to a different one. At the same time such resources offer considerable protection from imitation from firms outside the group. Table 4.2 shows a range of organizational resources which are potential sources of mobility barriers. McGee and Thomas (1986) suggest this is a helpful way of understanding the asymmetry in competition within an industry, since different strategic groups will be characterized by different mixtures of resources. Mobility barriers are also a cost penalty which a new entrant to the group must bear relative to the incumbents and as such are the potential costs of imitation.

In most industries there are a relatively small number of strategic groups, representing differences in strategy within that industry. To give an extreme example, in a pure monopoly situation the number of strategic groups in that industry will be just one. In more competitive marketplaces, it is still feasible that any particular strategic group could contain only one firm, although several in any group is more usual. Strategic group analysis offers a 'map' of an industry based on the most significant dimensions of competitive strategy

Table 4.2 Possible sources of mobility barriers

Market-related	**Industry supply characteristics**	**Characteristics of firms**
Product line	Economies of scale:	Ownership (e.g. public, private, state-owned)
User technologies	production	Organization structure
Market segmentation	marketing	Control system
Distribution channels	administration	Management skills
Brand names	Manufacturing process	Boundaries of firms:
Geographic cover	R&D capability	diversification
Distribution systems	Marketing and distribution systems	vertical integration
Firm size	Stakeholder relationships	Know-how, skills, expertise, routines

Source: Adapted from McGee and Thomas (1986)

within that industry. (Obviously these dimensions will vary from industry to industry, which means that the axes on strategic group maps will almost certainly be different for different industries. It is up to the strategist, using industry knowledge, to select those axes that most accurately capture the factors which drive their particular industry. For example, for a 'map' of the pharmaceutical industry, we might choose R&D expenditure as a percentage of sales and geographic spread as our two axes.)

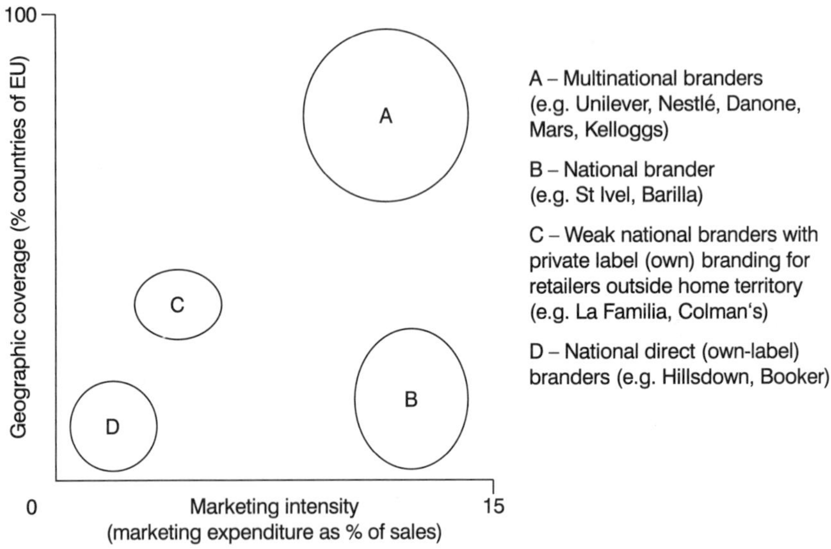

Figure 4.1 A 'map' of strategic groups in the European food-processing industry in the 1980s. *Source:* Adapted from McGee and Segal-Horn (1992)

Box 4.3 Key to the strategic groups in Figure 4.1

The four strategic groups represented in Figure 4.1 constitute very different competitive postures in the late 1980s:

Group A consists of the Multinational Branders, such as Mars, Unilever, Nestlé, Kraft, and PepsiCo. They are all multinational consumer packaged goods companies, which operated many related businesses throughout the world. All the businesses offered high product quality supported by robust branding. Reflecting the (then) nationally-

●●▶

cont.

determined patterns of demand in this industry, the structure of all these companies was 'multidomestic' rather than global, i.e. structuring all operations separately on a country by country basis.

Group B contains the National Branders, e.g. Ross Young, Verkade, St Ivel, Smiths/Walkers/Planters, Cote d'Or, Barilla. These firms were nationally based and nationally focused. They utilized proportionately as high a degree of marketing support as the multinationals for branded products which were primarily aimed at the domestic market, in which they occupied strong positions. Their product range was also more restricted than that of the Multinational Branders.

Group C is made up of the Weak National Branders (with some regional direct branding for retailers), such as Unigate, Colman's, and La Familia. These firms occupied lower ranking brand positions and were not normally leaders in any national markets. Their modest market strength led them to supplement their position and absorb underutilized capacity, by acting also as private-label suppliers for large retailers' own brands plus some exporting where possible. Groups B and C are not uniformly represented in all food sectors in all markets.

Group D consists of National Direct Branders (own-labellers) e.g. Hillsdown Holdings, Hazlewood Foods. Often utilizing advanced product and process technology, these private-label suppliers concentrated on highly efficient low-cost production, supplying mainly domestic retail chains. They incurred virtually no marketing and branding costs of their own. ■

Figure 4.1 provides an example of a strategic group 'map' for the European food-processing industry in the 1980s. (The two dimensions used by McGee and Segal-Horn (1992) for explaining competition within the European food-processing industry were derived: first, from the overwhelming importance of marketing spend to support brands within this industry, and second, the European geographic coverage of major brands.) The purpose of such a map is to indicate the positioning of the various strategic groups in the industry and to reflect the resources on which their positions are based. However, the value of such resources may be eroded. The power of mobility barriers may decay and others arise in their place. This building and decaying of resources and the mobility barriers which they support, provides the explanation of differences between industry structures over time (industry dynamics). It also provides opportunities for new strategies, based on different types and clusters of resources as new markets or new technologies emerge (see also Box 4.3).

Strategic space and industry dynamics

Starting from an analysis of an existing industry structure, the strategic group concept may be applied to help organizations map their strategies against the moving target of changing industry structures. This approach creates the concept of 'strategic space' (McGee and Segal-Horn, 1990, 1992). 'Strategic space' captures areas of potential opportunity within an industry, areas which are not yet available but whose potential under developing conditions becomes feasible. Viable 'strategic space' can change over time. That means that feasible strategies in an industry can also change over time. For example, banks with no bank branches were not feasible in the mid-1980s. By the 1990s they were not only feasible, they existed.

A strategic space is a currently unoccupied location on a strategic group map. Therefore what Figure 4.1 is telling us is which 'space' in the industry map is occupied and which is empty. Each space represents a possible strategy with a possible alternative cluster of resources. The task of the strategist is to determine which, if any, of the empty spaces can be occupied and provide the basis for a viable strategy, given the changes in industry conditions. Figure 4.2 helps us to carry out this analysis of the strategic space by turning the 'map' of Figure 4.1 into a grid. The grid gives us an overview of existing strategic groups (A, B, C, D) and possible new strategic groups in the empty spaces (V, W, X, Y, Z). Each of these represents a potential strategy in this industry. Not all of these potential strategies will be viable.

For example, given the information you now have on the developments in the European food-processing industry, would you consider that Group C in Figure

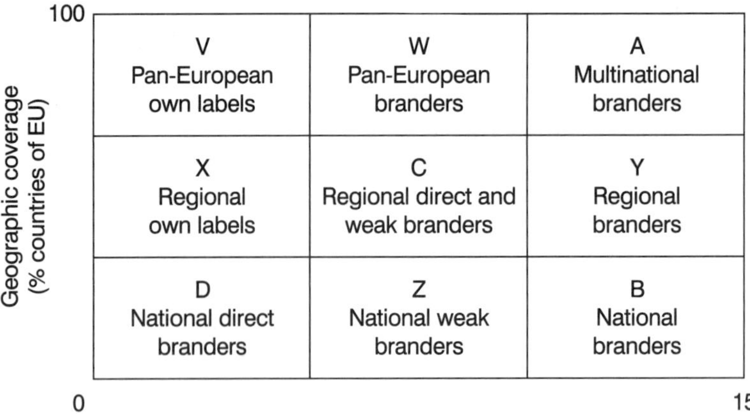

Figure 4.2 Strategic space analysis. *Source:* Adapted from McGee and Segal-Horn (1992)

4.1 is still in a viable position? Do firms in Group C have either scale efficiencies or strong brands? Would you expect Group B to disappear or become stronger? Would you expect Group A to disappear or become stronger? One of the companies named in Figure 4.1 is Colman's. In 1995 Colman's was sold to Unilever, a Group A company. As a Group C company Colman's was not big enough to survive alone since it lacked sufficient resources to build its brands internationally. In the longer term, Groups C and D are likely to disappear while A and B remain strong. V and W are likely to replace C and D.

These are real 'industry dynamics' affecting real firms in a real industry. This analysis should give you a better understanding of industry dynamics and the resources and capabilities of firms, and the relationship between the two.

MNC's ability to compete

The concept of strategic space is a way of showing new directions towards which investments can be channelled, but says nothing about the intensity of the competition in any of the spaces. However, if mobility barriers are changing, then they are no longer effectively blocking entry or exit to either new or existing spaces. Barriers to imitation may be weakened (e.g. because the amount of investment capital or lead time required is reduced), leapfrogged (e.g. by new types of distribution channels such as telephone banking which dispenses with the need for a high street property-based branch network or Internet booksellers who have no need for retail outlets), or simply disappear altogether ('free' long-distance telephone calls via the Internet threaten the long-term existence of traditional telephone companies). The relative profitability of different strategic groups in an industry cannot be protected by any firm's historic investments in resources already made, if these resources no longer provide relative competitive advantages because the nature of competition in the industry has changed.

Clearly the ability of firms to adapt will vary and can be understood as representing differences in the organizational capabilities of individual firms. Therefore the key to understanding long-term industry dynamics is how effectively, or indeed whether, firms are able to adjust their resources over time. Our analysis of the European food-processing industry has suggested that two new strategic groups are likely to emerge: the pan-European brander and the pan-European own-labeller. The resources supporting these two new competitive positions and the commercial logic behind then have already been described. What cannot be predetermined is which individual firms within these sectors (such as the competition between Diageo of the UK versus PepsiCo of the USA in the billion-dollar snack food sector) will be able to build the relevant capabilities for longer-term survival.

A method has been described for looking at industry dynamics and planning the future strategies of firms. Making sense of industries is difficult, partly because what we mean by an 'industry' is frequently unclear since industry boundaries change and become hard to define. For long-term dynamics, however, the strategic group concept can be more useful. 'Industry' is an imprecise concept with modest strategic significance (Rumelt, 1991). Competitive issues in international strategy are much more to do with the existence of firms and groups of firms, and the investment decisions that particular firms make. Strategic group analysis can offer insights into industry dynamics. Analysis of the strategic space can identify directions of migration and thus, an approach to future strategic direction. Although the industry used to illustrate the approach in this chapter is the European food-processing industry, the approach is transferable to other industries.

Summary

International strategy is developed and implemented in a dynamic hypercompetitive context. We have looked in some detail at two industries to illustrate this statement. For the global consumer electronics industry we compared the competitive strategies and structures of two global MNC competitors in that industry: Philips of Holland and Matsushita of Japan. To illustrate our analysis of the industry dynamics of the European food-processing industry and the competitor firms within it, we made use of the concepts of strategic groups, strategic group 'maps' and strategic space analysis.

We said earlier that the task of the international strategist was to assess whether a strategic space was viable and could be occupied. A space may be unoccupied because it does not represent a viable strategy (for example, the technology does not yet exist to provide the service in this way), or because the opportunity which it represents has not yet become apparent to firms within the industry (for example, that a market may exist for cheap, no-frills airline tickets to compete with full-service carriers). Most importantly, a space may be unoccupied for historical, cultural, structural, regulatory, market or technological reasons which, under changed conditions, no longer apply. In the European food-processing industry, long-standing assumptions about differences in consumer preferences had changed. Customers can now be found for pizza or hamburgers anywhere in eastern or western Europe. That does not mean that different nationalities have ceased to have different national cuisines. It means rather that MNCs such as Unilever can develop international strategies for selling frozen pizza in all European markets and that a pan-European segment for such a product exists.

5

The role of culture in international strategy

This chapter examines the impact of culture upon the implementation of international strategies. It shows how culture simultaneously can both create barriers to international strategies, and also provide a valuable input into the design of an international strategy. We explain the difference between organizational culture and national culture, why culture is relevant in international strategy, and we also look at some approaches to managing culture within international strategies. Cultural diversity is thus seen as creating both problems and opportunities in international strategy.

Culture is a much-used anthropological and sociological concept attempting to capture the intangible, but universal, aspects of human social life. Such aspects of culture usually include: knowledge, values, preferences, habits, customs, practices and behaviour, as well as more tangible things like artistic and architectural artefacts (Keesing, 1974). The ancient temples of Angkor Wat in Cambodia or Kyoto in Japan, the Arc de Triomphe in Paris, the Lincoln Memorial in Washington, USA, are all well-known examples of such architectural artefacts. They are not just buildings; they have significant emotional symbolism for the members of their respective societies. Similarly, the values, customs, behaviour, artefacts, etc. of modern work organizations represent more than just their face value to organizational members. They have the power to shape attitudes and behaviour within those organizations, between both organizational members and in the organization's external relations.

National culture and organizational culture

Within the management field, the seminal work which triggered immense interest in the relevance of culture to management practice was that of Hofstede (1980, 1991; Hofstede and Bond, 1988) arising from original research across different national divisions of IBM. Hofstede defined culture as 'the collective programming of the mind which distinguishes the members of one group or category of people from another' (1991, p.5). This definition focuses on the intangible aspects of culture and stresses that culture is learned and shared within social groups. Most people experience two major groups in their daily lives: the organizations in which they work and the society in which they live. These have given rise, respectively, to the concepts of 'organizational culture' and 'national culture'.

'Organizational' culture is usually taken to comprise shared values, beliefs and ways of behaving and thinking that are unique to a particular organization. Brown (1995) concluded that 'an organization's culture has a direct and significant impact on performance. Organizational strategies and structures and their implementation are shaped by the assumptions, beliefs and values which we have defined as a culture.' (p.198).

Schein (1985) distinguishes between the assumptions, values and artefacts which together make up an organizational culture. Assumptions are what the members of an organization take for granted and what they believe to be reality. Assumptions therefore influence what members of the organization think and how they behave. Organization members also have values, which are the internal beliefs they share and to which they attribute intrinsic worth. Artefacts are the tangible, external manifestations of a culture, such as an organization's physical style and dress code, its ceremonies, its stories and myths, its traditions, rewards and punishments. Organizations may also contain more than one culture. The dominant organization culture may be shared by all the members of an organization and may act as an integrating mechanism for a diverse set of organization members. However, often there are also organizational subcultures representing different groups within an organization such as the 'techies' versus the accountants; production versus sales; or headquarters versus the business units. Most common in international strategy are the differing organizational subcultures of groups of managers and staff from different geographic locations who either do not wish to work together, or perhaps do not understand each other well enough to do so effectively. Such common circumstances as a merger between multinational corporations (MNCs) of different parent nationalities, such as the acquisition of Zanussi (Italian) by Electrolux (Swedish) in the 1980s require procedures for international team-building, and time for such processes as the building of trust to develop.

Organizational culture may therefore be a positive means of integrating people around common purposes or a source of conflict which threatens the success of international activities when a particular organizational culture is so deeply embedded that it persists beyond a structural change, such as a change of ownership of the corporation.

'National' cultures are acquired during childhood and reinforced simply by living one's life in a particular society. The strength of national cultures can be illustrated by reflecting on how different they can become in only one or two generations, as in East and West Germany during the period of their separation by the Berlin Wall from 1945 to 1989. Similarly, national cultures may change equally rapidly in one or two generations. Recent research in China (cited by Child and Faulkner, 1998) found that the younger generation, which has grown up during the age of reform, displayed more individualistic and materialistic attitudes than the older generation. In international strategy terms this has made the younger generation of China more open to 'Western' products and services.

National cultures are a highly significant element in international strategy. They affect not only obvious things such as the variable meaning of particular brand names or corporate logos in different languages; they are also part of the mindset which the corporate headquarters brings to its dealings with staff, suppliers or customers in another country. To use Ohmae's (1989) concept, MNCs may act as either 'insiders' or 'outsiders' and be perceived as either by their local emloyees, their customers and the host government of the country in which they are located (Stopford and Strange, 1991). However, unsurprisingly, different definitions of the key attributes and dimensions of national culture exist. The two best-known typologies for modelling the effect of national culture on the behaviour of individuals in organizations (the aspect which affects strategic thinking) are those of Hofstede's (1980, 1991; Hofstede and Bond, 1988) five-dimensional model and Trompenaars's (1993) seven-dimensional model.

Hofstede's well-known typology of national culture is divided into five dimensions. First, *individualism versus collectivism*: individualism describes societies in which the ties between individuals are loose. Each individual is expected to look after himself or herself and his or her immediate family, rather than to belong to strong, cohesive groups. Second, *power distance*: this captures the extent to which the less powerful members of institutions and organizations within a country expect and accept that power is distributed unequally. Third, *uncertainty avoidance*: this dimension describes the extent to which the members of a culture feel threatened by uncertain or unknown situations. Fourth, *masculinity versus femininity*: the dominance in any given society of a set of values and attitudes usually associated with men (e.g. aggression or competitiveness) in contrast to those usually associated with women (e.g. concern for people and relationships). Fifth, *time-orientation*: an emphasis on either the long-term or the short-term gratification of needs. The former is more oriented towards the future. It gives high value to perseverance and thrift, together with ordered relationships and having a sense of shame or honour. (This dimension emerged from research among Chinese populations.)

Trompenaars's typology of national culture has seven dimensions. First, *universalism versus particularism*: which means always applying a standard rule as opposed to deciding on the basis of the specific case. Second, *individualism versus collectivism:* whether people regard themselves primarily as individuals or primarily as part of a group or community. Third, *neutral versus emotional*: the importance attached to being objective and detached as opposed to allowing emotions to affect one's judgement and decisions. Fourth, *specific versus diffuse:* confining business to the contractual as opposed to allowing personal involvements also. Fifth, *achievement versus ascription*: evaluating people on merit and achievement as opposed to evaluating them according to background and connections. Sixth, *attitudes towards time*: having an orientation towards the future as opposed to an orientation to the past; and how the relationship between past, present and future is viewed. Seventh, *attitudes towards the environment:* the view that individuals can shape the environment and other people ('inner-directed'), as opposed to the view that we have to live in harmony with the environment and with other people and should therefore behave in accordance with these considerations ('outer-directed').

Whilst there are both some overlaps, such as time-orientation and individualism/collectivism, between Hofstede's and Trompenaars's typologies, as well as differences, our concern in international strategy is to understand the effects such national cultural differences may have on organizational behaviour and strategic thinking, rather than a comparison of the typologies themselves.

Why culture is relevant to international strategy

MNC strategies bring together people from different national cultures into organizations within which they are expected to develop a working relationship. These MNC staff may themselves have been recruited from national organizations or overseas subsidiaries which have their own distinctive organization cultures. Thus, Forsgren *et al.* (1995) describe the impact of geographic location of a subsidiary on its power relations with corporate headquarters. They stress that the decisions of overseas subsidiary managers must be understood to be based 'on local or contextual rationality' (p.488).

The MNC may hope to benefit from such cultural diversity amongst its staff, especially from their national marketplace knowledge. In all international strategy decisions, such as new product development for overseas markets, many aspects of market entry strategy, the ability to carry out processes of negotiation and contracting, managing relationships with customers, suppliers, distributors, even whether to grow by acquisition or organically, and so on, the MNC needs to understand the people and the market and the institutions that it is dealing with. The MNC organizational culture will hope to gather some of that understanding from the distinct national cultures of its individual staff. However, sharing of knowledge and subsequent learning within the organization cannot take place until national cultural differences are understood, and any possible barriers to adaptation or integration have been removed or reduced.

Cultural barriers in international strategy

Finding ways of bridging distinctive organizational and national cultures which individuals and groups bring to MNCs is essential to the effective functioning of the MNC. National cultural differences can display themselves either as simple misunderstandings or at the more fundamental level of conflicts in values (Child and Faulkner, 1998). Misunderstandings about language and about the interpretation of behaviour are common. What is understood as humorous or ironic in one language, may be taken literally in another. Although in a fast-changing world some of these stereotypes may no longer be so typical, behaviour is still likely to be interpreted in contrasting ways by people from different national cultures. These may lead to misunderstandings or give great offence. Eye contact can signify respect in one culture but a lack of it in another. Physical touching may denote warmth in one culture and an unacceptable invasion of personal privacy in another. In Scandinavian culture it is polite to wait until another person has finished speaking before speaking oneself. In East Asian societies it is a mark of respect to pause before replying, thus indicating that what the other person has said is deserving of careful consideration.

Such external cultural differences, once they are appreciated, may be dealt with by MNCs briefing staff properly and encouraging a healthy attitude of mutual respect. However, beyond such surface behavioural factors, deeper cultural values may generate far more serious differences. Let us consider the implications of the first two of Trompenaars's (1993) dimensions of national culture: universalism versus particularism and individualism versus collectivism. As stated earlier, the definitions for these two dimensions are: *universalism versus particularism* – always applying a standard rule as opposed to deciding on the basis of the specific case; *individualism versus collectivism* - whether people regard themselves primarily as individuals or primarily as part of a group or community.

Decision-making on the basis of personal relationships is acceptable in *particularistic* societies but not acceptable in *universalistic* ones. So, in a particularistic culture, people will tend to support friends and relatives rather than an abstract universalist principle such as 'the rule of law'. Trompenaars questioned around 15 000 employees in many different countries, (75 per cent managers) about types of personal decisions likely to be made in different circumstances. He found the 'Anglo-Saxon' and 'northern' (Australia, Canada, Denmark, Finland, West Germany, Ireland, Japan, Norway, Sweden, Switzerland, UK, USA) countries to be the most universalistic; whilst China, South Korea, Indonesia, Russia, Venezuela and the former Yugoslavia, were the most particularistic countries. How then would this affect the managerial relationships or customer relations between a German and a Chinese company, or between the joint German and Chinese partners in a German joint venture in China, or indeed between the German managers of their own Chinese subsidiary? The two groups are likely to be suspicious of each other. The (German/Canadian/Danish/etc.) universalists would regard the other group as untrustworthy 'because they always help their friends first' and the (Chinese/Korean/Venezualan/etc.) particularists would regard the universalists as untrustworthy because 'they would not even help a friend'. The consequences of these types of universalist/particularist differences are discussed in the research on strategic alliances cited in Chapter 11. It shows the differences in criteria used in selection of an alliance partner by Chinese compared to their foreign partners. Most foreign companies selected on the (universalist) basis of the best available partner, according to their requirements, regardless of any personal connections they might have with existing managers or staff. Indeed, such personal connections were frowned upon as being potentially unethical, unfair or even corrupt. Whereas Chinese companies tended to favour the recruitment of family members, since it is a (particularist) Chinese social norm that members of an extended family should help each other, and managers also believe that recruitment on the basis of personal connections will encourage the employees concerned to be loyal members of the organization.

As far as *individualism* and *collectivism* are concerned, it is the highly industrialized countries which have high degrees of individualism, i.e. the 'Anglo-Saxon' nations; the Netherlands; some of eastern Europe; although Austria and Germany have less individualistic attitudes than other west European countries. The prime orientation of individualistic cultures is towards the self rather than the group or the community. Collectivism is stronger in the developing economies and in those sharing a Chinese cultural heritage. Interestingly, Hampden-Turner and Trompenaars (1993) found Japan to be the most collectivist among the highly industrialized countries.

Individualism and *collectivism* generate different management styles. Individualistic cultures value quick decisions, individual responsibility, expression of individual views and goals, competition between people for recognition and advancement, and individual incentives. Collectivist cultures have other decision-making processes. They value consultation to gain consent before decisions are made, group responsibility, sharing common organizational objectives, high levels of personal and departmental co-operation, and a system of rewards that does not single out individuals. The history of

MNC/subsidiary relationships is littered with examples of misunderstandings arising from such differences. The contrast between Japanese, Middle Eastern and Anglo-Saxon styles of negotiation and even what each regards as a 'successful' outcome, differ widely. It is perhaps not surprising that process innovations such as total quality management (TQM) or just-in-time (JIT) production and distribution systems were created in an individualist culture (USA), but adopted first and made to work effectively in a collectivist culture (Japan). Even in cross-cultural strategic alliances these individualist/collectivist cultural differences make themselves felt. As we shall discuss further in Chapter 12, some of the Japanese/US alliances came under strain because the Japanese learned more from them than did their American partners. Casson's (1995) explanation of this outcome is subtle. He suggests that the difference in learning benefit is due, at least in part, to cultural differences. The individualism and competitiveness of the Americans generated a sense of mistrust which prevented them from learning within the alliance, while the high-trust Japanese were more open to learning from their alliance partners, and did so notably more successfully.

Given the national cultural differences already discussed, we might expect there to be significant differences in management practices in different countries. Box 5.1 lists the dominant management characteristics of the main industrialized nations. We may particularly note the contrast between US and Japanese practice.

Box 5. 1 Characteristics of Different National Management Practices

Japanese management practice

Policies and practices associated with Japanese companies are:

- Long-term orientation
  - strategic rather than financial
  - emphasis on growth
  - long-term employment commitment
- Rewards based primarily on seniority and superior's evaluation
- Internal training and seniority system; heavy investment in training
- Collective orientation
  - collective participation in, and responsibility for, decision-making and knowledge creation
- Flexible tasks with low specialization
- Emphasis on lean production and continuous improvement

• • ▶

cont.

Management practice in the USA

Policies and practices associated with US companies are:

- Short-term financial orientation
- Rewards related to specific performance indicators
- High rate of job change and inter-company mobility
- Rationalist approach: emphasis on analysis and planning
- Reliance on formalization and systems
- Delegation down extended hierarchies

German management practice

There is some disagreement between investigators over the key characteristics of (West) German management – these may reflect differences in sampling (for example, large versus *Mittelstand* firms) and methodology (Ebster-Grosz and Pugh, 1996). However, while the picture which emerges of German management policies and practices is not so clear-cut as that portrayed for American and Japanese management, its main contours are the following:

- Long-term business orientation
  - toward production improvement rather than short-term profit distribution
  - but orientation towards employment is not necessarily long term
- Strong technical and production emphasis, including a substantial investment in training
- Managers and staff tend to remain within one functional area during their career
- Emphasis on planning, procedures and rules
- Preference for participation and collective action

French management practice

France is also a difficult country to categorize, and the same applies to its management practice. Hampden-Turner and Trompenaars (1993, p.333) comment that 'France defies easy categorization. It requires a sense of irony, for which the French are famous, to make sense of seemingly contradictory results'. Bearing this caution in mind, the policies and practices which have been described of French companies are:

- Strategic rather than financial orientation

●●▶

cont.

- Tall organizational hierarchies, with a large proportion of managerial personnel
- High degree of specialization
- Widespread use of written media
- Individual rather than collective working and decision-making
- Centralization of decison-making

UK management practice

Policies and practices associated with British companies have some similarity with those associated with US companies, but with far less emphasis on formal systems and records:

- Short-term financial orientation
- Large general management superstructures
- Low level of functional specialization
- High mobility of managers between functions
- Use of formal meetings, especially committees
- Interactive informality – limited formal and paper-based reporting
- Limited importance attached to systems

Source: Child, Faulkner and Pitkethly (1998). ■

Problems with culture in international strategy

Cultural differences increase the chances of mutual misunderstanding and even personal offence. They therefore have to be transcended before a basis for trust can be established. That is usually a time-consumimg process. Cultural distance may be associated with a preference for modes of overseas market entry which offer MNCs higher control. For example, Shane (1994) found that US manufacturing MNCs preferred foreign direct investment (FDI) to licensing as their mode of new foreign market entry. That was because FDI allowed for higher levels of monitoring and higher levels of interaction with foreign personnel than did licensing. The issue was one of levels of trust. Hofstede (1980) found that the dimension of power distance (i.e. the extent to which the less powerful members of institutions and organizations within a country expect and accept that power is distributed unequally) also represented societal trust. He found that power distant societies exhibited low interpersonal trust and a high need for controls on the behaviour of individuals, especially hierarchical organizational controls. Acceptance of such hierarchical monitoring varies across cultures. Cultural differences may also lead to operational problems. Such problems are common, particularly in sensitive situations like MNC mergers or cross-border acquisitions. These frequently generate fear and mistrust as to what the future may hold for the staff of the acquired company and misinterpretation of signals between acquirers and acquired. Cultural differences will reinforce this unless considerable effort is made to overcome them.

MNCs are communication intensive and relationship dependent, and they therefore cannot function well if they are internally divided by substantial cultural barriers. If cultural distance is not reduced, or at least channelled into a form that avoids conflict, it is likely to give rise to serious breakdowns in communication of information and integration. This may matter less in the multidomestic and international exporter forms of MNC, where little cross-border integration is being attempted. It is, however, critical in global and transnational MNCs, where cross-border integration of processes, operations and information are mandatory.

Cultural accommodation to buying behaviour of overseas customers or wholly-owned overseas subsidiaries may require acceptance of what appear to be inefficiencies in their managerial practice. Whereas a Western company is likely to operate individualistic, universalistic, and short-term performance norms, an East Asian company is likely to operate collectivistic, particularistic and longer-term performance norms. The Western parent may view the East Asian subsidiary as inefficient because it sees what appear to be protracted decision-making processes and a lack of individual accountability and performance measurement. East Asian managers will take into account the employee's commitment and loyalty to the company, as evaluated by their manager, rather than apparently more objective information. Western managers are expected to take little account of personal circumstances, but to evaluate and reward in terms of purely task-specific criteria.

Benefiting from cultural differences

Although these international differences in management practice can create many difficulties in the management of MNCs, cultural diversity also creates opportunities to use the competencies and knowledge contained in different cultures for the benefit of the MNC as a whole. Recognition by some Western MNCs of the value attached to collectivism in the host society can, for example, result in a modification of human resource management (HRM) policies in ways that might increase the commitment of local employees (e.g. from individual to group assessment and reward). Indeed, these modifications may, in time, be extended to the 'home' staff.

MNCs seek to benefit from having a diversity of cultures amongst its organizational members. At best this should provide a stimulus to learning and sensitivity to local markets. This does not happen by accident. Organizational cultures need to be managed so that they become forces for integration rather than division. There is a parallel here with effective organizational learning (discussed further in Chapter 13). Learning arises from synthesis: selecting strands from the diversity present within the organization and integrating them to create shared understandings and eventually a shared commitment. Both the management of culture and of learning within MNCs require a reconciliation and integration of differences.

Corporate cultures can be an important resource available to the leaders of organizations (Brown, 1995; Deal and Kennedy, 1982; Hampden-Turner, 1990). They can promote social cohesion and act as the 'glue' that bonds an organization together. Because a shared culture encourages people to accept common goals and to identify with each other, it can also facilitate the processes of co-ordination and control within a complex organization. MNCs are by nature very complex organizations. By giving the members of such organizations some common reference points and shared ways of interpreting their working reality, a common organizational culture can reduce uncertainty and promote cross-border consistency of best practice, both internally (across departments or country groupings) and externally (to customers and other stakeholders). In providing meaning to their work and to their membership of an organization, an appropriate and cohesive culture can also be an important source of motivation for employees.

Managing cultural diversity within international strategy

Cultural diversity is becoming commonplace with regionalization, globalization and the continually increasing levels of international trade. How MNCs manage to achieve integration between their various national and international divisions, or successfully integrate a cross-border acquisition, or even get an internal multicultural team to work together effectively, depends on their ability to achieve a 'fit' between these various cultures. Fit refers to the extent to which different cultures are brought into a workable relationship that permits them to operate without undue misunderstanding and tension between their divisions, their alliance partners, their businesses or their staff teams.

The active management of cultural diversity is aimed at the achievement of a 'cultural fit' between groups, divisions or teams. Cultural fit means that cultures are combined in a mutually acceptable manner. 'Fit' does not necessarily mean integration of the cultures; there may be other ways in which they can be accommodated. There are a number of broad options for the management of cultural diversity. Some will provide a better cultural fit than others.

The two basic choices in the management of MNC cultural diversity are:

- whether headquarters MNC culture should *dominate* or whether to strive for a balance of contributions from the subsidiaries' cultures;
- whether to attempt an *integration* of headquarters/subsidiaries' cultures (with the aim of deriving synergy from them) or to segregate the various subsidiary cultures (with the aim of avoiding possible conflict and reducing the effort devoted toward cultural management).

These two dimensions of choice give rise to the four broad possibilities shown in Figure 5.1. Following Perlmutter (1969) we have drawn on his well-known cultural typology which offers the following MNC organizational types: *Ethnocentric* – all key positions filled by parent company nationals; *Polycentric* – host country managers in domestic subsidiaries while parent company nationals dominate HQ; *Geocentric* – best people for jobs regardless of nationality. Perlmutter has thus provided the vocabulary for describing our four MNC options given in Figure 5.1.The first three are all options offering a basis for cultural fit, though not generating the same level of benefit from the different cultures. The fourth possibility is one of failure, likely to lead to parent–subsidiary conflict and, at best, suboptimal performance.

1. *'Geocentric'* – a policy aimed at cultural integration of both or all headquarters/subsidiary cultures.
2. *'Ethnocentric'* – a policy aimed at cultural integration on the basis of dominance by the headquarters' culture.
3. *'Polycentric'* – a policy aimed at an acceptable balance between the influence within the MNC of various subsidiary/divisional cultures, but not striving for integration between them.
4. *'Culture clash'* – which may occur when headquarters seeks domination but fails to secure integration or acceptance.

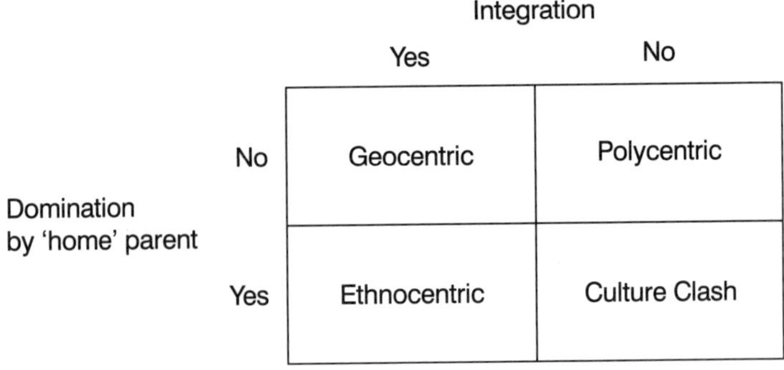

Figure 5.1 Management of cultural diversity in MNCs: four options

Geocentric aims at achieving the fullest possible fit between cultures. It is the policy best suited to optimizing and promoting learning between the different constituent parts of the MNC. With synergy, elements from each participant culture are combined to bring about an effective management system and deployment of resources. The idea of synergy is that the whole is greater than the sum of its parts. The key idea is that the 'positive aspects of the various cultures are preserved, combined, and expanded upon to create a new whole' (Tung, 1993, p.465). The achievement of synergy does not ignore or suppress cultural differences, but requires that time and effort be devoted to discussing them openly.

An MNC may be recognized as having a general superiority in technical and managerial know-how from which the whole company and all its subsidiaries could benefit. In these circumstances, an *ethnocentric* policy will be adopted, a policy aiming at integration on the basis of dominance by the headquarters culture.

Polycentric is a policy which aims at an acceptable balance between the cultural inputs of subsidiaries, teams, alliance partners or divisions, but does not attempt any integration or synthesis between them. In an international joint venture say, one partner may introduce its own systems for production and quality control, while the other partner continues to manage external transactions in the field of supply, distribution and government relations as before. This form of accommodation, whilst aceptable, clearly can be a suboptimal solution in other respects. Cultural segregation between subsidiaries means a separation of tasks which each business unit will manage itself. Such an approach obviously reduces the opportunities for mutual learning to a very low level. It may also lead to a poorly integrated and inefficient management system for the MNC as a whole, with unnecesary duplication of effort and with continuing problems due to limited communications, and a sense of rivalry, between different functions within the organization.

Polycentrism may also give rise to personal problems for individual managers who are sent to work in the overseas subsidiary, especially if they are expatriates. It can create difficulties for an expatriate to acquire the local language or understand the behavioural norms of the country where the subsidiary is located. The expatriate and his or her family will tend to be isolated, possibly in their own foreign 'ghetto', with a high chance of family stress and personal failure in the role.

The fourth possibility is of *culture clash.* This situation can arise if headquarters attempts to pursue a policy of domination without securing adequate levels of operational co-operation and co-ordination. Tension and conflict will result, with performance adversely affected. Such clashes can develop out of the MNC headquarters (perhaps after an overseas acquisition) unilaterally introducing its own norms and practices, derived from its own culture. If this situation is handled badly, then culture clash, and eventual possible breakdown, is the more likely outcome. In this surprisingly common situation, a divestment is likely to occur in due course after this type of disastrous post-acquisition management process.

Achieving cultural fit

Much of the responsibility for improving cultural fit within an MNC lies with its chief executive and other senior managers. The senior management team is responsible for generating a sense of common purpose within the organization. The idea of cultural fit only makes sense if some genuine understanding exists amongst the MNCs managerial groups as to the style and content of the various cultures co-existing within it. Therefore the content of cultures within an MNC need to be assessed, so that actual degrees of difference between them may be appreciated. Only in this way can the MNC harness the resources offered by each culture and attempt to develop realistic policies for constructive integration.

Some cultural attributes are more deeply rooted than others, and although all organizational cultures are supported by 'cultural webs' (Johnson, 1990), these will differ considerably in their responsiveness to change. Johnson (1990) described the cultural web of an organization as consisting of the structures of power and authority, control systems, routines and rituals, symbols, stories and myths which represent the reality to which the members of that organization have become accustomed, and which in turn act to maintain and reinforce its dominant cultural paradigm. Just as the elements of the cultural web for a steel manufacturer or an oil exploration company are likely to be different from that of a law firm or a fashion designer, so will cultural web characteristics vary by nation. For example, within an individualist culture, common organizational stories might include those about organization 'mavericks', i.e. those individuals who do not conform and who often acquire heroic stature as a result of their non-conformist exploits, although perhaps this would be more acceptable in a fashion house than in a bank. In a collectivist culture such stories would make little sense and may be virtually incomprehensible. If they existed at all, they would more likely to be describing bad role models rather than organizational heroes.

Such an analysis may be similarly applied to the web of a national culture: its political structures, institutional bodies, rituals, symbols, historical stories, and so on. The general principle here is that the more deeply entrenched is the web reinforcing a culture, the greater will be the resistance of its constituent individuals and groups (such as shareholders, financial institutional stakeholders, professional associations, labour representatives, the separate nationalities, government agencies) to cultural change. The more a given culture is perceived by stakeholders to serve their personal interests, the more entrenched it is likely to be. The constituent parts of a cultural web will indicate which elements need to be addressed as part of the process of bringing the divergent cultures closer, as in the context of a cross-border acquisition discussed earlier, or in MNC headquarters managers gradually learning how to help make an overseas subsidiary work effectively. This process of a mutual (although asymmetrical) acculturation process has been common for Japanese parent company managers learning how to manage local European or American subsidiaries throughout the 1970s and 1980s. Pure Japanese management systems and practices did not take root; they were adapted to absorb some of elements of local working practices. This process of cultural adaptation of course also needs to occur for European and US firms operating in Japan, East Asia, the Middle East and Africa.

Achieving personal cultural fit

The cross-cultural adjustment of individual managers is a huge problem for MNCs. Black and Mendenhall (1990) found that between 16 and 40 per cent of all expatriate managers given foreign assignments ended them early either because of their poor performance or their inability to adjust to the foreign environment. They also found that up to 50 per cent of those who stayed were functioning poorly. They estimated the cost of each failed expatriate assignment to be between $50 000 and $150 000, and further estimated that the direct costs of failed expatriate assignments to US MNCs is over $2 billion a year. This estimate did not include intangible costs such as reputation effects or loss of potential business. Their data are now about 10 years old and in the intervening period, both the volume of international trade and the frequency of such international assignments and their associated costs have continued to rise.

Two policies frequently adopted to reduce such adjustment problems are: selecting for such assignments people with previous international experience and anticipatory training. Neither policy has been shown to be universally effective. For example, for executives with experience of previous international roles, the nature of that previous experience is relevant. Many expatriate managers and their families simply withdraw into an expatriate community, thus avoiding much real cross-cultural contact. Such expatriate ghettos not only prevent any real adjustment, they also may encourage the wholesale application of 'home' practices (i.e. doing things according to the expatriate's own national or organizational norms). MNCs need to choose staff for such roles who have demonstrated a positive approach during their previous experience.

Anticipatory training must offer language proficiency to an appropriate standard, since a high standard of communication skills is necessary to avoid misunderstandings, as well as to enhance relationships. Any general and specific cultural information must be well-informed, realistic and up-to-date.

Although these points may be obvious, many such training programmes convey inaccurate knowledge. The trainer should therefore be someone who is from the relevant country and who has maintained regular contact with it. Such training is costly and time-consuming. Increasingly, where possible, MNCs try to draw on their existing staff who themselves come from mixed cultural backgrounds and who may therefore already be bilingual, such as Chinese-Americans. Longer-term anticipatory socialization (rather than just short-term training) is intended when entrepreneurs or executives send their children to study abroad as part of the development of future international management skills for the firm.

Achieving inter-cultural communication

MNC communication takes place between the divisions and subsidiaries, between the staff working within these business units and between all levels of business units and the parent headquarters. Each of these lines of communication may cross boundaries both of organizational and national cultures. Many MNCs have begun to develop roles which are conceived as 'boundary spanners' (Newman, 1992a, 1992b). He defines this role as follows:

> 'The process of boundary spanning builds a bridge between two different organizations or between two or more people coming from different cultures. Boundary spanners – the persons who perform the bridging activity – need several talents: 1) An empathetic understanding of the customs, values, beliefs, resources, and commitments of people and organizations on each side of the boundary; 2) understanding of the technical issues involved in the relationship; and 3) ability to explain and interpret both 1) and 2) to people on both sides of the boundary.' (1992a, p.149).

The key role played by boundary spanners in contributing to the requirements of global integration in MNCs is described in the example of the global account manager's (GAM) role as developed within Hewlett-Packard (described in Chapter 9). A different type of boundary spanning role may be that of the chief executive of a cross-border joint venture, whose political and communication skills are often key in smoothing the difficulties that arise. In the cross-border strategic alliance between the Royal Bank of Scotland and the Banco Santander of Spain, the role of the boundary-spanners Walter Stewart (Royal Bank of Scotland) and Jose Saavedra (Banco Santander) was key. Their joint ability to identify cultural differences between the partners and deal with them sensitively has been a major factor in the success of that alliance between the two banks (see also Chapter 11, Box 11.1) The availability of boundary spanners, together with relevant anticipatory training and people with relevant experience, are all management practices which can enhance opportunities for positive cultural fit and cultural learning.

Achieving effective multicultural teams

In practical terms, cultural integration often consists of getting multicultural teams to operate effectively. Such teams arise in meetings between managers and staff within and between MNC subsidiaries, as well as internal groups at headquarters or specially constructed and dedicated project teams or task forces.

In the alliance between the two car companies Rover (UK) and Honda (Japan), the alliance teams experienced early problems with cultural differences and cultural stereotyping. However, relations within the teams evolved in different ways over time, dependent on a number of contextual factors. Particularly relevant was Rover's poor financial position which emphasized its need to make the teams work and achieve the necessary learning experience. The pressure was less insistent on Honda, but its Japanese cultural socialization pattern made it a naturally good team player anyway. Interaction between senior managers and team members appeared to have a beneficial effect, as did the passage of time, since the alliance was accompanied by increasingly successful learning during its lifespan.

Summary

Culture is an important aspect of organizational life. MNCs will contain a complex mix of organizational cultures and national cultures. The differences between national cultures may strongly affect the ability of different parts of the MNC to work together effectively and to sensitively avoid misunderstanding, both internally and externally. Cultures give rise to differences in typical management practices and policy orientations. All these differences have to be accommodated within the various subsidiaries, divisions and teams that make up an MNC.

Cultural diversity reveals itself in many ways, from forms of polite address to fundamental values. Although people rarely change their underlying values, possibilities do exist for achieving cultural adaptation and accommodation between individuals and groups who come from very different cultural backgrounds. Organizational cultures may, and do, adapt to different national cultures.

A mixture of national and organizational cultures is not always a problem for MNCs. It may also bring positive benefits to the organization, since cultural diversity creates opportunities for adaptation and learning. Managerial practices throughout the MNC may benefit from the organization's absorption of different cultural practices. Indeed, these may be competencies from which the organization as a whole may learn.

We have described some ways of accommodating cultural differences and differences in managerial practices within organizations. It is possible to adopt the MNC parent culture as the dominant mode. Alternatively, the subsidiary cultures and practices can co-exist, applied to optimum effect in different parts of the MNC's operations. Yet another approach is to attempt to integrate differing practices and to derive synergy from this integration. We also gave some guidelines for improving cultural fit within the MNC. These would assist individual adjustment to different cultures, promote better communication between staff from different cultures, and improve the effectiveness of cross-cultural teams.

Part 2

Issues of co-ordination

6

The international corporate structure model

The multinational corporation (MNC) has dominated the international business environment at least since World War Two. One of the most popular academic rationales for the MNC is that of Dunning's (1974) eclectic paradigm described in Chapter 2. Rugman (in Rugman *et al.*, 1985) provides a different characterization of the same ownership, localization, internalization (OLI) elements used by Dunning. However, Rugman combines the three elements into two factors: firm-specific advantages (FSAs – which include 'O' and 'I') and country-specific advantages (CSAs – which incorporates 'L'). Rugman sees international strategy formation by MNCs as an outcome of the balance of benefits to the MNC of sets of FSAs and CSAs within each firm. Both Dunning's and Rugman's approaches to explaining the strategic decision-making of international firms assumes that decision-making is based on rationality, and hence on the attempt to minimize transaction costs and factor costs. These are not always justifiable assumptions. Porter (1986) identifies the two key tasks of the would-be international firm as: first, to achieve the optimal form of *configuration* (where to locate value chain activities, which would include CSA issues); and second, type and degree of *co-ordination* (how to set up the appropriate organization structure and systems to support the actual choice of configuration of the MNC, which would incorporate FSA issues).

In Figure 6.1 *dispersed configuration* means having value chain activities in many countries; while *concentrated configuration* means having value chain activities mostly in the home country. Obviously an array of possibilities exists along that continuum. On the other axis, we use *high co-ordination* to mean mainly centralized decision-making and *low co-ordination* to mean mainly decentralized decision-making. The company examples used on the matrix in this figure are all MNCs which feature in various chapters of this book. Thus, in Figure 6.1 Gillette has a globally dispersed configuration with high centralization of decision-making at MNC headquarters. Nestlé is

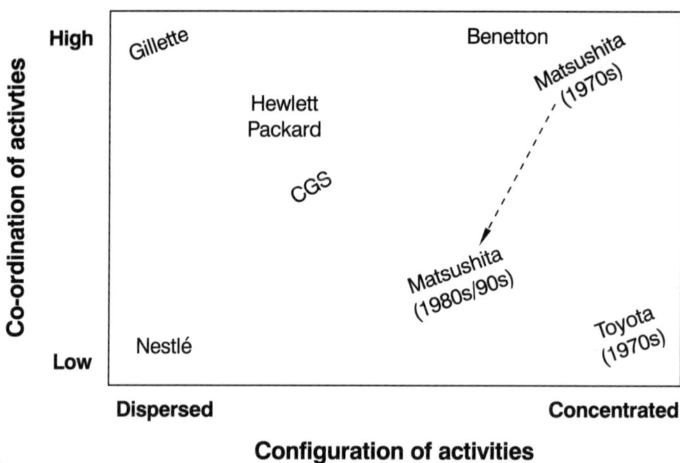

Figure 6.1 Configuration/co-ordination matrix. *Source:* Adapted from Porter (1986)

shown with a dispersed configuration and low co-ordination; a way of capturing in the matrix Nestlé's multidomestic MNC structure. We have shown Matsushita of Japan twice: first (top right) as it was structured in the 1970s, with a concentrated configuration and high co-ordination, which means that it was very centralized in its decision-making and resource-allocation processes at that time; and second (bottom right) as it was by the late 1980s/early 1990s, with a more dispersed configuration and more decentralization of decision-making. The reasons for this shift were discussed in Chapter 4 (Box 4.2) in explaining the drivers (Yip, 1992) behind Matsushita's global to 'glocal' international strategy.

It would probably be more accurate in discussing the concept of MNC *co-ordination* to move away from simple alternatives such as centralization or decentralization, since such dichotomies are rather old-fashioned and do not capture well enough the fluid but clear objective of co-ordination – to get dispersed activities such as disaggregated R&D departments, production plants and marketing teams, to truly work together (Birkinshaw *et al.*, 1995; De Koning *et al.*, 1997; Porter, 1986). The configuration and co-ordination of the activities of a multinational corporation on a global scale certainly provides a more daunting and more complex task than is involved in carrying out such activities on a purely national scale. However, as is implicit in the concept of the strategic flexibility of the MNC (Buckley and Casson, 1998a; Kogut, 1985), MNCs have more choices and options with regard to configuration than are available to a national firm. International strategy choices by an MNC are complex and involve the search for competitive advantage from global configuration/co-ordination choices throughout the entire value chain of the firm.

This chapter attempts to provide some answers to the question of how MNCs configure and co-ordinate their international strategies, by examining various approaches to internationalization as a strategy process (Buckley and Casson, 1998b; Melin, 1992). These will include stages models of internationalization, studies of the link between strategy and structure in MNCs, and more recent organizational models of MNCs. Finally, we will introduce a model to summarize and discuss the four basic MNC forms described.

The stage models of internationalization

Vernon's (1966) product lifecycle model of the internationalization of a firm suggested that the process should take place in stages. First of all, a product is developed and sold domestically. In stage two it is exported and then, as scale develops in stage three exporting will be replaced by foreign direct investment (FDI). That will lead to its being produced in the countries in which demand for it has proved large. This stage three is thus the growth stage of the lifecycle. In the maturity stage, stage four, production moves to lower wage cost developing economies, and the final stage is decline where the product is imported into the country from which it originally emerged. This is a very stylized model, which assumes that the firm with the new product is starting out from scratch with no existing international organization. Its basic contribution to theory is to demonstrate how internationalization can cause production to gradually move from the home country.

A somewhat similar stage model was developed in Uppsala by Johanson and Vahlne (1977). They envisaged a firm gradually internationalizing through increased commitment to and knowledge of foreign markets. The firm is therefore most likely to enter markets with successively greater psychic distance (Perlmutter, 1969). Thus, at the outset it sells to countries culturally similar to itself. The model depends on the notion that uncertainty, and hence risk, increases with increasing psychic distance and unfamiliarity. The problem with this model is that there are many examples of internationalizing companies who have merely gone for the large rather than the familiar markets and many markets at the same time, e.g. Sony Walkman, McDonald's, Levis. The contrast is between the so-called 'waterfall' model of global expansion (one country at a time) and the contrasting 'sprinkler' model (many countries at a time). In current markets with ever shortening product lifecycles, and the strategic importance of 'time-to-market', there is often insufficient time to adopt the waterfall approach. At all events both of the popular stage models are highly sequential in the stages they describe and are both very deterministic.

Studies of the link between strategy and structure in MNCs

The first major theory linking strategy and structure in MNCs is identified with Alfred Chandler. This 'structure follows strategy' school first emerged from Chandler's seminal book *Strategy and Structure* (1962) in which he described how a number of major US companies adopted the 'M-form' (multi-divisional) organization in order to better cope with the need to co-ordinate activities around the globe. Stopford and Wells (1972), following in Chandler's path, developed a simple descriptive model to illustrate the typical stages of development for companies progressively moving towards an international organization structure. They saw this as a process driven by two dimensions: the number of products sold internationally, i.e. foreign product diversity; and the importance of international sales to the company, i.e. foreign sales as a percentage of total sales.

Stopford and Wells (1972) suggested that international divisions were set up at an early stage of internationalization when the figures for both product diversity and percentage of foreign sales were both low. Then, those companies which found that international expansion led to substantial foreign product diversity tended to adopt a worldwide product division structure (pathway (a) on Figure 6.2). Or if companies expanded overseas without increasing product diversity, they tended to adopt a geographical area structure (pathway (b) on Figure 6.2). Finally, when both foreign sales and the diversity of products were high a global matrix emerged. Thus the grid structure of the MNC with a geographic axis and a product group axis emerged. Bjorkman (1990),

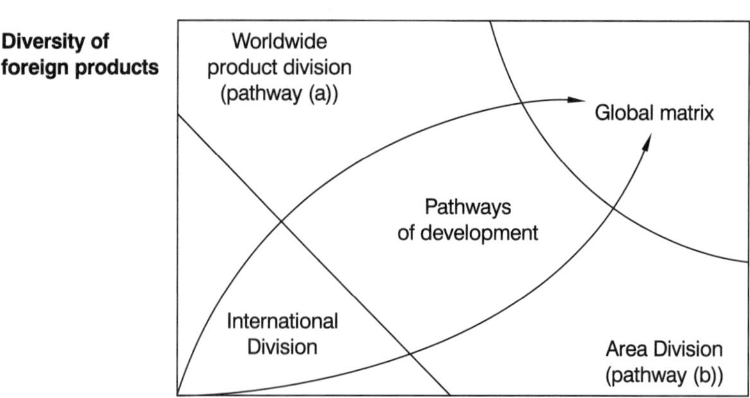

Figure 6.2 The Stopford and Wells matrix: pathways for international development. *Source:* Adapted from Stopford and Wells (1972)

however, was unable in his research to correlate structures with performance. He therefore concluded that the adoption of new structures was more a matter of fashion than anything else and resulted from firms copying current organizational trends at any specific time.

Recent organizational models of MNCs

Bartlett and Ghoshal (1989) and Prahalad and Doz (1987) are of the newer 'process' school of MNC management. They emphasize control through socialization and the creation of a verbal information network to develop a corporate culture that transcends national boundaries. This school emphasizes *global integration* combined with *local responsiveness*. Both sets of authors have used variations of a *global integration/local responsiveness* framework in their work. Bartlett (1986) described these two major forces and their organizational effect on shaping the international strategies of MNCs as follows:

> Some (forces), such as the increasing manufacturing economies associated with global or regional scale demand, or the need to spread escalating technological development costs over shorter product life cycles, tend to create the need for greater global co-ordination of effort and integration of operations. Other forces, such as national differences in consumer taste or market structure, or host government protectionism or regulation, increase the need for more local differentiation and responsiveness. It is the balance and interrelationship of these two forces that is influential in shaping the organizational task of the MNC. (1986, p.369)

All international strategy decisions are made with this trade-off in mind. This approach is not at all deterministic or prescriptive of organization structure; it is contingent. The emphasis is on the optimal functioning of MNCs in the markets in which they operate. Figure 6.3 illustrates how the balance of these forces for global integration and national responsiveness can vary from one industry to another.

Figure 6.3 shows how these different industry forces influence the strategic task and hence the appropriate response of the firm. For example, there is little incentive to build a global scale plant for the manufacture of corrugated cardboard (bottom left in grid) and little basis for differentiating this basic commodity product by national market. By contrast, consumer electronics (top left in grid – together with batteries and razor blades) offers high R&D and manufacturing scale economies, together with standard design opportunities and little need for differentiation by national market. Food products, soaps, detergents, together with some services such as insurance (bottom right in grid), all need to be adapted to meet local consumer preferences and differences in distribution channels per market, as well as various regulatory requirements.

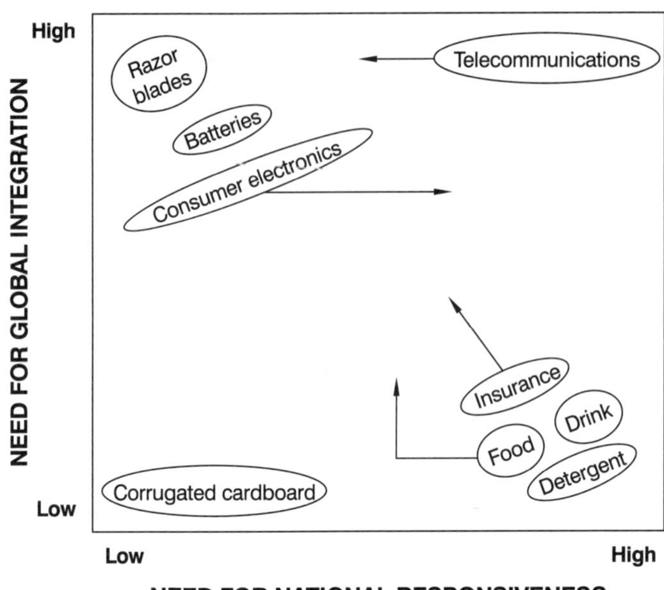

Figure 6.3 An 'integration-responsiveness' grid. *Source:* Adapted from Bartlett and Ghoshal (1989)

Telecommunications (top right in grid) requires high capital investment and massive R&D costs, but still must meet the variation in technical standards and service levels required by the different national and regional markets. In addition, you will note the direction of the arrows attached to many of these industry positions. They indicate directions of movement over time for the different industries illustrated, as the forces shaping the industry dynamics shift and change. Each movement around the grid denotes the need for a review of the existing configuration of the MNC, and a corresponding change in its levels of global or regional co-ordination and integration.

It should be obvious that each of the four extreme corners of Figure 6.3 represents one of the four approaches to being international described in Chapter 1 (Table 1.1). Working clockwise around the integration-responsiveness grid from bottom left, these are: international exporter, global, transnational and multidomestic.

Strategic issues affecting the four approaches

All international competitors have to be at least as good as a local firm providing a product or a service in the local market. Poorly organized international competitors may bear higher costs than local competitors, given their more complex structures and systems. Initially also local companies are likely to be equipped with better knowledge of the local market. Therefore one of the key issues in operating globally is how to organize one's enterprise so that it is possible to compete with local companies in terms of both demand and supply.

In some ways the development of an international competitive strategy is no different from the development of a domestic market competitive strategy. Competitive strategy is about being able to achieve the highest level of customer satisfaction or 'perceived use value' (PUV) at the lowest cost in relation to one's competitors in each product/market, whether the market is national or international. 'PUV' is a term used to identify the dimensions and attributes that customers value in a product or a service, and which influence their customer buying behaviour (Bowman and Faulkner, 1997). Similarly, international corporate strategy is about selecting, resourcing and controlling the businesses within the corporation. Corporate strategy is about the mix of businesses within the corporation according to market attractiveness and the risk profile of the firm; the overarching organizational structures, systems and processes to support those businesses; and the investment in necessary firm-wide resources and capabilities either by investing internally or acquired by merger and acquisition activity or through participating in alliances with partner organizations. This is so whether the firm is competing nationally or internationally. However, in international strategy there are both additional problems, such as the management of cultural diversity across the organization, and greater opportunities and options, from either leverage or arbitrage as identified by Kogut (1985) and discussed in Chapter 1.

How then is a market defined as national or global? That decision is made by the preferences of customers and the cost structures of the operating firms. If Sony is able to bring its electronic products to the UK at competitive prices, and UK customers find them acceptable as alternative sources of PUV to those of local suppliers, then the consumer electronic market has become international. This will not of course apply to all products. The market for corrugated cardboard is said to have a radius of about 50 miles. It is a low value commodity in which little differentiation is possible, and once 50 miles have been travelled the local producer is able to realize lower costs than the travelling producer. The same applies to building aggregates. This explains the position of corrugated cardboard on Figure 6.3.

There is then a *strategic market* (Barwise and Robertson, 1992) which is defined by the relative homogeneity of consumer tastes, and the possible cost structure of the company that enables it to be a credible competitor over varying distances. Since Levitt's (1983) opening remarks in the debate about global consumers, followed by Sheth (1983), Ohmae (1985, 1989) and others more recently (Makhija *et al.*, 1997), it is accepted that with the passing of each year more and more products and services fall into the category of global competition, as similar products and services are sold around the world, as technologies too become global, and as transportation costs become a smaller and smaller percentage of delivered costs.

Strategic issues affecting the four approaches to international strategy fall into three categories:

1. Those that determine which segment to select, and whether or not they involve global competition.
2. Those that affect the company's ability to resource and deliver the product at a competitive price anywhere in the world, i.e. political factors and cost structures (configuration issues).
3. Those that are concerned with how a company should organize itself to control its international activities (co-ordination issues).

We will deal with each of these in turn.

Selecting where to compete

A useful framework to help managers decide how to approach the selection, and eventually, the configuration task in their international strategy, is that provided by Ghoshal (1987). He identifies three strategic objectives of any global strategy and three key bases of potential competitive advantage derivable from a global strategy. The resulting framework is given in Table 6.1.

Table 6.1 Global strategy: an organizing framework

	Sources of competitive advantage		
Strategic objectives	**Country differences**	**Scale economies**	**Scope economies**
Efficiency in current operations	Factor cost differences, e.g. wages and cost of capital	Potential scale economies in each value chain activity	Sharing of resources and capabilities across products, markets and businesses
Risk management	Assessment of risk by country	Balancing scale with strategic and operational flexibility	Portfolio diversification
Innovation and learning	Learning from cultural variety in process and practice	Opportunities for technology-based cost reduction	Shared organizational learning

Source: Adapted from Ghoshal (1987)

The three basic strategic objectives of a global strategy in Table 6.1 are seen as:

1. *Efficiency*, i.e. carrying out all value chain activities to a required quality at lowest cost. This is the most frequently emphasized objective in the literature. Indeed, it is often the only objective mentioned. Each of the OLI (or FSA/CSA) factors need to be considered when reaching decisions about the optimal efficiency of any specific activity.
2. *Risk management*, i.e. managing and balancing the risks inherent in operating in a number of diverse countries, e.g. exchange rate risks, political risks, or raw material sourcing risks. This is very strongly concerned with L (location) or CSA factors.
3. *Innovation learning and adaptation*, i.e. the opportunity to learn from the different societies, cultures and markets in which one operates.

Ghoshal's organizing framework takes the three types of strategic objective identified above and relates them to what are identified as the three key sources of competitive advantage, namely:

1. National differences, i.e. competitive advantage can come from exploiting differences in input and output markets in different countries, e.g. low wage countries are perhaps the most commonly cited examples of such factors, but every other type of national difference should also be considered as part of the strategic flexibility of the MNC. That should include for example relative cost of capital, tax regimes, and so on.
2. Scale economies provide a source of competitive advantage if one firm is able to adopt a configuration of its activities such that each activity is able to operate at the optimal economic scale for minimum unit costs, especially if competitors fail to do this. Of course, achieving optimal scale economies globally may sometimes lead to dangerous inflexibility. This creates higher rather than lower risk if fluctuating exchange rates alter or destroy these potential economies after plant has been brought on line to take advantage of them.
3. Scope economies are the third source of global competitive advantage. These have been more fully discussed in Chapter 1. Simple illustrations of economies of scope are found in the use of global brand names like Coca-Cola or McDonald's, but can be found in any area of the firm's activities where resources used to produce or market one product in one country can be reused, virtually without cost, to do the same for other products and in other countries. Technology, IT, any learning or skills are further examples of areas of potential scope economies.

This organizing framework enables the global decision-taker to identify the potential sources of global competitive advantage available to the firm, and to cross-reference them to the three basic types of strategic objective – achieving efficiency, managing risk and enabling learning – with the ultimate objective of deciding where, why and how to compete internationally.

Resourcing global production

Further decisions regarding the configuration of activities on a global scale are concerned with the issue of what parts of the value chain for a product or service should be produced within the company, and what should be outsourced. Configuration also means deciding where such production or other activities should take place – in the home country, the Far East or elsewhere.

The configuration profile is influenced by a number of barriers that have historically ensured that most markets remained local. As already discussed, however, many of these are becoming progressively less important. Global products had traditionally been considered to have limited potential in many industries, since people in different parts of the world living in very diverse cultures were assumed to have different tastes and values, and therefore to require different products and services to satisfy them. To some extent that is still true; more soft drinks are sold in the USA per head than any other country in the world; more tea per head in the UK than elsewhere; the Far East consumes more rice than the West; and the West more potatoes than the Far East. Yet such variations are far less common in the manufactured products area. Levitt's (1983) comments that:

> ...the same single standardized products – autos, steel, chemicals, petroleum, cement, agricultural commodities and equipment, industrial and commercial construction, banking, insurance, computers, semiconductors, transport, electronic instruments, pharmaceuticals, and telecommunications (are sold) largely in the same single ways everywhere.

while over-generalized to make his point in a dramatic way, are nevertheless less controversial and more accurate with each passing year.

If the limitations on demand for would-be global products are less, we should also consider barriers to the supply of global products and services. The traditional supply-side barriers that make cross-border strategies more difficult were referred to in Chapter 1; for example tariffs, government regulations, different languages and cultures, and exchange rates. Some of the drivers behind the perceived regionalization and globalization of markets during the 1980s and 1990s have brought about the marginalization of, or complete elimination of, many of the traditional barriers to trade.

A range of these traditional barriers to cross-border trade were discussed in Chapter 3. The spread of 'Western' culture through films, videos, travel, and satellite television, and the greater interest in Eastern food, clothing styles, art and music, has done much to homogenize tastes. Many of the effects of the formation of larger trading blocs on the supply side have been significant. We have noted such international trade agreements by the EU, ASEAN, GATT, Mercosur and NAFTA set up to reduce the levels of tariffs, and where possible eliminate quotas and domestic subsidies (outside agriculture). Fewer countries now require local majority shareholdings in joint ventures set up with foreign companies, and where they do, the foreign companies have learnt to live with this and operate in a multicultural way. Language barriers remain to some degree although, for good or ill, English is becoming the language of MNCs and of international business, and any company wishing to operate globally has to ensure that its senior executives are proficient in it.

The remaining traditional barriers are transport costs and exchange rates. Transport costs are reducing, but they remain an inhibitor to competitive global trade, the importance of which varies with the value and volume of the article traded. Transport costs are virtually irrelevant to international trade in diamonds, but of considerable importance in limiting such trade in corrugated cardboard. Exchange rates, however, will remain of considerable importance, whilst every nation maintains a unique currency and retains the right to devalue or revalue it against other currencies, when the government or the market deems this advisable. To be caught with cash or debtors in a newly devalued or depreciated currency can wipe out any profit at a stroke. Against this background one can appreciate the move to a Europe-wide currency (the 'euro') in the EU, which enables European trading nations to get rid of internal exchange rate transaction costs across a market size similar to that of the USA or Japan, neither of which have carried these additional costs of trade in their internal market.

Since these barriers to global trade are now so reduced in strength, corporate strategy decisions concerning cross-border trade must be taken as it would be for domestic products, but within the mindset of international strategy. By this we mean fully utilizing the insights of Kogut's (1985) arbitrage and leverage opportunities, Dunning's (1989, 1998) OLI factors, Rugman *et al*'s (1985) FSA/CSA balance, Porter's (1986) configuration/co-ordination framework, Bartlett's (1986), Bartlett and Ghoshal's (1989) integration-responsiveness grid, and so on, to inform your approach to each industry and market.

One approach to general corporate strategy decision-making uses a 'customer matrix' and a 'producer matrix' (Bowman and Faulkner, 1997), each of which should be constructed for the strategic market of each product/market. The 'customer matrix' is a tool developed by Bowman and Faulkner (1997) with two axes on the matrix (PUV and price) to assess the market's view of the relative strength of the company's products compared to those of its competitors. Similarly, the 'producer matrix' has axes of effectiveness (arising from competencies) and unit costs. It assesses the 'real' underlying strength of the company in relation to its competitors in terms of its competencies and factor costs. These analyses will show for which markets the company has attractive products. The market size should also be assessed to ensure it is sufficiently interesting for the firm. Since the dimensions of PUV are likely to be different by country, or at least to have different weightings, a separate set of matrices will need to be developed for each country. Perceived price is also likely to be different for each country for reasons of exchange rate, local taxation and cost of living, and the impact of transport, and perhaps other costs will need to be factored into the producer matrix.

Controlling the international corporation

It is not just the configuration of the value chain that is the key to international competitiveness, it is also the way in which it is co-ordinated and controlled. In fact since outsourcing, virtual corporations and networks are in the ascendant as modern organizational forms, the MNCs international co-ordination and control capabilities may well be the key to its international effectiveness.

Ghoshal and Nohria (1993) used the integration-responsiveness grid to identify four appropriate organizational forms for coping with our four basic types of MNC environments: global, international exporter, multidomestic and transnational. Their research placed the following industries in the *global* box: construction and mining, non-ferrous metals, industrial chemicals, scientific measuring instruments and engines. Little national responsiveness was seen as necessary in these industries. *International exporter* industries low on global scale economies and national responsiveness were: metal industries, machinery, paper, textiles and printing and publishing . *Multidomestic* industries high on the need for local adaptation were beverages, food, rubber, household appliances and tobacco, and the *transnational* industries high on both national adaptation and global scale were seen to include drugs and pharmaceuticals, photographic equipment, computers and automobiles. Of course as particular industries evolve they may well move boxes. Automobiles, for example, may well be moving into the global box.

Ghoshal and Nohria highlight organizational process as being as important as organization structure. They claim that when process environment and organizational form are correctly aligned, MNC performance is higher than when there is a 'misfit' between them. On the process side they identify structural uniformity as best suited to global environments and organizational forms. Differentiated structures to fit multidomestic environments, integrated variety to fit with the transnational form and *ad hoc* variety to fit with international environments.

The international corporate structure model

The four possible configurations described above are illustrated in the matrix shown in Figure 6.4. This matrix follows a tradition in international business research used and developed by Bartlett, Ghoshal, Doz, Prahalad and Stopford, amongst others, and already cited in this book. Although most authors vary their definitions to some extent, the underlying principles remain the same. In international business there is always a tension between the production efficiency need to make a standard product and ship it around the world with as little variation as possible at lowest cost, and the marketing need to offer a product to a local market that takes into account possible local tastes and culture. This tension exists of course in all business beyond the very local at all times, but it is most in evidence across borders.

The existence of this tension, and the resultant perceived trade-off between global standardization and local adaptation applies in a number of areas. It applies in varying degrees to different industries, e.g. commodities need no local adaptation, wheat is wheat, oil is oil but a car is not yet an undifferentiated product. It applies also to individual countries. If there is a market for a product in the USA, a similar market may exist in Europe, but more adaptation may be needed for India, Africa or the Far East. For example, McDonald's do not sell pure beef hamburgers in India for religious and cultural reasons.

A similar tension exists between business functions. It is possible for a pharmaceutical company marketing worldwide to carry out all its R&D in one major research site in its home base country. This achieves the greatest economies of scale in terms of running teams of research scientists, and having the hardware resources for them to carry out their research. However, if the company is big enough, it may need more than one R&D establishment in different parts of the world. This is not for reasons of scale economies but for market intelligence-gathering and to give it the necessary flexibility when the market environment changes unexpectedly. The same company may need a small number of production units sited regionally around the world to achieve the minimum economic size for scale economies in production. It may well need one sales force per country to develop and use the local market knowledge needed to achieve effective global reach with its portfolio of products, and to gain national and local acceptance.

These tensions exist for industries, for markets and for functions. Relevant balances and trade-off needs to be solved differentially for each contingent set of circumstances; international strategy to be effective must respond to contingency. How then should a multiproduct, multimarket global company be organized? There is not one response, but a number of responses to this issue, and as environmental circumstances change so will the organizational pressures, and the optimal solutions. Figure 6.4 shows the four most common organizational forms in response to each set of global/local contingencies.

There is some confusion in the international business literature over the appropriate term for firms in the bottom left-hand box. Bartlett and Ghoshal (1989) describe the relevant configurations for the global and the international

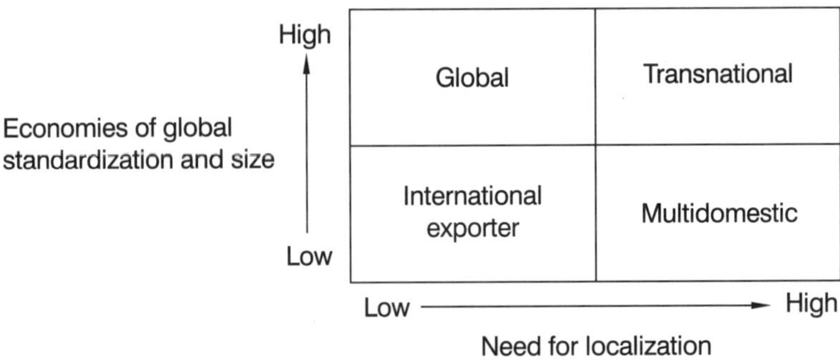

Figure 6.4 The international corporate structure model

models in terms which fit this box. The difference is that in their view there may be knowledge transfer from the headquarters unit to local companies in the international model, whereas their global model has a mentality that treats overseas operations as no more than delivery pipelines. What we call multidomestic, Bartlett and Ghoshal call their multinational; a company that operates with strong overseas companies and a portfolio mentality.

We believe that the term multinational should be the umbrella term to describe all company forms that trade internationally, and have a presence in a number of countries. In terms of our matrix this includes the company forms in all boxes of the matrix other than the bottom left-hand box. Let us look at each of the four types in Figure 6.4, starting with the global type.

The global company

In the top left-hand box is the *global* company producing standardized products for sale around the world such as Gillette razors. As a global company, Gillette may not have a major problem. Razor blades need little local adaptation, have an established technological production function, have an easily understandable marketing message, and therefore only sales need to be handled locally. In this model, the global corporation treats overseas operations as delivery pipelines to a unified global market. Most strategic decisions are centralized at the home country base, and there is tight operational control from the centre. There is likely to be very little adaptation of products to meet local needs. Gillette, Coca-Cola or Johnson and Johnson's Band-Aid division are all examples of this type of company.

The classical global organization model was one of the earliest international corporate forms that developed, after it became apparent that scale and scope economies were key to international competitiveness in many industries (Chandler, 1962, 1990a and 1990b). The global company built scale facilities to produce standard products, and shipped them worldwide. It is based on the centralization of assets, with overseas demand operations used to achieve global scale in home-base production.

The global corporation may have an international division in order to increase its foreign sales, but the international division is very much the poor relation of the domestic divisions, which are probably further subdivided into product group divisions. The company ships from its home base whenever possible, with very little regard for the differing tastes and preferences of the countries to which it is exporting. This form of organization was typical of the Japanese exporting companies of the 1970s, and is still common in many current USA corporations; the Spalding Sports group is an example of this mode.

The predominance in the international strategy literature of a focus on this simple model of the global firm is criticized by Yetton, Davis and Craig (1994). They target Porter's (1990) work, and the assumptions implicit in his 'diamond' framework in particular:

> Porter's primary concern with the capacity of the US to compete with Japan leads to a preoccupation with the globally exporting firm, which is the principal form by which Japanese manufacturing firms have competed internationally. He focuses not on the complexity of international operations, but on the characteristics of the home base market as a platform for a successful export strategy. Consequently the global MNC is his primary interest.

The international exporter

By contrast, the firm in the bottom left hand box, the *international exporter*, may not even think of itself as an international company. It exports opportunistically. Domestic customers are its lifeblood, but it will sell abroad if approached by an international customer, and in times of recession, when overcapacity looms, it may actively solicit international sales to fill its factories. Generally, however, the percentage of its home-based production exported is low, as a percentage of total sales. For many companies this may indeed be a transitional form, as its markets internationalize.

The multidomestic

In the bottom right-hand box is the *multidomestic company*. Its key characteristics are that of a portfolio of independent subsidiaries, one per country. Such a firm adopts country-centred strategies, and there is relatively little international co-ordination. To survive as a multidomestic it is important that there be unique product features required per country market and few opportunities for scale economies, since if such economies do exist in large measure the domestic subsidiary will be out-competed by the integrated global firm. In a rapidly globalizing world, traditional multidomestic firms are becoming rarer, since producing on a global scale and getting local acceptance for a global product is becoming the more powerful competitive stance. An illustration of the old style multidomestic is the pre-1970s Philips (as described in Chapter 4). The multidomestic form is sensitive to local needs but may not always achieve possible production scale economies. Although the same company name may be used in all countries in which the firm operates, this may be all that is in common between the various country operations. The products are fashioned to meet local demand and meet local tastes.

A more sophisticated, innovative form of multidomestic may now be observed. This *modern multidomestic* can provide an alternative effective form to the transnational if it concentrates on achieving scale and scope economies that are available to a large corporation. This involves the corporate centre playing a very positive value-adding role to ensure that best practice in one country is successfully transferred to the other countries in which the corporation operates (Anand and Delios, 1997). To compete successfully as a multinational organizational form the multidomestic must of course excel in responding sensitively to local PUV needs. In addition, however, the multidomestic operates best where the centre is able to establish a degree of 'friendly' competition between country units, where benchmarking is rigorously employed, and where process learning in one country is spread rapidly to the others (Yetton *et al.*, 1994).

Innovation must be similarly spread around the group with vigour, and incentives established for executives to think beyond the confines of their own country business unit for the good of the corporation. Unlike the traditional multidomestic, the successful modern multidomestic also has an active centre which carries out its selection task carefully, only entering markets where there is a clear demand for its (standard) products. In Yetton *et al.*'s (1994) words:

> Successful multidomestic corporations decouple the local, constrained product responsiveness from the global, integrated process and production platforms and manage them separately. In addition they minimize the risk by entering only friendly rather than relatively hostile markets, and outsourcing the local responsibilities to then local management...

which may be through an acquisition by takeover or a joint venture partner.

Traditional multidomestic forms that sacrifice production economies of scale, yet do not achieve economies of scope, or of learning, innovation, and process do now increasingly appear to be an endangered species. The Philips Group was an example of such a company prior to its repeated reorganizations from the late 1980s on. Management at the centre regarded overseas operations as a portfolio of independent businesses, and the corporate centre did not add value, as in other MNC organizational forms including the modern multidomestic, it is in a unique position to do.

The transnational organization form

Bartlett and Ghoshal (1989) suggested the concept of the *'transnational'* enterprise, a modern form for the MNC with some of the loose network characteristics of a strategic alliance, although ownership is all within the same firm. It is located in the top right-hand box of the Figure 6.4 matrix. Although it does have some home-based exports, it also has a high percentage of foreign production. However, it is not strongly directed from the home-base country. As Bartlett and Ghoshal (1989) explain: 'Managers are being forced to shift their thinking from the traditional task of controlling a hierarchy to managing a network'.

The transnational organization seeks to overcome the weaknesses of more traditional models by moving beyond the global integration/local responsiveness trade-off implicit in the traditional models. To be globally competitive now requires both. Bartlett and Ghoshal (1989, 1990, 1993) have argued that all MNCs must now be locally responsive, with learning as a key requirement for success, whilst also achieving optimal global scale and scope efficiencies. This can only be done by adopting new attitudes to capture knowledge from all parts of the MNC organization and enable it to pass in all directions as appropriate. They also support Ohmae's (1989) view of the desirability of a 'borderless' mindset within the firm. It should be global in mindset rather than, say, a Japanese or USA company with foreign subsidiaries. It may indeed have three or more head offices like NEC, as suggested by Nonaka (1989).

To succeed, the transnational form must integrate three flows: first, the company has to co-ordinate its internal flow of parts, components, and finished goods; second, it must manage the flow of funds, skills and other scarce resources among units; third, it must link the flow of intelligence, ideas and knowledge that are central to its innovation and learning capabilities. The transnational may exist more as an aspirational form than a real one as yet, although some organizations, such as the Swedish/Swiss ABB or the Japanese NEC, are often quoted as examples of the form. It is, however, the model which attempts to show the real complexity of the optimal co-ordination processes to achieve global competitive advantage for an MNC. The transnational represents a truly global enterprise, neither owned in one country, nor controlled from one unified corporate headquarters. It is therefore a genuine attempt to find a modern style of MNC capable of embracing the management of complexity, diversity, and change which is the central issue facing all MNCs.

Formal organization charts are only one aspect of what binds the transnational organization together. It is held together more strongly by managerial decision-making processes, which depend on information flows. Bartlett and Ghoshal believe it is not a new organizational form as such that will be needed to meet future global competition, but rather, a new philosophy towards achieving global competitive advantage by transforming existing thinking about local differentiation and global learning in the global enterprise. Clearly, the transnational is a new and more sophisticated concept than earlier organizational forms for the international enterprise. With its emphasis on a network philosophy and the absence of domination by a home-country-based head office, the philosophy can embrace equally well the enterprise based on a network of alliances as it can the integrated corporation. It can be seen, for example, in the approach taken by Fujitsu of Japan to the development of the global Fujitsu 'family' of companies.

Interestingly a similar philosophy is emerging amongst strategic theorists in Japan. Nonaka (1989) talks of the need to manage globalization as a self-renewing process in which information is the key to success:

> Globalization comes about through the interaction of articulated globalized knowledge and tacit localized knowledge, partly through the hybridization of personnel and consequent internalization of learning. (Nonaka, 1989)

Nonaka calls this 'compressive management', an interesting echo of Ansoff's (1984) 'accordion' management, similarly devised to deal with the uncertainties of the modern turbulent environment. This process can also lead quite acceptably to a hybridization of the company's headquarters, with perhaps one headquarters in Japan, another in the USA and maybe a third in Europe. As Contractor and Lorange (1988) have pointed out:

> One model of the MNC sees it as a closed internalized administrative system that straddles national boundaries. An alternative paradigm is to view the international firm as a member of various open and shifting coalitions, each with a specific strategic purpose.

There is considerable congruity between the philosophical standpoints of Bartlett and Ghoshal, of Contractor and Lorange, and of Nonaka in their rejection for the future of the rigid hierarchy of the traditional MNC, strongly controlled from its home base, even when allowing for local product variation. A world of sometimes shifting but continually renewing informal networks, cross-border partnerships and teams, and strategic alliances, fits well within this philosophy.

An illustration of the four organizational forms

Few companies meet all the criteria for the pure stereotypes, and there are transitional paths whereby companies restructure themselves from one form to another to meet the changing needs of their global market. The illustration in Box 6.1 may help, however, to clarify the mindsets behind each of the four stylized forms. We use the international strategy consulting firm McKinsey as our illustrative case.

Box 6.1 McKinsey as an Illustration of the Four Organizational Forms

Let us suppose that a financial services company in the City of London approaches the McKinsey London office with a 'request for proposal' mandate for a reorganization study. If this were to have happened in the early 1960s, it may have reached the firm when it was basically an 'international exporter' company (Figure 6.4 – bottom left-hand box). The request would have been transmitted to the New York head office. If the proposal were successful, the project would then have been staffed from New York and led by a New York consultant. US analytical models would have been used, largely unadjusted for local conditions, and London people would have been used to provide the necessary local intelligence.

If McKinsey were a 'global' firm (Figure 6.4 – top left-hand box), the UK office manager would negotiate the job and global models would be used, i.e. not purely US ones but certainly standardized ones. A New York engagement manager would probably come over with his team to run the study. UK consultants would be invited to New York for training and socialization in the ways and products of the firm. This was largely the situation when one of the authors was a member of the firm in the early 1970s.

If the firm were a largely multidomestic company (Figure 6.4 – bottom right-hand box), the McKinsey name would be used to get the study, but it would then be staffed and run from London, developing a specifically British solution of a bespoke nature without necessarily any contact with the USA. The performance of the London office would be judged by its sales and profits record. Firm-wide training programmes would not be held.

Currently, by the late 1990s however, McKinsey fits fairly closely with the criteria for a transnational firm (Figure 6.4 – top right-hand box). In this case there is complex multi-path information flow globally. Projects are staffed from wherever the expertise exists worldwide within the firm. Centres of excellence in particular specialist areas have developed around the world, led by expert individuals and teams. Technological and marketing centres of gravity move, often as a result of forces exogenous to the corporation, in search of any better fit (even if only short term) with particular markets.

In our imaginary illustration the City assignment would be negotiated from London with an international expert on hand. It would

••▶

cont.

then be internationally staffed with the 'best' resources available who would be personally 'bonded' by their identification with the firm culture as developed in particular through international training meetings and work on international project teams. The recommendations would be sensitively tailored to the specific situation but based on firm-wide expertise and experience.

Source: Authors. ■

Transitional pathways of development

As can be seen from the illustration in Box 6.1, for any MNC the development from one international organizational form to another is path dependent; most forms can be transitional. The arrows on the matrix in Figure 6.5 illustrate the most common directions of transition.

The transition from international exporter to global, and then on to transnational, is perfectly possible as the need for local adjustments becomes apparent as a key requirement for international success. Similarly, a multidomestic can become a transnational as the country units develop a recognition of, and uses for, each other's skills and abilities, and as shifts in various markets create a need for greater scale economies in certain areas (Malnight, 1996). Global to transnational is also feasible. This shift is about moving from simple global to complex global responses to greater complexity across

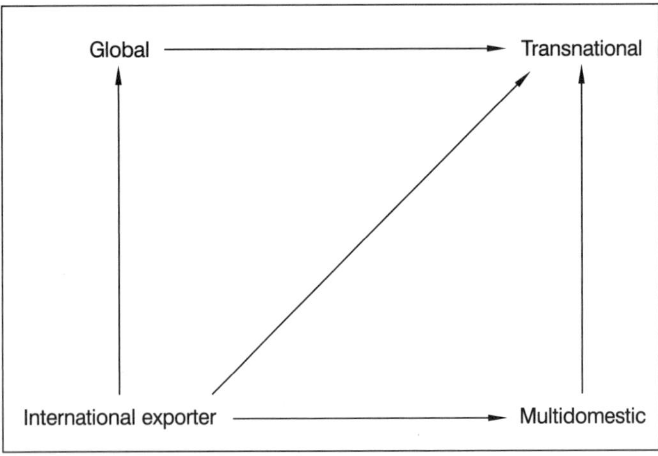

Figure 6.5 Common transitional pathways. *Source:* Authors

markets, and less tolerance for simple standardized global products and services. It is also a more efficient use of scarce resources if the organization has the internal capabilities to manage this complex process effectively.

Some transitions would be more improbable. A multidomestic would find transmutation into a global company or an international one with the required standardization very traumatic, and the corporation might find extreme difficulty in surviving the trauma. Should the transnational form be found to be strategically inappropriate it would also be very difficult to move from a transnational mindset into any of the more centralized hierarchical forms, which are structured to provide lower levels of personal autonomy. However all four forms need not be transitional. In a more stable environment they may each represent the optimal organizational form, at least for a period of time.

Summary

We have suggested that a firm will adopt an international strategy if it believes that it can achieve a competitive position with any of its businesses in any of the countries it decides to target. Also, that it should do so if an international strategy will provide it with better ways of achieving efficiency, managing risks or enabling innovation and learning within the firm. Ghoshal's (1987) organizing framework is helpful in deciding what potential sources of advantage are available for different international strategy configurations, where to compete and where to locate different value chain activities.

Although in all corporate strategy decisions the firm will need to carry out the tasks of selecting, resourcing and controlling, in carrying out those tasks for international corporate strategy, a greater number of factors would need to be considered, related to both patterns of demand and sources of supply. In relation to basic costs or potential costs, it will need to consider carefully transport (including insurance) costs, and the costs of hedging against the movement of exchange rates. In terms of its overall strength compared with local companies and other international companies operating in the target countries, it will need to evaluate the strength of the various components of its national diamond (Porter, 1990) as a source of potential advantage or disadvantage.

We discussed at length the possible relationships between the configuration of the activities of an MNC and how it manages their co-ordination. In order to consider how to configure and co-ordinate its activities internationally, Dunning's OLI framework will assist in determining what activities should be carried out at home, and what in other countries. Finally, in co-ordinating and controlling activities it will need to consider the steps necessary to become an organization structured to succeed in a world with increasingly regionalized or globalized markets, achieving optimal levels of efficiencies, knowledge transfer and local product sensitivities. In terms of product or service adaptation, it must review the practicalities and costs involved in such organizational adaptation. There is no simple solution offered here. The transnational form, and the modern process-integrated multidomestic, provide alternative solutions to the fundamental problem of configuring global integration to achieve the optimal levels of scale and scope economies coupled with sensitive local responsiveness. The centralized, standardized global organization still has a powerful role to play meeting clear universal needs.

These frameworks of course describe contrasting paradigms. Few actual MNCs fit neatly into one or another. Indeed, the decision of where to locate and how to manage each function will be made by the MNC's top management on the basis of contingent circumstances and specific cost benefit trade-offs. The likelihood of their arriving at a precise organizational form which fits neatly into one of the particular 'boxes' we have described is low. However, each of these paradigms, describing the different organizational forms, is appropriate for certain specific conditions and offers certain advantages for those conditions. The next three chapters consider each paradigm in more detail.

7

The multidomestic form

The traditional multidomestic model of the multinational corporation is described by Bartlett and Ghoshal (1989) as:

> a decentralized federation of assets and responsibilities, a management process defined by simple financial control systems overlaid on informal personal co-ordination, and a dominant strategic mentality that views the company's world-wide operations as a portfolio of national businesses.

The multidomestic was a very early form of MNC. It followed a pattern adopted by many European and North American companies expanding in the early decades of the twentieth century, mostly in the period up to World War Two. In industries where there were well-established consumer preferences which were different, national market by national market, and where often strong local competitor firms existed, there was a positive logic to setting up independent subsidiaries to compete strongly and directly, in each national market.

Politics had an important role to play too in the reasons for the expansion of this type of international organizational form, early in this century. Pre-1914 those European countries with large overseas empires, such as France, Germany, UK and the Netherlands, dominated world foreign direct investment (FDI) expansion. The UK alone accounted for half the total of foreign investment abroad and France, Germany and the Netherlands for a further 43 per cent, with the USA at just 6 per cent in 1914 (quoted in Bartlett and Ghoshal, 1989, p.46). Politics of a different kind were at work during the 1930s and 1940s, with high levels of government protectionism common around the world. Protectionism in general and World War Two in particular, had led many MNCs to set up their overseas subsidiaries as separate legal entities. The amount of control exercised by the corporate parent as a result of this combination of factors was greatly diminished, whilst the independence of the national subsidiary organizations greatly increased.

Although in some of the international strategy literature this traditional form of international organizational structure is called the multinational organization model (Bartlett, 1986; Bartlett and Ghoshal, 1989), in this book we have adopted Porter's (1986) terminology and called it by the less confusing, more self-explanatory name of the multidomestic enterprise. 'Multidomestic' seems a self-explanatory term since it is being used to describe an organizational model in which the MNC has a presence in a 'multitude' of 'domestic' markets and is operationally fully integrated within each of those domestic markets. In terms of resource-allocation and co-ordination, the role of the centre in a multidomestic is largely residual, rather than central. Personal relationships between country general managers may have a disproportionate importance in getting things done, since these individuals are very powerful within such an MNC.

The pure multidomestic form

The traditional multidomestic form is usually described as a historically early one which, together with the international exporter form, was most common before the onset of globalization and when major economies of scale and scope were not key to determining competitive advantage in international business. However, the multidomestic is not necessarily an outdated form where local responsiveness is key, and few if any scale economies exist.

In terms of selection, resourcing and controlling, MNC headquarters of a pure multidomestic was initially responsible for the selection of the industry and business portfolio. However, in subsequent development, it was less so, as each country subsidiary has a lot of control over its own resource allocation. MNC headquarters is also responsible for resourcing overall corporate MNC growth by whatever means, and certainly through organic development. Acquisitions and alliances usually need central approval depending on the size of the deal. As regards control, the centre is most visible in its financial role, for setting financial targets and taking responsibility for financial control. Control of human resource management is very largely in the hands of the country units. All of this makes complete sense if the MNC sees no benefit in integrating any of the activities of its subsidiaries across international markets. To seek to do so would be counter to the source of advantage for which a pure multidomestic MNC has been designed: dedicated knowledge and resources to a specific domestic market. For this strategic objective, cross-border integration may be positively disadvantageous.

The characteristics of the multidomestic in its pure form are those of a federation of companies each operating in separate countries, but under a common brand name. The centre's role is akin to that of a holding company with the limited purpose of monitoring financial performance in its subsidiaries around the world, deciding when and where to increase or decrease its portfolio of companies, and maintaining often largely informal contact with the subsidiaries in a largely political way.

In Porter's (1986) view the multidomestic corporation can choose where to compete internationally as its strategies will be a series of domestic strategies:

> In a multidomestic industry, a multinational firm may enjoy a competitive advantage from the one-time transfer of know-how from its home base to foreign countries. However, the firm modifies and adapts its intangible assets in order to employ them in each country; and the competitive outcome over time is then determined by conditions in each country. (Porter, 1986, p.18)

Its pattern of communication and decision-making is captured in Figure 7.1.

Each of the black circles in Figure 7.1 represents a country subsidiary. Each is therefore a repository of a set of resources and functions fit for its unique competitive marketplace. Decision-making and resource-allocation reside with the country subsidiary. The most significant element of the communication and decision-making pathway represented by Figure 7.1 is that in a pure multidomestic MNC organization, the dominant direction of movement is from the subsidiary to MNC headquarters ('bottom-up') rather than top-down from headquarters to subsidiary. The reason for this is that if each national subsidiary in, say, France, Italy, Greece, Turkey, Philippines, South

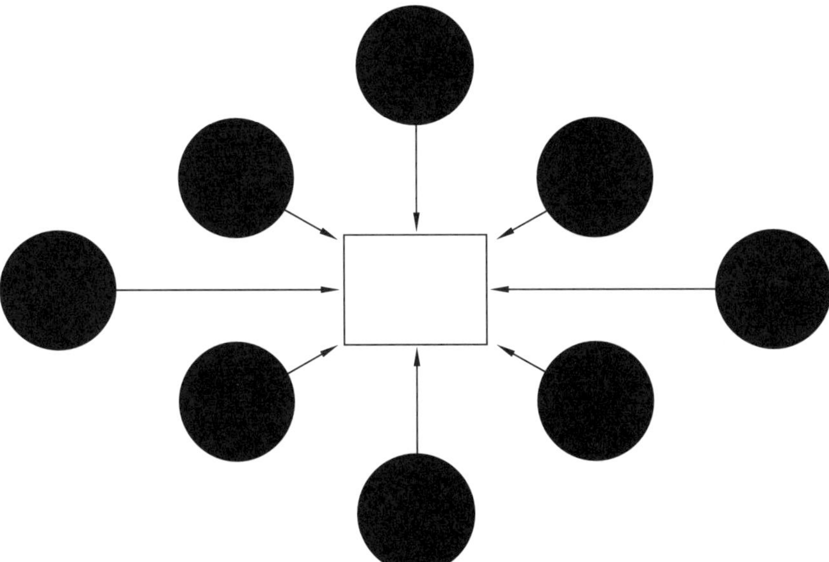

Figure 7.1 Multidomestic communication and decision-making. *Source:* Adapted from Bartlett and Ghoshal (1989)

Korea, Indonesia, Canada, USA, Mexico, Brazil, Argentina, and so on, faces a unique marketplace, the relevance of information, skills and experience acquired in one marketplace, to any of the others, is minimal. Little lateral communication is either relevant or necessary; equally, the centre has little to offer the domestic subsidiaries, except occasional financial or technical support for specific projects.

Thus, the pure multidomestic corporation develops responsiveness worldwide on a country-by-country basis through the dispersal of resources, initiatives and authority to each country subsidiary. It is also important to understand other general factors that influence strategy in the multidomestic MNC. It exhibits few extra-national scale economies or experience curve effects, or locational economies (Hill, 1997). Therefore the minimum economic size of production plants will also be relatively small, as each will serve only its local market. For the MNC as a whole, market shares in one location are independent of those in another. In industries for which this MNC form is suitable, such as consumer branded goods, food, beverages, household appliances (Ghoshal and Nohria, 1993), R&D and overall capital intensity are relatively low, so that the duplication of facilities in each country which is a necessary feature of this form of MNC, is not too costly. Levels of both product and process standardization are likely to be low as each country centre will have high autonomy and little co-ordination with the other country subsidiaries in the group. Since their markets are different, there is no need for it.

If we think of international strategy as on a continuum with pure differentiation per country market at one end, and pure global standardization strategy at the other end (Douglas and Wind, 1987), the multidomestic corporation will be at the extreme differentiation end of the continuum. This means that for MNC competitor firms in that particular industry, each country will demand and receive a different product specific to its needs, even if the brand name is the same. Figure 7.2 gives a stylized representation of such a 'standardization – differentiation' continuum. A strategy may be 'differentiated' in each of its elements: in segmentation of the market and market positioning within that market (e.g. Benetton sweatshirts may be middle-market priced in Italy or France but high-priced in the USA, whereas The Gap merchandise may be low-priced in the USA but high-priced in the UK); in the characteristics of the product itself (e.g. low temperature detergents for the USA market, but high temperature detergents for Italy or Spain); in its marketing in terms of packaging, advertising and PR and customer and trade promotion. It may even be distributed by different channels from one market to another. For example, washing-machines may be sold mainly through department stores in one country, through discount stores in another or through specialist chains or by mail order in another. Figure 7.2 captures these different marketing activities that may be standardized or differentiated per market.

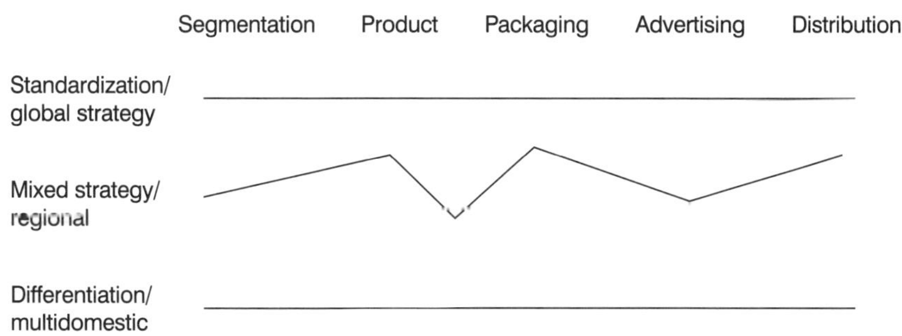

Figure 7.2 The standardization-differentiation spectrum. *Source:* Adapted From Douglas and Wind (1987)

As Ellis and Williams (1995) put it, the dominant power group of executives within the corporation is the country-based national managers, as they are in control of the delegated resources, and profits are not normally repatriated to the centre (only dividends) and the country managers are therefore in a position to allocate resources for future intra-country development and growth. In many companies they are known as the country barons. The corporate culture inevitably places strong emphasis on the subsidiary's independence from the centre.

Hill (1997) describes the structure and culture of multidomestics in the following way. In terms of vertical differentiation they are decentralized; in terms of horizontal differentiation they have a worldwide area structure. Their need for internal co-ordination is low. They therefore have few if any integrating mechanisms, have little need for cultural control and little if any performance ambiguity. The performance of each unit is there for all to see and measure due to their high autonomy. This is a picture of a set of separate companies linked together only by use of common corporate names and symbols, and formal reporting to a common head office.

Ellis and Williams (1995) distinguish multinational organizational forms along four dimensions:

1. Product or service offering.
2. Resources, responsibilities and control.
3. Dominant power group and culture.
4. Location of R&D and source of innovation.

On these criteria the multidomestic has products developed for local markets, has local autonomy and control of resources, has a power group of country managers and a local culture, and has supporting national R&D facilities and local sources of innovation. This gives a succinct summary of the nature and style of a multidomestic MNC.

Particular merits of the multidomestic corporate form are that they are good at 'sensing' future possible trends in global products by identifying them at an early stage in their local market. They also provide good environments for the advancement of foreign nationals within the corporation, although there may be a 'glass ceiling' inhibiting them from reaching the corporate board at the subsidiary headquarters in the 'home' country.

This organizational form was particularly appropriate for a world beset by high levels of trade barriers and conditioned by high global transport costs as a percentage of total costs. When these factors are coupled with only moderate scale economies the attraction of the form with its high motivational characteristics for local managers is clear to see. Hence its proliferation until approximately the 1960s. In more recent times, however, for the multidomestic to survive in the modern world it needs to evolve into a less pure form and pay due deference to the needs of scale economies and merging market tastes and technologies.

As described in Chapter 4, companies like Philips experienced severe problems in the 1960s with their multidomestic form, as Japanese competitors (such as Sony, Hitachi. Sharp or Matsushita) entered their markets with lower costs brought about by a more integrated global approach to business and the scale economies following from this. As is to be expected, given the power of country general managers within this type of MNC, the multidomestic form also made it difficult for Philips to develop a unified global strategy to fight back at its Japanese competitors. Individual country barons concentrating on their individual markets were unable to perceive the global threat from the Japanese. In any case, that was not how their own performance was measured: they were judged on performance in their own country market and not on performance measures of the MNC worldwide, such as world market share in each product category and sector. A culture founded on the supremacy of the national organizations, self-sufficiency, sales rather than profit orientation and at corporate level the need for consensus and collective responsibility among the barons, was ill suited to fight the global Japanese, and the necessary restructuring was painful. As we saw the account of this battle in Chapter 4, the transition from multidomestic to global is not an easy one.

Nevertheless, these issues do not operate in only one direction. We have described the multidomestic/global battle in the consumer electronics industry, which is a global industry. If we looked instead at a very different industry, such as cosmetics, we would find almost the opposite story. Many of the products in cosmetics are still heavily differentiated, if not still by country, then certainly still by region. What sells in Asia is different from what sells in Europe, partly because of differences in hair colouring, skin types, and so on, which require different colour palettes and treatments. In that industry it was the Japanese companies such as Kao, Shiseido and Kanebo which, on their initial unsuccessful attempts to enter the lucrative European and American cosmetics markets, at first tried to sell undifferentiated products in a highly differentiated marketplace.

The modern multidomestic

Yip (1992) characterizes the modern multidomestic as having a corporate organization with dispersed national authority, no domestic – international split, and a strong geographical dimension relative to business and functional dimensions, i.e. country managers are kings, or at least princes. In terms of management processes there is the transfer of technology from headquarters outwards, but national information systems, and national strategic planning, national budgets, national performance review and national compensation systems. Senior executive ranks are populated by professional expatriates, whereas nationals tend to run the local businesses. There is only limited international travel. The culture is very varied and reflects the strong autonomy of the subsidiaries.

In terms of the role of the centre, the modern multidomestic concedes more power to the centre where this seems likely to enhance competitive strength. So the white box at the centre of Figure 7.1 might have to be re-shaded grey. Thus, the centre is likely to play a stronger role than traditionally in resource allocation and the selection of markets. It is certainly likely to have a strong say in technology matters, in R&D and in anything concerning strategic alliances and mergers and acquisitions. Its corresponding role in control is therefore also likely to be enhanced. It will not only receive financial reports but allocate to itself the power to take action if the information in them is a cause for concern. The modern multidomestic is therefore not as much a loose confederation as its traditional predecessor. Rather, it is becoming a more centralized corporation, albeit one within which a strong culture of operational decentralization and product differentiation exists.

The advantages of the multidomestic are that it enables a fully local product to be designed and produced; it retains the resources necessary for product development; and it tends to develop local managers strongly committed to the local organization. However, the problem is that it has an inherent inability to exploit competitive interdependencies and global efficiencies. It sometimes needlessly duplicates facilities when one larger regional or global one would be preferable on a cost basis, and it is not well suited to new product diffusion on account of the independence of the subsidiaries. The failure of Philips to establish its V2000 VCR format as the dominant design paradigm in the video industry in the late 1970s, in opposition to Matsushita's VHS design, is laid at the door of the independence (or possibly intransigence) of its own US subsidiary (Hill, 1997).

To overcome these deficiencies, some corporations organized historically on a multidomestic basis have made adjustments to their structure to avoid some of the weaknesses of the multidomestic in a modern global environment. Where applied sensitively, these adjustments can preserve the multidomestic as a viable organizational form even in conditions where globalization is becoming increasingly prevalent. Nestlé of Switzerland is an example of a multidomestic MNC that has made such adjustments, and thereby retained its international competitiveness. We have already examined the European food industry in Chapter 4, and seen how deregulation and European harmonization have made cross-border strategies viable, and thus created feasible new strategic space. In our analysis, one of the two dominant strategic groups predicted for strong growth in the post-1992 Single Market European food industry was 'the multinational branders', of which Nestlé is a conspicuous example (see Box 7.1).

Box 7.1 Nestlé – A Modern Multidomestic

Nestlé, the Swiss-based international food and beverages company, has over 200 operating subsidiaries. It has a philosophy of decentralization and dispersion of activities. The company has nearly 500 factories around the world and sells its products in over 100 countries. Less than 2 per cent of its sales are in Switzerland.

The original Nestlé business was based on milk and children's beverages, but over time numerous other products have been added, some outside the food business entirely. Nestlé produces pharmaceutical and cosmetics products, for example.

The company's organization structure, systems and culture emphasize the importance of local responsiveness, and the considerable autonomy of local managers. As is traditional in multidomestic companies, the subsidiaries are bonded to the centre by close personal relationships. Nestlé's corporate management is, however, responsible for giving strategic direction to the organization overall. Nestlé is a modern multidomestic, however, and its corporate management is responsible in addition for major resource allocation decisions, selection of markets, and the initial management of all acquisitions. R&D are also strongly centralized.

Nestlé recognizes the increasing convergence of tastes and national regulations in many regions of the world and has developed co-ordinating mechanisms on a regional basis between its subsidiaries for some product groups. It thus maintains its multidomestic philosophy

••▶

cont.

of local responsiveness, whilst adapting where appropriate to the needs of the forces of globalization. Local managers continue to have considerable discretion, and the company continues to have many more factories than would be the case if it were organized as a 'global' company.

Source: Adapted from Ellis and Williams (1995). ■

A principal part of the adaptation of the traditional multidomestic to meet modern needs is, then, the strengthening of its central controls, particularly in the area of resource allocation, staffing and performance measurement. Another area in which it has also adapted is that of developing the capability for transferring skills developed in one subsidiary to other subsidiaries as appropriate, throughout the group. Yetton *et al.* (1994) emphasize this feature in their empirical research into the viability of the multidomestic form in Australian MNCs. They contrast the modern Australian multidomestic with the global form on four dimensions:

1. The distinction between inter- and intra-firm competition. Intra-subsidiary competition can, they claim, be developed amongst the multidomestic units of a corporation to establish which units are the most efficient. This competition would be rewarded by promotion of executives and allocation of resources to the most successful business units.
2. The distinction between single and multiple point learning. Organizational learning from units in numerous different environments would be large. A prime determinant of the opportunity to learn is the heterogeneity of the environment. Heterogeneity can come from a variety of customer needs, from different factor endowments and from local competitive rivalry. The modern multidomestic firm needs to be able to learn from the variety of different environments in which it operates and to transfer knowledge between units.
3. The distinction between continuous and discontinuous change. Incremental change can be achieved across all multidomestic locations in a piecemeal fashion. By spreading change both over time and over different locations, the risk of major discontinuous change would be mitigated, and the firm would be protected from its possible adverse effects.
4. The distinction between responding to, and selecting, an environment. Operating environments can be selected on the criterion of only entering those that offer the potential for competitive advantage.

Multidomestics in which the corporate centre focuses on achieving the four benefits described above may, Yetton *et al*, believe, achieve competitive advantage from their multidomestic form on three counts.

1. Although they may not achieve production scale economies, they do achieve other economies through multiple plant learning.
2. They may also achieve reduced costs through incremental change and reduced risk of careful environment selection.
3. There are also motivational and other benefits from the decoupling of the global functions at the centre, from the local ones in the multidomestic units.

Firms that adopt this organizational form operate in industries where the efficient plant scale is small to medium-sized, and therefore the existence of multiple plants in multiple locations does not destroy the possibility of achieving the relevant level of scale economies in that industry.

The other key criterion for success is that local responsiveness does not damage the firms' abilities to achieve global learning or to operate worldwide strategies. As Yetton *et al.* (1994) put it.

> The global component for these firms is the process technology, and not as commonly assumed, the product characteristics. The introduction, maintenance and development of process are co-ordinated and regulated on a global basis, and various mechanisms ensure that the learning that occurs in one location is transferred throughout the network of plants.

Their argument then is that multidomestics need not necessarily be firms at an early stage of international evolution, that will later become global or transnational firms. Rather they see the multidomestic as a form that, in certain environmental circumstances, is one which is competitive in support of the global expansion of the MNC. It will work if certain adjustments are made to the traditionally passive role of the corporate centre to ensure that the benefits described are achieved corporation-wide.

It is most appropriate in product areas with low tradeability, low scale economies, and where firms have the option of selecting suitable friendly national environments to roll-out a proven formula with low risk.

Another important factor needs to be taken into account if the multidomestic is to be maintained as a modern international organizational form, namely that of flexibility (Buckley and Casson, 1998a). The history of its own administrative heritage (Bartlett,1986) plays a large part in the organizational form of all large companies, including MNCs. Buckley and Casson discuss the development of new approaches to MNC organization since the end of what they call the MNC 'golden age', which terminated suddenly with the oil price rise shock of 1973 (Marglin and Schor, 1990).

A new dynamic agenda, they claim, incorporates an understanding of:

1. Global market turbulence.
2. The resultant need for MNC strategic flexibility.

3. The growth of co-operative strategy.
4. Entrepreneurship, competencies and corporate culture.
5. Organizational change including mandating subsidiaries and the empowerment of individuals.

After 1973, and the second oil price shock in 1978, there was a time lag as MNCs adjusted to the fact that they would be operating in future in a world in which the global balance of power between developed and developing nations and firms, had permanently shifted. Subsequently flexibility, i.e. the ability to reallocate resources quickly in response to change, became the dominant strategic objective for MNCs from the 1980s onwards. They claim the main factors responsible for this growth of volatility since the end of the 1970s to be:

1. The diffusion of modern production technology, and the increase in the number of industrial powers and hence potential sources of political and social disruption.
2. The liberalization of trade and capital markets.
3. The improvement of communications that means news travels more quickly.
4. The increase in exchange rate volatility, following the breakdown of the international monetary system of fixed exchange rates agreed at Bretton Woods, USA, shortly after the end of World War Two.

So every MNC subsidiary experiences more shocks from around the world than in the pre-1970s era, not just from its own national economy but from new import competition, new export competition and new opportunities for international co-operation.

Increased organizational flexibility is therefore needed to deal with these shocks. The need for increased flexibility has led to the growth of MNCs with federal structures of operating divisions, drawing on a common source of specialist skills but empowered to go outside if it chooses to do so, sometimes leading to a growth of virtual firms, networks and coalitions. The issue of managing mandates to subsidiaries (Birkinshaw, 1996) is part of this exploration of MNC flexibility. Given such developments, the reassertion of the multidomestic form but with these additional modern adjustments, is clearly one option. It is viable only if the traditional extreme isolation of the country subsidiaries from one another, a characteristic of the traditional multidomestic, can be overcome.

Many of the older, historically well-established MNCs, which grew out of the early industrial expansion of Europe and the USA, have become overmature and somewhat set in their ways and their structures. They have also gradually lost many factor cost advantages and their early strength in entrepreneurship, a major source of early comparative advantage. Dynamic levels of entrepreneurship are now more often visible in the Asian, and recently, South American economies.

Buckley and Casson (1998a) describe the typical US MNC of their 'golden age' as vertically, as well as horizontally, integrated. The modern need for flexibility has long discouraged such vertical integration, since lowest cost supply (consistent with acceptable quality) is vital to competitiveness, and this may be best available from outside the firm. Open markets both internally, and externally through outsourcing, have now become more common, and managers are able to bypass parts of their own firm if they judge them to be inefficient. So we see a movement towards the firm becoming the hub of a network of interlocking internal and external joint ventures, but with the operating parts still able to tap into headquarters expertise as required. Buckley and Casson see sharing information of this type as playing an important part in dealing with environmental turbulence since: 'Collecting, storing and analyzing information therefore enhances flexibility because, by improving forecasts, it reduces the costs of change' (1998a, p.33).

Other organizational effects of this quest for flexibility have led to investment in plant becoming more based on modular structures; the principle of modularity allows the greatest level of flexibility to be maintained to enhance flexibility. Organizationally, as turbulence increases, so lateral consultation needs to be increased and the hierarchy somewhat flattened to speed communication, but with some hierarchy retained to ensure cohesion of decision-making. Greater flexibility may imply greater effort and greater costs, both financially and managerially, in promoting a corporate culture that reinforces trust, since trust is necessary for operating in more loosely bound corporate environments.

Many of these incremental changes, including those elements which shift the traditional multidomestic to a modern multidomestic, are likely to involve 'unlearning' organizational methods that have served well in the past but are no longer relevant.

> In general the growth of MNCs may be understood as a sequence of investments undertaken in a volatile environment, where each investment feeds back information which can be used to improve the quality of subsequent decisions. In this sense, the expansion of the firm is a path dependent process. (Kogut and Zander, 1993).

By contrast, some of the changes involved here, such as wresting power from the absolute control of subsidiary country general managers in traditional multidomestics are more path-breaking than path-dependent. Consider how some traditional multidomestics are moving some of their activities onto a basis of some regional co-ordination. Regional, rather than national, distribution hubs, for example, offer a compromise location strategy for modern multidomestics, helping them to deal with situations in which volatile markets lead to varying market demand year on year.

It is emphasized in the international strategy literature (Bartlett and Ghoshal, 1989; Ghoshal and Nohria, 1993) that very closely tailored organizational/

environmental fit is necessary for optimal performance, although the empirical evidence for this is modest. We argue therefore, that a particularly complex environment, as is often found in world markets, needs an MNC organizational structure which mirrors the requisite level of complexity faced by the MNC. This means that the simplistic models of traditional analysis are only useful in order to explore what specific solutions may be necessary for a particular situation. Bearing this in mind, the pure multidomestic form in the modern sense is almost bound to have characteristics of other forms within it, when translated into a real life situation. Otherwise it could not cope with the requisite level of complexity faced by the majority of modern MNC organizations in most of their markets. However, except where specific market conditions dictate otherwise, the multidomestic will not be the traditional autonomous country unit sharing only a common corporate name with its peers in other countries, but is much more likely to have the characteristics we have described for the modern multidomestic instead.

Summary

The multidomestic organizational form of the modern MNC is still a viable one in certain circumstances and with certain adjustments to its original pure multidomestic, largely autonomous, form.

It will still be the most appropriate form where efficient production methods yield only limited scale economies, and where local niche demand requires specific locally tailored products or services. However, flexible manufacturing systems and the growth of outsourcing are making scale economies less important than they were in many industries, while few industries exhibit global uniformity of tastes. Local cultures remain important in many markets and make the bottom right-hand box of the global integration/local responsiveness matrix (Figure 6.3 in Chapter 6) a far from empty one.

Where the traditional local autonomy of multidomestic units can be adjusted successfully to allow an enhanced role for the centre headquarters, the multidomestic form becomes potentially competitively viable for modern purposes. The centre needs principally to allocate resources effectively, ensure the transfer of skills and new knowledge throughout the group, and ensure flexibility of operation, sometimes with the assistance of an occasional regional hub, for example as a supply centre. If it is able to do this is, it can at the same time modify the absolute isolation of subsidiaries in the pure multidomestic form, whilst preserving its strengths in motivating local staff, and forming the basis for understanding local conditions and the bases of national competitiveness.

8

The global and international exporter forms

This chapter discusses the global and the international exporter forms of international organization. Both these forms are able to deliver varying levels of scale economies, but neither achieves local responsiveness or differentiation in their standard products; nor is such local differentiation their major purpose.

Unlike the early part of the twentieth century in which international expansion was dominated by European-based multinational corporations (MNCs), after World War Two international expansion was led by US-based MNCs. Not only were they relatively undamaged by the ravages of war, unlike the European MNCs, but they also dominated the development of new technologies and new management practices (especially in marketing of branded goods) which began to change the bases of international competition. Throughout the 1960s and 1970s, protectionism went into reverse and the series of important GATT rounds began which contributed to a freer world trade system. This made further operational changes more feasible, such as global sourcing. Changed technologies, such as miniaturization and containerization, contributed to a dramatic reduction in transportation costs, whilst production and process technologies exerted pressure for seeking yet larger scale economies. Under these circumstances, the organizational trend began to move away from the multidomestic, and towards the global, organizational form.

The global form

The global company resides in the top left-hand box of the global integration/local responsiveness matrix (Figure 6.4 in Chapter 6), and is philosophically the antithesis of the multidomestic company. It is founded on the belief, promulgated first by Levitt (1983), that if a product meets a need at a low price and is of acceptable quality, then customers in whatever market will be prepared to forgo their particular local consumer preferences in favour of purchasing the lower price product of reasonable quality. If this were indeed found to be the case, then local (national) market tastes and preferences would soon cease to matter. Many modern industries do indeed sell global products in this way, although Birkinshaw *et al.* (1995) consider many industries to be, if anything, under-globalized in their global integration. The examples of such global products most commonly quoted come from such industries as the consumer electronics industry (Sony Walkman, camcorders, stereophonic hi-fi systems) or the clothing (Levi jeans or Benetton sweatshirts), sportswear (Nike or Reebok trainers), leisure (Club Med holidays or Sheraton hotels) and drinks (Coca-Cola or Heineken lager or Guinness) industries. All seem to bear out Levitt's hypothesis. We return to the US-based MNC Gillette (first encountered in Chapter 1, Box 1.1) for their Chief Executive's view on these matters and how it is implemented. Box 8.1 illustrates the Gillette style of global strategy.

Box 8.1 Gillette – A Global Corporation

Al Zeien, chief executive of Gillette, refuses to pay tribute to cultural differences. He believes Gillette is a 'global' company in the way few corporations are... 'We know Argentina and France are different, but we treat them the same. We sell them the same products, we use the same production methods, and we have the same corporate policies. We even use the same advertising, in a different language, of course'. The company's one-size-fits-all strategy has been effective. Gillette's net income has grown 16 per cent a year in the past five years, and its share price has risen by an average of 33 per cent a year since 1987. The group makes items almost everyone in the world buys at one time or another, including shavers, batteries and pens. It aims to dominate the markets it operates in: its share of the worldwide shaving market, for example is 70 per cent, which the company hopes to increase by the launch next week of a new razor for men. Scale and flexibility are the main advantages of reverse parochialism, says Mr Zeien. R&D cost less when applied to a world market. Global companies may be better positioned to leverage intellectual capital as well. Good ideas are worth more when applied to global operations rather than to a single factory. Globalization also makes the company more nimble. For instance it responded to the Asian crisis by slicing spending on marketing there... There are few

••▶

cont.

companies, says Mr. Zeien, that take globalization as seriously as Gillette – perhaps Coca-Cola, and the Band Aid division of Johnson and Johnson... To make sure the managers world-wide are on the same wave-length, Mr. Zeien insists they move from country to country and division to division...The company's commitment to standardization, moreover, costs it customers in niche markets within countries. Mr. Zeien long ago decided the drawbacks were worth suffering.

Source: Financial Times Tuesday, 7 April, 1998. ■

In the global form of MNC, the corporate headquarters plays a very hands-on role. It is instrumental in selecting the businesses and markets to be in, or those it wishes to stay out of. The centre decides where the various functions are carried out, i.e. the global configuration for the firm, its locations for production, R&D and the other activities of the value-added chain. In short, it determines the configuration and the methods of co-ordination of all activities and corporate assets and resources. It also decides on how resources and activities are to be acquired and maintained, whether through internal development, alliances or acquisitions. Thus, the global MNC headquarters exercises control not just in a financial way, but also through a centrally determined and administered human resources policy. Strategic and major operational decisions all emanate from the centre.

To be a leader in an industry with a global strategy for global products, a firm must develop and implement a strategy that integrates its activities across countries. Such cross-border integration is the key to a global strategy, although some activities, usually sales and perhaps some marketing activities, must have a presence in each individual country. Generally in global industries, competition in one country will be strongly influenced by competition in others. This contrasts with the multidomestic with its decentralized federation of semi-autonomous units. The global company can instead be thought of as a centralized hub organization with spokes radiating from the centre, building and exploiting global efficiencies through the centralization of resource allocation, strategic objectives and decision-making. This type of global MNC is depicted in Figure 8.1.

In the global form, as given in Figure 8.1, the white circles each represent a division or a subsidiary and the black square in the centre is corporate headquarters. This is the reverse of Figure 7.1 (Chapter 7) depicting the multidomestic. In the global form it is largely the centre which makes decisions and allocates resources. Lines of communication and decision-making therefore flow from the centre outwards.

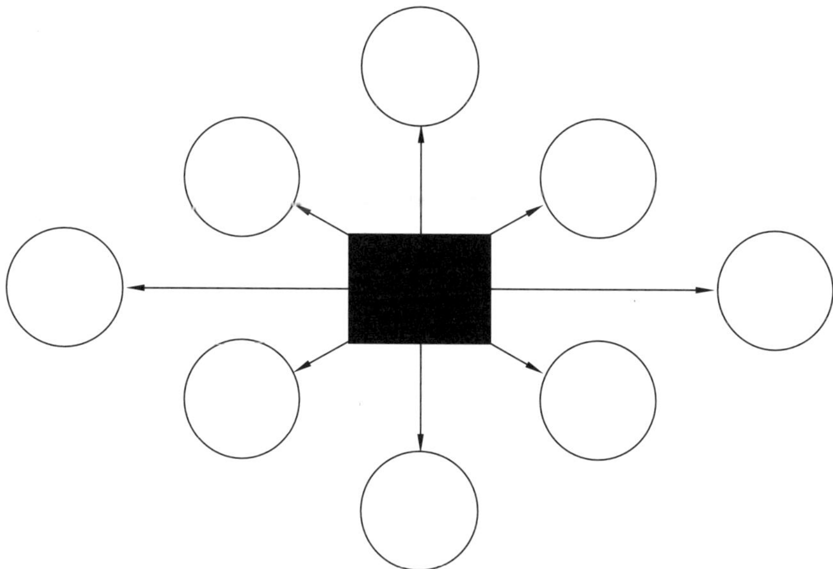

Figure 8.1 The global form. *Source:* Adapted from Bartlett and Ghoshal (1989)

The conditions most appropriate for a global configuration are those in which a standard product is recognizable and acceptable in all or most markets worldwide, and in which there are substantial cost economies to be achieved from large-scale production. Although a strong brand name may well be important to sales, as it is with Gillette, the product sells on price in the last resort, and thus the advantages of scale and often scope are critical to competitive advantage. In comparison with the multidomestic form described in the previous chapter, the global business typically operates in markets that have a high level of interdependence, that are capital intensive and require a high level of research and development (R&D) expenditure. Both product and process standardization is likely to be high and activities are directed and co-ordinated strongly from the centre, i.e. the company's 'home' country.

Birkinshaw (1996) described how globalization has led MNCs to integrate their globally dispersed activities. Thus where foreign subsidiaries had been set up as miniature replicas of the parent as in the multidomestic form, under the new global philosophy they have taken on specialized roles reflecting their competencies and sometimes including a global product mandate. Thus, over time an MNC reconfigures itself from a multidomestic to a global form to meet the needs of the new globalized environment where scale economies and standardization of product offering lead to competitive advantage.

Yip (1992) identified four categories of benefits that come from global product standardization:

1. *Cost reduction*: these include development, purchasing, production and inventory costs. The greater the development costs, e.g. ethical pharmaceuticals, the greater the drive to market the product worldwide. Considerable economies can also be achieved by standardizing and hence reducing product lines, gaining large purchasing discounts for volume items, and minimizing inventory through standardized product ranges.
2. *Improved quality*: the fewer the lines in which quality needs to be achieved and maintained the greater the focus that can be applied to each line. Multiple product lines incur quality risks.
3. *Enhanced customer preference*: where customers prefer to find the same product when travelling as they find at home, their preference is enhanced by access to standardized global products, e.g. Louis Vuitton luggage, McDonald's fast food, or American Express travel services.
4. *Competitive leverage*: the possession of global low cost products helps companies increase their global reach to achieve market entry to new countries easily. Their brand names are already recognized.

In Douglas and Wind's (1987) terminology, the global corporation tends to have a uniform segmentation of its market and consistent positioning within it. The product is standard, as is the packaging. Indeed, as consumers we are now so accustomed to multilingual packaging on everything from food items to cosmetics to electrical goods, that even the continuation of different languages in different country markets is no longer a barrier to globalization. Advertising and PR, and customer and trade promotion methods vary little from country to country, and even distribution methods are likely to be uniform.

The traditional global corporation

The classical global form in modern times was to be found most typically in the Japanese corporations of the 1970s which caused so much anxiety for their European and North American MNC competitors, and often for their governments too. These early Japanese global MNCs took advantage of vast production scale economies and, together with (then) very innovative production processes such as lean production and just in time (JIT) inventory methods, captured dominant world market shares with very reliable, low priced consumer goods, particularly in the automobile, motorcycle, electronics, home entertainment and reprographics industries. However, industrial goods sectors, rather more than the consumer good sectors, are the most obviously appropriate target for global corporations as they meet a consistent need rather than satisfy a potentially variable taste. Thus Intel, Texas

Instruments and Motorola are all characterized by global organizational forms, since they sell basically standard products in all markets.

In the archetypal Japanese global corporation, strategy and control were strongly centralized. Overseas units were sales outlets used to build global scale. The mindset in the global corporation was to regard the world as a single economic entity serviced through delivery pipelines (Bartlett and Ghoshal, 1989) The culture of the corporation tends to be clearly identified, usually set from the centre. Many of the Japanese global MNCs had very strong central cultures. For example, as we mentioned in our earlier discussion of Matsushita (in Chapter 4, Box 4.2) its founder created a set of 'spiritual precepts' for the management of the corporation. Matsushita placed great emphasis on these precepts as part of the additional training it gave any of its executives who were to work outside Japan in any of its overseas subsidiaries, in which key positions until the late 1980s were always held by internal Japanese expatriate senior managers.

Hill's (1997) analysis of the global corporation is that it will be likely to be organized into worldwide product markets, to be high in its need for co-ordination, to have many formal and informal integrating mechanisms to make it operate effectively, to tolerate a high level of performance ambiguity and to exhibit a high need for cultural controls.

In the traditional global corporation production was concentrated principally in the home country for ease of control and quality assurance, although this factor has been considerably relaxed in recent years. R&D tends to be centralized also and, following on from the R&D, also new product development. This is the simple global strategy, exemplified by global MNCs such as Toyota in the 1960s and 1970s, as it sought to achieve the advantages of low cost production as its major source of 'global reach' (Emmott, 1991) i.e. of international competitive advantage. At that period Toyota capitalized in particular on the automobile industry's (then) huge potential for manufacturing scale economies, leading it to develop a tightly co-ordinated, centrally controlled operation, that emphasized worldwide export of fairly standardized models from global-scale plants in Toyota City, Japan (Bartlett, 1986).

With concentrated production facilities reporting to the centre, and with a role limited to simple assembly, the traditional global corporation had the advantages of low costs due to scale economies, and global scale efficiencies. In addition, its centralized functional organization enabled resources to be so concentrated that new products could be quickly developed, and then equally speedily diffused worldwide (Ellis and Williams, 1995). However, it also suffered from corresponding limitations. It was not able sensitively to reflect local tastes and, due to its single 'home' culture and great distance from point of sale to decision-takers, the traditional global corporation found it difficult to react in a timely fashion to external stimuli for any new products identified in foreign markets.

As the forces for globalization have gathered and grown since the 1980s, the concept of global strategy has moved on from that of the traditional centralized global corporation. To have a global strategy it is no longer necessary to have an organizational form with vast scale factories located in an equivalent of Toyota city, and a culture which spanned the world, yet nevertheless still clearly emanated from the 'home' country. The need for standardization and low cost is still the primary driver of a global strategy, but the watchword of the modern global corporation is no longer ethnocentrism but polycentrism (Perlmutter, 1969). It will continue to have strong co-ordinating mechanisms able to achieve low cost, but will have added a varied global configuration of activities by no means always dominated by the original 'home' country. Such adjustments mark the move from the traditional to the modern global corporation.

The modern global corporation

With the dramatic general improvement in information and communications technology (ICT), and in flexible manufacturing systems, plus the growing volatility of world economic conditions as global deregulation takes place in many markets, the rigid paradigm of the global corporation has been transformed. Porter (1990) pointed out the advantage of operating from a strong national 'diamond'. This may be thought of as a late twentieth-century restatement of the eighteenth-century Ricardian concept of national comparative advantage. However, if the USA represents a strong diamond in a given industry, there is nothing to prevent a Japanese 'transplant' taking advantage of it, and exporting back into world markets. Similarly the cost advantages of assembly in South East Asian countries can be taken advantage of by USA-based global corporations. As Kogut (1989) points out, succeeding internationally comes from locating functional activities in countries with comparative advantage in order to achieve a value-added chain able to give international competitive advantage. As he succinctly puts it:

> ... to ask what is the analytical value of prefacing strategy with word global. What is distinctive in the international context, besides larger market size, is the variance in country environments and the ability to profit through the system-wide management of this variance. (Kogut, 1989, p.388)

The meaning of the 'global' corporation then is changing. Until the 1980s it was focused on operational integration from a home base founded on four dominant concepts:

- a strong and low-cost sourcing platform;
- efficient factor costs;
- global scale;
- product standardization.

Since then it has become more sophisticated, focusing on strategic co-ordination, with the integration of skills and disciplines worldwide as the key factors for global success, while factors such as scale and home country control, become less critical considerations. Thus, it has come to be recognized that even in the global corporation all functions are not equally international in scope. A global corporation may appear as shown as shown in Figure 8.2.

Figure 8.2 suggests that some activities may be centralized global (R&D, product design), others regional (manufacturing, distribution, some marketing) and still others local (sales). The value chain configuration will depend on the benefits to be gained from each particular set of variations for that industry. Not only may it be appropriate to locate a particular function in a country or countries other than the 'home' country, but some activities, e.g. sales, may need for greatest effect to be duplicated country-by-country even in so-called 'global' corporations. Unlike in the traditional global corporation, in the modern global corporation, as Yip (1992) puts it:

> Global activity location means deploying one integrated, but globally dispersed, value chain or network that serves the entire worldwide business rather than separate country value chains or one home based value chain....(p.104)

Yip (1992) characterizes the modern global corporation as having an organization structure based on a centralized global authority, no domestic – international split and strong business dimensions relative to geography and function. Management processes involve extensive co-ordination processes, global sharing of technology, global strategic information systems and global strategic planning, budgets, and performance review and compensation systems. Its employees have multi-country careers. Foreign nationals operate both in home and third countries and are involved in extensive travel. The

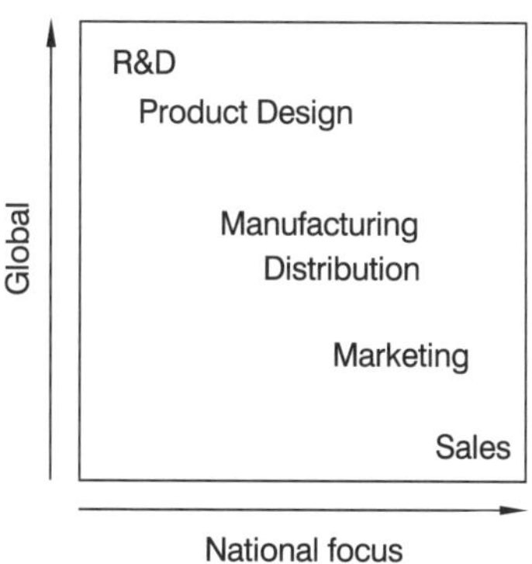

Figure 8.2 Different degrees of global integration for different functions.
Source: Authors

culture is one involving a global identity and strong interdependence; far removed from the single country culture of the traditional global corporation.

This concept reveals a distinct change from the origins of the traditional global corporation where the activities and power of the home country were dominant. The growing volatility of world markets in the 1980s and 1990s has led to the need for the global corporation to disperse production around the globe. This ensured flexibility in the face of changing exchange rates, varying factor costs for labour and raw materials and the inevitable political risks inherent in global operation. If Ford encounters high labour and social costs in Germany, it can switch production to Portugal, Spain or the Czech republic or Poland, or at least threaten to do so. Even the Japanese MNCs which constituted the archetypal centralized global role model, have found it increasingly appropriate to locate 'transplants' in overseas locations and have been doing steadily more of this throughout the 1980s and 1990s. They have set about building offshore supply networks to mirror their domestic keiretsu, with the additional benefit that to locate plants in the USA or the EU also had the advantage of enabling them to duck under USA or EU import tariff barriers. From the USA viewpoint locating factories in the Far East enabled the global corporation to take advantage of the lower wage rates prevailing in that part of the world. Indeed had they not done so, they would have found it impossible to compete on price with Far East products in international markets (Andersson and Fredriksson, 1996).

Rangan (1998) demonstrates through empirical research that MNCs do in fact change their production locations to take note of changes in exchange rates that they consider to be long term. He adds however, that such changes are only at the margin, probably because of the influence of sunk costs in already established locations. His research does confirm the influence of CSAs (Rugman *et al.*, 1985) or Dunning's 'L' factor, i.e. country-specific advantages, in the minds of decision takers in global companies faced with the issue of incremental functional activity location. The expansion of the firm is inevitably a path-dependent process (Kogut and Zander, 1993). An alternative route to this same end of production flexibility, or to take advantage of the best exchange rates, is to subcontract a significant proportion of production (Buckley and Casson, 1998a). Reflecting the point made by Figure 8.2, dealing with the volatility of globalized business may lead global companies to establish warehousing hubs in nodal points of transport networks, thus enabling them to withdraw from particular markets and enter others as economic conditions and opportunities fluctuate.

Casson, Pearce and Singh (1991) also extend this functional dispersion to R&D laboratories. They claim that in many global MNCs the central research laboratories of high-technology MNCs were either closed down, shifted to the divisions or forced to operate as suppliers to 'internal customers' in competition with outside bodies such as universities, although this movement is by no means universal.

For service businesses these issues may affect less the location of a production plant or R&D grouping, and more the infrastructure to deliver the service worldwide and the development of a global mindset for servicing the global customer. For example, the rapid and continuing globalization of the international airlines has provoked competitive moves to control access to routes, airport hubs in good locations to get high international passenger throughput, and control of the best times of take-off and landing slots. In a geographic sense, obviously airlines are international businesses, but they have had nationally-based structures controlling national routes for most of their history until the rounds of deregulation began in the US in the 1970s and have been continuing in Europe. National 'flag-carriers' like Lufthansa of Germany, Air France, Alitalia, Qantas, Singapore Airlines are all strongly identified with their national home-base cultures. Their management structures have been wholly national and their current involvement in massive global alliances has created tremendous pressures for change from local to global.

All of the above suggests a considerable movement of the mindset of the global company, and recognition of decision-making options in relation to its mode and nature of operation at the end of the twentieth century. Porter's (1986) categorization of the configuration and co-ordination issues facing the MNC (see Figure 6.1, Chapter 6) offers a useful framework for understanding these changes and their organizational effects.

Modern global configuration issues

A modern global configuration will take into account the perceived nature of FSAs and CSAs (firm-specific and country/location-specific advantages) in identifying the best way to achieve global competitive advantage, and this will be considered individually by function.

Thus, to take production as an example, in deciding how to configure production worldwide, the global corporation will assess the optimal size production unit required to achieve the greatest scale economies, as cost remains the critical factor for a global company. It will then choose locations that give the best balance between factor costs, not only labour costs. It may attempt to cope with volatile exchange rates by selecting locations with the best rates in relation to the alternative of home country production, and will handle the inflexibilities resulting from sunk costs by ensuring that a sizeable proportion of production is subcontracted. It will ensure flexibility and cost efficiency of distribution by operating through regional warehousing hubs. It will pay strong attention to FSAs in deciding on the location of R&D facilities and would be unlikely (for Dunning's 'I' internalization reasons) to subcontract these, although it may consider the option of limited dispersion to the divisions. New product development and product design may not be uniformly carried out in the home country, as was traditionally the case.

Downstream, sales will usually remain a country responsibility, although in the case of smaller markets there may be some grouping of activity here into sales teams for country clusters; similarly in marketing. The modern global corporation recognizes that even if tastes are converging they still vary by market and in most cases note still needs to be taken of this. In the USA, ketchup is vinegary; in continental Europe, it is spicy; in the UK, ketchup is sweet (Riesenbeck and Freeling, 1991). Margarine is made to taste as close to butter as possible in the UK, but not in the Netherlands. The variants are endless. To reflect this, some marketing activity may be local, but the thinking will be carried out on a global scale and the message will be developed and co-ordinated globally to enhance the corporation's global image. With regard to personnel, modern global firms are beginning to better reflect their own natures in the variety of their personnel and will not, as previously, be dominated by personnel from the 'home' country.

Modern global co-ordination issues

Modern global co-ordination is still likely to be based on the traditional M-form of organization, i.e. the multidivisional form (Chandler, 1962, 1990b). The dominant grouping is that of worldwide product groups, as compared with the country general managers of the multidomestic. There is likely, however, to be some loosening of the degree of control from the centre to allow the development of networks and alliances outside the firm in key markets where this appears valuable for the achievement of competitive advantage in any area. Global MNCs are still, however, predominantly vertically integrated. Andersson and Fredriksson (1996) found that the level of export from subsidiaries of MNCs depends crucially on whether the MNCs are vertically or horizontally integrated: multidomestics are seen as horizontally integrated, and global companies as vertically integrated. Their research shows that exports are generally higher from vertically integrated global MNCs as these evince greater specialization and competitive advantage through scale economies.

Systems remain strongly tied to the centre, since the central headquarters regards itself as responsible for global positioning of the firm. The strategic objective of headquarters is to develop an identity, a mission and key products that are recognizable in all markets, as the Gillette illustration in Box 8.1 demonstrates. That means central strategic planning, backed up by monitoring of performance, and executive career development and compensation run from the centre. It also means the ability to disseminate around the worldwide corporation, information skills and new methods developed in specific areas, but recognized as having more general applicability.

The international exporter form

The international exporter company is frequently one with aspirations to become global. Currently it has only a well-developed domestic infrastructure but possesses an adequate capacity to make exporting, and ultimately distribution, attractive to it. It is placed in the bottom left box of the global integration/local responsiveness matrix (Figure 6.3 in Chapter 6). That box is also, of course, home to the local-for-local company operating in the domestic market only, with low scale economies, but a sufficiently specific or niche product to survive in its domestic market.

The international exporter form was typical of many USA companies in the post-war period. They had a strong domestic base, but developed small, mainly sales outfits, in many countries around the world. These subsidiaries depended heavily on their American parent for products and the transfer of knowledge, and were generally heavily patronized by the parent, which was dominant in all forms of control. As well as largely standardized products, the parent sought to control any transfer of technology, marketing skills or managerial capabilities to its subsidiaries (Andersson and Fredriksson, 1996). As a result, the home-base functional managers became the major power brokers in the company. The organization could be drawn as shown in Figure 8.3.

In this form the corporate centre is based in the 'home' country and is the power-base. There are no country-based national subsidiaries, only sales and marketing affiliates. The dominant decision flow is from the centre to the affiliates.

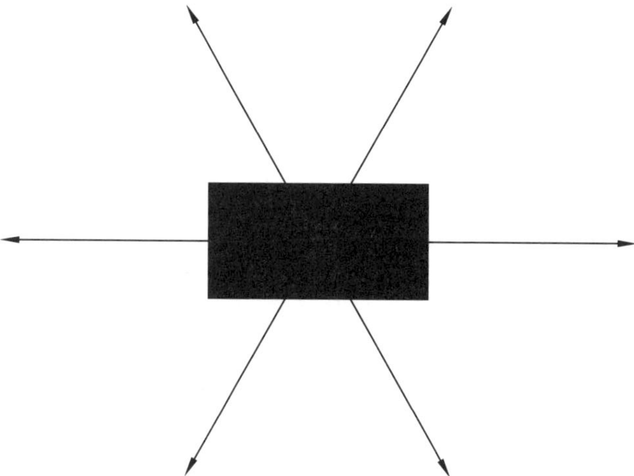

Figure 8.3 The international exporter form. *Source:* Authors

The characteristic of the international exporter form is to enable a domestic company to become a worldwide one without the need to change its culture. It is strongly ethnocentric in Perlmutter's (1969) terms, not because a product has global homogeneous demand as in the case of modern global companies, but because the home country saw international exporting as the only sensible way to expand, given its lack of international market knowledge and its modest resource base. The result was generally products focused on the home market; parochial home country managers operating abroad in an unintegrated way; and home country hegemony not allied to local sensitivity.

The international exporter form is a rather unsophisticated way of becoming international. Since it does not necessarily attempt to suit its products appropriately to the non-home market, it is likely to be an unstable and transitory organizational form, leading either to structural transformation into a global corporation or, less likely, into a modern multidomestic or transnational form (see again Figure 6.5, Chapter 6 – for common transitional pathways from one MNC form to another).

Box 8.2 illustrates the development of an embryonic international exporter corporation out of the domestic Proton car company in Malaysia.

Box 8.2 Proton – An International Car Company

Proton is Malaysia's only 'made in Malaysia' car company. It is majority owned and controlled by the Malaysian government as a joint venture with Mitsubishi Motors Corporation of Japan, which provides the engine and technological expertise.

Proton dominates the car market in Malaysia as it is heavily subsidized by the government, and imported cars are subject to substantial tariffs, and are therefore not price competitive with Proton. This situation is based on the argument for government protection for infant industries, and it is intended that eventually Proton will be able to stand on its own feet economically.

The company is used as an experiment for training local Malays in industrial skills both at executive and shop floor level. It is expected that Malays will be able to take over management from the current Japanese executives in time.

Proton has 40 direct sales outlets in Malaysia, 42 independent dealers and 6 franchise dealers to distribute the car. An international marketing division has been established to develop the export market, and to set up a sales network on an international basis. Sales to the UK are currently encouraging, and at competitive prices

●●▶

cont.

(although still subsidized by the Malaysian government). Proton is also sold in the USA, Hungary, Japan, Germany, New Zealand, Turkey and Bangladesh. Foreign sales units are, however, totally dependent upon the Malaysian parent and still need the substantial subsidy to be price competitive in their respective markets.

Proton is selling into a domestic market in Malaysia just beginning its love affair with car. The car is therefore specified for the domestic Malaysian market and overseas sales are still very much seen as simply a supplement to domestic demand. Little effort is therefore made currently to understand the particular needs of overseas markets, but merely to produce a reliable budget-priced car for the low to middle-price market. The company has no specific international strategy except to meet price competition, and sell as hard as possible.

Source: Compiled by authors from press articles. ■

The Proton car company is at the international exporter stage, and has possibilities for moving to a traditional global strategy. When it begins to devote more attention to operating successfully and profitably in international markets, it is likely to convert itself into a genuinely global company selling varieties of its standard models throughout the world in an increasingly 'Gillette'-style way. This transition will, however, take time to effect and the company is currently a very weak player on the international scene. This is for a number of reasons including its poor brand name and the existing overcapacity in the world car market. However, it is also weak because it has an inappropriate international organizational form for further international expansion and has not clearly identified possible sources of comparative and competitive advantage for its product.

Summary

In some respects the modern multidomestic and the modern global corporation are moving together. The modern multidomestic is developing a centre that is able to: ensure best practice throughout the corporation; allocate major resources when appropriate; and declare worldwide products if this makes sense (see Nestlé as discussed in Box 7.1). It is therefore far more than the traditional holding company for receiving subsidiary dividends. The modern global corporation, on the other hand, is far more flexible with regard to production location and, sometimes, R&D, and is likely to take note of major area differences of culture in marketing and sales. Yet despite some appearance of convergence, the two polar forms remain distinct archetypes, although many corporations may combine elements of both in their actual configuration and co-ordination.

Ultimately the multidomestic will always be the most appropriate form, where scale economies are limited and local tastes are paramount in maintaining market share. Correspondingly, the global corporation will remain the most appropriate form where scale economies dominate, and the nature of the market need varies little from country to country. Thus, some industries (like cardboard) are more appropriately handled on a multidomestic basis, and others (like computer chips) on a global one. Meanwhile the international exporter form is becoming increasingly dated, and for success in world markets needs to transform itself to a variant of one of the other three major forms, dependent upon which has the best environmental and technological fit. In many industries the needs of local responsiveness and of global integration are both important, and not biased towards one or other polar form. The next chapter describes the case of the relatively newly developed form of the transnational organization which has a more complex response to this organizational balancing act.

9

The transnational form

In Chapters 7 and 8 we discussed two contrasting but dominant models of the multinational corporation (MNC): the multidomestic (Porter, 1986) and the global (Yip, 1992) as well as the transitional international exporter form. In this chapter we continue our review of strategy and organization structure for MNCs by exploring a different type of organizational model for multinationals which began to emerge in the late 1980s and has driven forward the debate on the most effective strategies and structures for competing across borders in the turbulent environment of the twenty-first century. This is an approach within international strategy which most closely resembles the contingent, conditional school of management research. This emergent model has become known as the 'transnational'.

Introducing the idea of the transnational

Developed first in the work of Bartlett and Ghoshal (1989), it is perhaps more useful to think of a 'transnational' as an idea or a philosophy rather than an organization structure. Thus the transnational is probably best understood as a state of mind. It is a state of mind which is adaptable and which sees efficiency across international boundaries as something that companies achieve through responsiveness, flexibility and the ability to learn. Thus, decision-making is approached at whatever level, and in whatever geographic context is most appropriate for the international objectives of the firm. Achievement of goals, rather than protection of turf, country managers' pet assumptions, or the historical traditions of the firm, is what should influence decisions.

The notion of contingency theory as a framework for making sense of the management of international organizations has a deep appeal given the permanent fluidity, changeability and the fundamental dynamic character of the international business context. It is, however, an approach which rejects certainties and prescriptions and thereby it places great strains on international business managers. It is natural to seek for certainty as the reassuring basis for action, and deeply disconcerting to find only continuous uncertainty. But to seek to impose certainties where few exist is a recipe for failure in any business context. It remains more helpful therefore to accept the discomfort and try to find more and better ways of interpreting and acting within it. It is in response to these uncertainties that the transnational form has emerged.

A simple way of illustrating this continuous dynamic of uncertainty, and therefore of the need for an organizational model that can transform itself as the requirements of its context change, is to state how much the idea of globalization itself has changed. The issues that are debated with regard to global strategies have moved on. As discussed in Chapter 8 the meaning of 'global' has changed from an emphasis on *operational integration* to its current emphasis on *strategic co-ordination and local responsiveness*. In the earlier simple globalization phase, the focus was on globalization affecting products and components. The dominant concepts in this phase were global operational scale advantages, factor costs, product standardization and global sourcing platforms. In its later complex globalization phase, the focus was on globalization of skills and capabilities. The dominant concepts in this later phase were flexibility: systems to give variety at low cost; regional autonomy; risk avoidance; and deep understanding of customer needs. This shift in emphasis as globalization became more complex meant that in place of the centralized hubs of the early simple global organization structures, more complex decentralized structures were emerging to meet the need to operate locally, regionally and globally *simultaneously*, for different sets of market and industry conditions. Gradually then, an organizational form has been emerging which Bartlett and Ghoshal (1989) have christened 'the transnational solution'.

Being truly multinational

The phrase 'truly global' has been popularized by Kenichi Ohmae (1989) in developing his view of what he sees as an increasingly and inexorably 'borderless world'. In the 1990s, global and globalizing firms became more significant than ever before. In part this is because there are so many of them: about 38 000 transnational companies at the last count by the United Nations Commission for Trade and Development (UNCTAD). These companies control about a third of all private-sector assets in the world and have worldwide sales of about \$5.5 trillion, which is not much less than the GDP of the USA. The other important development for modern MNCs is how they see themselves as organizations and how they are attempting to organize themselves. Their objective is to be able to fully utilize any resource, wherever it is located, against its competitors and for its customers. That means not only moving production facilities around to benefit from the best expertise or the most productive labour anywhere in the world (what Ghoshal's framework, Table 6.1 in Chapter 6, would have called 'benefiting from local differences'), but it also means breaking down internal barriers to the free movement of people and, particularly, of ideas (e.g. to benefit from economies of scope in learning).

This new approach to being multinational is based upon two ideas about modern business life. First, that if continuous innovation is the key to long-term success an organization that relies on one culture for its ideas and treats its foreign subsidiaries just as output locations, might as well hire subcontractors or outsource. Second, that technology is making geographic space and physical distance irrelevant. Software writers in Bangalore, India and Palo Alto, West Coast USA, work together on programmes in different time zones, and the programmes may then be specially tailored for local markets.

All this has huge implications for company management and organization structures. Most MNCs are having to think through massive reorganization programmes to reach these changed objectives for the organization and enabling different internal ways of operating to establish themselves. AT&T (US telecommunications giant) paid $347 million in consultants' fees in 1994 to help with its global reorganization. Gillette (US consumer-goods firm) has developed a 'federalized' global management system which the company thinks of as operating in 'over 500 states'. Matsushita and Sony (both Japanese consumer electronics giants) announced publicly that to become 'truly global' they must have cultural diversity in their top management. Sony began appointing non-Japanese to its board of directors in 1989 and now aims to give the top job in each of its subsidiaries to a manager from that country. Ford (US motor company) has spent most of the 1990s on a massive worldwide restructuring to turn itself into a borderless firm.

European firms such as ABB (Swedish-Swiss electrical-engineering conglomerate) have been at the forefront of such organizational experiments. Yet its senior managers still feel that 'the truly global multicultural company does not yet exist' (quoted in *The Economist* 30/7/94) since few MNCs produce more than 20 per cent of their goods and services outside their immediate or wider home market and most boards are still ethnocentric and come predominantly from the company's 'home' culture.

Since ABB is itself a company endlessly cited in the management literature as an impeccable example of a truly global transnational, theirs is an interesting viewpoint. ABB is a firm with a board of eight directors comprising four different nationalities; English is its corporate language; and its financial results are reported in dollars. Until 1998, its executive committee contained eight people from five countries; but after another reorganization abandoning its regional matrix in favour of flattening its structure even further (see Box 9.2), ABB no longer has any Germans or Americans on its executive board, only Swedes, Swiss and one Norwegian. Philips has begun to open its top ranks in Holland to non-Dutchmen. Royal Dutch/Shell (Dutch/UK oil giant) is another MNC often regarded as truly multicultural, with about 38 nationalities at its head office in London and having announced in 1998 its intended closure of its most prestigious European offices (including the flagship London headquarters) in favour of their dispersal to a larger spread of smaller locations closer to its refineries. Royal Dutch/Shell, like other MNCs such as Citicorp, rotates managers around its businesses in different parts of the globe to develop a more international frame of reference. However, it is still noticeable within Royal Dutch/Shell that to get to very senior positions it certainly helps to be either Dutch or British.

Bertelsmann, the German global media and entertainment MNC, despite its global positioning, is at a much earlier stage in struggling with how to be 'truly multinational' (see Box 9.1).

Box 9.1 Multinationalizing Bertelsmann's German Supertanker

Two-thirds of Bertelsmann's revenues are now generated outside Germany. Since it acquired the huge US publisher Random House in 1998, it has become the world's second-largest media company. Its business interests cover books, magazines, television, music and the Internet. Unlike other media MNCs, which are focusing their efforts across business divisions to maximize the number of uses to be made of each bit of company 'software' (i.e. the TV programmes, record, film and video libraries, stories or characters that can be repackaged in other media formats), Bertelsmann is still organized as a set of fiercely independent business units.

A new chairman was appointed in 1998 to head the Bertelsmann management board and attempt to change the company's rather isolationist, and certainly overwhelmingly German, culture. There are no non-Germans on its management board and Germans are overwhelmingly represented in the senior management ranks. Its headquarters is located in Gutersloh, North-Rhine Westphalia, which is in effect a company town and where Bertelsmann has had its corporate centre for 163 years. It is a considerable psychological distance from the media mindset of New York.

Two recent strategic disasters have exposed the shortcomings of the company's totally independent, highly entrepreneurial, divisional structure (typical of the type Matsushita used to have and has been moving away from for the last five years). In a situation which

••▶

cont.

mirrors closely the one experienced by Philips and its attempted international launch of its VCR format (discussed in Chapter 7), Bertelsmann's decentralization and the failure of its divisions to co-operate led to the following two recent major opportunities missed by the company. First, Bertelsmann's biggest magazine *Stern* put a CD-ROM on its cover which gave access to T-Online, which is Deutsche Telekom's Internet service and the direct rival of AOL, Bertelsmann's own on-line joint venture partner. Needless to say, Bertelsmann's magazine publishing division and its multimedia division do not speak to each other. The second example had even more drastic long-term consequences for the company. Although the whole company was aware that the Internet is growing *across* all its product lines, the independent divisional heads on Bertelsmann's management board debated book retailing on the Internet for two years without resolving to do anything about it. Meanwhile Amazon established itself as the world's leading on-line book retailer, leaving Bertelsmann with a tough task of catching-up, given the rapid development cycles on the Internet. It bought 50 per cent of the Barnes and Noble (USA) website business for $200 million in 1998 to begin the fight back.

The need to work together is recognized , but the structure to enable that co-operation is missing, and possibly also the will to create such a structure. The powerful heads of Bertelsmann's divisions are all present on the management board and have so far not consented to any dilution in their own independence. Nor do they appear any more willing to co-operate with each other. The head of Bertelsmann's magazine division was recently quoted as saying that he would not necessarily co-operate with the music division to promote a new artist through his magazines: 'only if it were interesting for our readers' (quoted in *The Economist* 7/11/98).

Source: Compiled by authors from various press articles. ■

The central dilemma

These companies, as well as all the others not as far down the multicultural road, are all struggling with the global/local dilemma. Global firms can shift huge volumes of goods at high speed, whilst standardization offers huge advantages of scale, speed and lower unit costs. Their standardized products require fewer plants, they buy from fewer suppliers and reduce duplication. This can cut unit costs by 20–30 per cent. However, local knowledge is also essential, as we have already seen in earlier examples of the size of Procter and

Gamble's baby diapers for the Japanese market or Johnson Wax's wrong-smelling cleaning polish. As a result of its international experiences, Procter and Gamble no longer imposes managers from headquarters on overseas subsidiaries. Local knowledge is essential not only to tailor products and services to local market preferences and conditions, but also to get access to local expertise. Few of the patents granted to US or European MNCs are granted for work done by overseas operations, representing a wasted knowledge resource opportunity to the parents.

Because this global/local dilemma will not disappear (Caves, 1998; Rangan, 1998), MNCs must find sophisticated ways of surmounting it or, preferably, harnessing it to their advantage, which is where the search for the transnational organization begins. It is an organizational approach based on complexity and flexibility, so much so that many managers have claimed it to be hopelessly unworkable in practice. However, it is at the very least an approach which accepts, and attempts to face head on, the challenges of combining the strengths of global with the strengths of local at the same time, rather than regarding them as trade-offs.

Most multinationals have adopted matrix structures, in which each unit reports simultaneously to a product-group headquarters and a country headquarters. It is a structure designed to avoid the dangers of parochialism or NIH ('not invented here') often occurring in multidomestic organizations. Such multidomestic structures frequently developed powerful country general managers often with vested interests in providing minimal co-operation to other national subsidiaries. Professional service firm (PSF) partnership structures often exhibited similar symptoms, as when one national practice refuses to make a star consultant with a valuable specialist expertise available to another national practice to assist on a particular client project. The reason for this non-co-operation was usually to be found in the two separate profit pools of the two separate national practices. They constituted a disincentive to lending a high-yield senior consultant to improve their national profit pool rather than yours. Under these systems inevitably the need to staff up to meet client expectations of service levels to international clients, and the structure of the national practices, were on a collision course. Following these experiences, many MNC professional service firms are abandoning their cherished partnership structures to transform themselves into corporations, with their inherently different possibilities for corporate governance.

Matrix structures were intended to address these multidomestic organizational psychoses. Following from Stopford and Wells' (1972) descriptive research described in Chapter 6, MNCs and consultants started to apply their ideas prescriptively, and the matrix structure was the result. Matrix structures emerged at the point in international expansion of the firm when it had both high presence in a range of international markets and extensive spread of international product range, as a means of simultaneously managing the demands of both. As an organization structure, the matrix is an arrangement that combines two (or sometimes three) types of responsibility: geographic regions and product groups, or product groupings and functional responsibilities. Table 9.1 illustrates a straightforward, very basic, geographic matrix structure.

This is a structure that relies on a dual command system which is intended to facilitate the development of a more globally or regionally oriented management mindset than the national domestic market mindset often fostered by the multidomestic multinational. As regional managers have responsibility for total levels of business within their region covering all of the MNC's products or services, and product managers have responsibility for the profitability of a particular product line or group of products; their responsibilities are different but require co-ordination if either is to achieve its objectives. Most operational managers within such a system therefore report to two bosses. That illustration describes only the simplest of matrices. Often they may be three-dimensional covering lines of responsibility for products, regions and functions. One of the major potential benefits of such a multidimensional matrix structure is that it forces the company to face up to the balancing acts often required to deal with complex business issues such as a decision concerning location of a global production function, whilst simultaneously trying to appreciate the effect this will have on a regional market and the company's ability to resource particular product lines for its individual business units. Prahalad and Doz (1987) argued for the matrix structure as the solution to the MNC's central dilemma of the need for efficient global integration of functions and processes, combined with the need for flexible responsiveness to national needs.

Problems with the matrix structure in MNCs lie in its complexity. In particular, the dual reporting structure rather than facilitating frequently leads to confusion over responsibilities and decision-making. Avoiding such confusion requires a great many meetings between the groups and individuals involved in each decision. Bartlett and Ghoshal (1990) suggest that clarity of the firm's basic objectives, continuity in the company's commitment to those objectives over time, and consistency in how the various divisions of the organization work together, are what is needed for good matrix management. If these three 'C's are present then the matrix structure can be very effective.

Table 9.1 A geographic matrix structure

	Country/Regions		
Product/Group	**Country 'A'**	**Country 'B'**	**Country 'C'**
Product group 1			
Product group 2			
Product group 3			

ABB has always been referred to as an exemplary, well-managed matrix MNC, whereas Philips has historically had problems managing its matrix, whether it was geographically or product division focused. The classic story of problems Philips had with lack of corporate consistency, already cited in Chapter 7, was the rejection (in the 1970s) by its own North American subsidiary of Philips videocassette format, in favour of the rival VHS format from Philips' Japanese rival Matsushita. The subsidiary (geographic region) simply refused to support the parent company's international VCR (product) strategy. That destroyed any chance of establishing Philips' videocassette format in the huge American market. Matsushita's VHS format became the industry standard. We have also described (see Box 9.1) a much more recent similar situation faced by Bertelsmann in 1998 concerning book retailing on the Internet.

Not surprisingly, another problem with this type of structure is the amount of management time taken by meetings and the elapsed time managers need to understand how the structure works in order to contribute to it effectively. If the MNC experiences a high degree of staff turnover, this can exacerbate such difficulties. Some MNCs have abandoned the matrix structure and gone back to more simple reporting lines, with clear responsibility being given to geographic managers. Citicorp (US global financial conglomerate which merged in 1998 with US Travellers Group to become Citigroup) was a well-known example of a company which had invested years of management time and billions of dollars in building its matrix, only finally to abandon the structure. Instead of a flexible structure, containing multiple perspectives and able to shift the balance of power between products, markets and functions as commercial need required, the matrix amplified any differences in perspective. Digital Equipment Co. (DEC, US computing MNC) also abandoned its matrix system in 1994 and spent $1 billion (and shedding 20 000 jobs in the process) in moving to a global structure. The dual reporting structure of the matrix often prevented resolution of differences between managers of different views but overlapping responsibilities (see Bartlett and Ghoshal, 1989 Ch. 2). Even ABB in 1998 decided to restructure (see Box 9.2).

Box 9.2 Changes at ABB

ABB, probably the world's most admired 'matrixer', announced in 1998 that it would dissolve its regional management structure, under which three members of its executive board shared operational responsibilities with the three executives heading its three core businesses (power generation; power transmission and distribution; and industrial and building systems). Instead ABB would restructure into eight core businesses,

• • ▶

cont.

all of which would be represented on the (reorganized) executive board. Percy Barnevik, ABB's first chief executive after the merger between Sweden's Asea and Switzerland's Brown Boveri in 1988, established the matrix when he removed the then country general managers from the executive board. Mr Barnevik's successor, Goran Lindahl, 10 years later, removed the regional managers from the executive board, filling it instead purely with business heads of the (reorganized) core businesses. The objective of the organizational restructuring was said to be greater speed and efficiency by further focusing and flattening of the organization. It also provided greater transparency both internally, and externally to the marketplace, of the balance of businesses within this large corporate group, especially of newer growth businesses.

Source: Compiled by authors from various press articles. ■

A matrix then, may sometimes be a route through which the MNC can move to another, different form of hybrid organization which it may find more effective in managing across borders.

Some organizations have constructed networks of different clusters of specialist local firms in order to benefit from local variations (Ghoshal's 'benefiting from local differences' again). One example is Nike (US sportswear manufacturer) which subcontracts the manufacture of its athletic shoes and clothing to 40 separate locations, mostly in Asia, using a technology-mediated network. Designs are sent to a plant in Taiwan; a prototype is then built; the final plans are faxed to subcontractors throughout Asia. Rather than attempting to meet all global/local requirements internally, some MNCs have opted to build external networks of strategic alliances. However, like all other complex organizational forms, these too are difficult to manage on a global scale and require their own knowledge and experience to work effectively. We will return to the management of strategic alliances in Chapters 11 and 12. Running a 'borderless corporation' in a borderless world is about endlessly struggling to resolve the paradox of our central dilemma.

The transnational

In their article 'Beyond the M-form', Bartlett and Ghoshal (1993) are attempting to develop a new managerial theory of the firm able to incorporate the management of high degrees of complexity and flexibility, and new ways of integrating activities and resources across borders.

Figure 9.1 illustrates the difference between the two earlier dominant organizational structural types in international strategy: the centralized hubs of

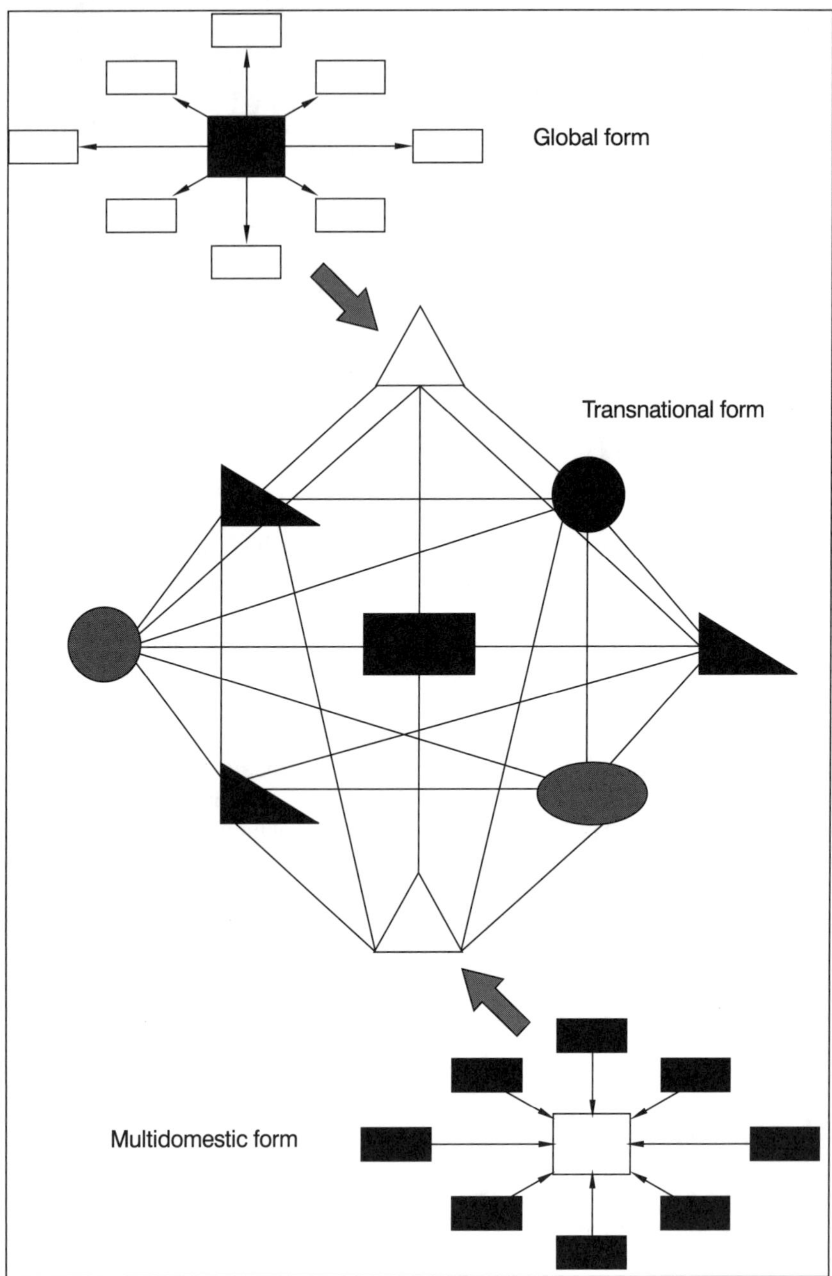

Figure 9.1 A transnational network organization. *Source:* Adapted from Bartlett and Ghoshal (1989)

the global form (top left); the decentralized portfolios of national subsidiary businesses of the multidomestic form (bottom right); and the transnational organization – defined here as an integrated network (the N-form). The diagrammatic representation in Figure 9.1 is intended to highlight two particular differences in the new form compared to the old: multilateral communications between all levels and layers, replacing top-down or bottom-up communication; and the idea that resources, responsibilities and decision-making are dispersed across all types of units, not just concentrated either at the centre (central headquarters) or at the periphery (autonomous national subsidiaries). Each separate circle, triangle or box shape, large or small, in the main diagram might represent an entirely different type and size of resource unit. One may be a global distribution hub based in Europe, while another may be a small project team working on the design of a new product or service, staffed by employees from a mix of international locations. The project team may be disbanded after six months and a different unit formed, for a different purpose, somewhere else in the organization. These resource units are thus *asymmetrical* in both size and duration.

That is what Bartlett and Ghoshal (1993) mean by 'beyond the M-form', where 'M' stands for 'multidivisional'. Instead an 'N-form' organization appears to be emerging, with 'N' standing for 'network'. Particularly noteworthy are the stress they place on: first, the importance of 'co-ordinating mechanisms' in the N-form; and second, the changed role of senior management.

There are many diverse examples of 'co-ordinating mechanisms'. Many firms are, for example, redesigning incentive systems to reward employees who help sister companies. IBM has introduces performance measures which reward managers for co-operating with colleagues around the world. Procedures for global account management are a sophisticated illustration of one type of 'co-ordinating mechanism'. They illustrate the internal consequences of network management and the capabilities required by managers in terms of systems and processes for dealing with it. These must ensure alignment of both the internal and the customer-facing processes. Box 9.3 discusses the triggers for creating such a system at Hewlett-Packard.

Box 9.3 Hewlett-Packard – Global Account Management System

The issue for Hewlett-Packard (HP) was how well it was managing the accounts of its multinational customers. As one of the world's largest computer products and systems suppliers, the US-based firm had more than 600 sales and service offices in 110 countries. The challenge for

cont.

HP was to get national sales managers in its different national subsidiaries to co-operate. Apart from the national sales managers, to make the proposed system work, buy-in was also needed from HP's country general managers. Until 1990, the nationally-based sales and account management programme blocked co-ordination across geographic lines. While some major accounts were looked after by senior level executives, others had no such relationship.

International customers were increasingly expecting not merely product standardization, but also service standardization to give them greater consistency of customer support worldwide. HP's MNC customers wanted confidential strategic partnerships with vendors who were more than simply suppliers. Customers wanted vendor support for their complex, networked global systems. Internally HP needed to speed up its own development as a global organization: it needed co-ordination across its businesses in the Americas, Asia-Pacific and Europe. Barriers to co-operation across these regions was blocking not only service consistency but also new business development opportunities. Also, HP's internal performance measurement system was based on product quotas per region. This meant that there were no incentives for managers to co-ordinate or to pursue joint initiatives for global business opportunities outside their region.

The proposal for Global Account Management Systems emerged in outline in 1991 to address the demand for more consistent worldwide support and service. The objective was to co-ordinate on global lines, balancing geographic, product and customer focus. A new role of Global Account Manager was established (GAM) to be located near the customer's headquarters and to be directly responsible for managing HP's relationship with the global account. The GAM's responsibilities were as follows:

- worldwide customer sales, support and satisfaction;
- assuring that HP is perceived as one company at all customer locations;
- working with HP's senior management to ensure that HP is organized and resourced to service opportunities identified in the global account;
- establishing close working rapport with the senior managers assigned to support the account.

GAMs are evaluated on the worldwide performance of the global account, whilst country managers are evaluated on the worldwide

••▶

cont.

performance of global accounts headquartered in their country and on overall country performance. This approach to evaluation provides necessary incentives to country managers to co-operate with the GAMs.

More than 30 global accounts were in place by 1994; senior executives estimated that around 50 such accounts might be the optimal number for the company worldwide.

Source: Adapted from Yip and Madsen, 1996. ■

In addition to the emphasis on co-ordinating mechanisms, the N-form promotes a changed role for senior management: to provide shared corporate purpose. This echoes points made by Senge (1992) concerning the new role of the corporate leader: as designer, teacher and steward, surfacing, designing , challenging and building new mental models and complex systems. Table 9.2 summarizes this view of the 'new model' of the roles of management appropriate to N-form network organizations, contrasting it to requirements in earlier organizational forms.

There is consistency in the new approach to managerial tasks and responsibilities in transnational MNCs exemplified in Table 9.2, between Bartlett and Ghoshal's work and that of Senge. They are searching after simple ways of capturing the behavioural complexity, the structural complexity and the organizational complexity that are essential in a transnational MNC. Now that centralized headquarters bureaucracies have fallen into disfavour

> ... the favoured form of the firm has become a federal structure of operating divisions drawing on a common source of internal expertise, but where each division belonging to the federation is free to outsource expertise if it so desires. (Buckley and Casson, 1998a, p.28)

Table 9.2 Roles and tasks of management: the transnational

Top management	Middle management	Front-line management
Then Resource allocator	*Then* Administrative controller	*Then* Optional implementor
Now Creator of purpose and challenger of *status quo*	*Now* Horizontal information broker and capability integrator	*Now* Entrepreuner and performance driver

Source: Adapted from Bartlett and Ghoshal (1993)

Building global flexibility and national responsiveness within the transnational

Greater transparency of information has created an increasing requirement for uniformity and consistency in quality, delivery and marketing of products and services across borders. Not all companies will be able to allocate the resources or develop the capabilities for such management of quality and responsiveness across geographic boundaries. Integration and co-ordination bring great benefits, but many companies are insufficiently skilled to implement them effectively. We will now introduce two examples of companies in quite different businesses who have both been attempting in the context of their own business needs to implement the ideas of flexibility, responsiveness and shared resources firm-wide that are at the heart of the discussion in this chapter. Interestingly, both Cap Gemini Sogeti (CGS) and Novotel are service businesses.

As will be developed in more detail in the next chapter, service firms are characterized by particular combinations of resources and capabilities different from those characteristic of manufacturing firms, the most obvious difference being the importance in assessments about quality in service organizations of the interface between the front-line staff and the customer. Also noteworthy in both these examples is the importance of the creation and sharing of knowledge-based resources. Knowledge-sharing and organizational learning is regarded increasingly as one of the most critical capabilities for all MNCs, not only generating knowledge, but just as importantly, spreading it through the organization (as an economy of scope). It is particularly helpful for service industries, since most services are heavily dependent on knowledge-based resources in both the design and delivery of the service, and especially on the tacit knowledge underpinning the routines of the staff, whether software consultants (in CGS) or hotel receptionists (in Novotel). See Box 9.4.

Box 9.4 Cap Gemini Sogeti – A Transnational Organization

Cap Gemini Sogeti (CGS) is Europe's biggest computer-software and services group. Since 1975 CGS has grown to Europe's number one position in computer services and consulting. It has taken all available means to pursue growth, developing by means of organic growth and acquisitions, as well as by alliances. It has a complex organization structure that reflects the nature of its history, its varied requirements and tensions, and its aim to be a modern transnational company.

••▶

cont.

CGS grew from a merger of Cap, a computer services group, and Sogeti, a business management and information processing company. This merger brought with it operations in the UK, the Netherlands, Switzerland and Germany, with a head office in France. It then acquired a large number of small groups in Europe and some in the USA. This expanded its service coverage to IT consulting, customized software, and education and training. The acquisition of SESA in 1987 broadened its culture from its origins as a computer 'body-shop'. Its current mission is to assist clients to get the highest possible benefit from the opportunities afforded by state of the art information technology.

As an organization CGS is strongly decentralized, and when any of its branches reaches 150 personnel, it splits it in two. In order to be able to respond to variations in local demand, it has gradually extended its range of business services to cover the full range of computer services. These divide into four distinct businesses:

1. *Facilities management*, spearheaded by its acquisition of Hoskyns based in the UK.
2. *Systems integration*, which develops packages of hardware and software to meet the client's needs, e.g. it will automate a factory, or computerize an invoicing process.
3. *IT consultancy*, which was the original service base of CGS.
4. *Management consultancy*, which is led by Gemini. This was created as a professionally independent group by bringing together three leading consultancy firms, the MAC group, United Research and Gamma International. Gemini has been structured to be legally, organizationally, and culturally separate from CGS, although obviously part of its 'family'.

CGS has developed information pooling systems to ensure that innovative solutions developed in one country or business are rapidly communicated to the others. These include electronic bulletin boards, and extensive electronic and voice mail facilities. In addition to these, there are also the informal networks developed by committed professionals working frequently together, repeatedly, in project teams, within the context of a deliberately enabling culture.

A major part of CGS's growth strategy is to increase its representation in a greater number of international markets. To facilitate this, and strengthen existing international operations, it has created an international support division. In 1991 CGS developed a strategic

••▶

cont.

alliance with Mercedes-Benz, in which the German company took a 34 per cent holding in CGS for $585 million, and which includes a joint venture with Debis Systemhaus, Daimler-Benz's software company. In 1992, CGS established a Benelux presence through an alliance with Volmac. It created Cap Volmac with 4000 staff and annual turnover of about $500 million.

For this fast growing transnational, the challenges are to integrate its wide variety of organizations into a group capable of acknowledging a complex web of ownership relationships, whilst benefiting from the strengths of its 'family' of semi-autonomous professionals. The reinforcement of a common culture, the creation of effective cross-selling activities, and the leveraging of its wide range of professional expertise across the firm to meet the needs of cross-border clients, all represent tasks of considerable magnitude and complexity.

In pursuit of those objectives, and despite extremely tough competitive conditions and poor business results throughout the mid-1990s, CGS's managers pushed ahead with a major internal overhaul. Nicknamed 'Genesis', it was intended to turn CGS from a loose federation of companies into a tightly-knit global group. In particular, it involved giving worldwide responsibility for particular industries to country managers. Thus CGS's French operation now handle telecoms while its American operation handles oil and gas. Though Genesis took much longer to implement than expected (nearly two years), its business purpose was to help the disparate group find the most appropriate way of meeting both internal and external pressures. Internally, the need was for better clarity and co-ordination in roles, objectives, systems and the use of resources, especially of its skilled professional staff. Externally, the need was to meet both market and industry changes, and to be able to meet the needs of its clients more responsively. This could be taken as the goal for all 'transnational solutions'.

Source: Compiled by the authors from various press articles. ■

The example which follows analyses the process of long-term capability-building within a multinational hotel chain – Novotel. It looks at the accumulation of skills and learning mechanisms within the firm. The analysis provides an illustration of the organizational structures, processes and routines which attempt to create both consistency and flexibility across the company's international operations. The international strategy task for Novotel is to create processes for meeting customer expectations in all its hotels worldwide. It must therefore achieve consistency plus responsiveness, i.e. enabling all front-line and managerial staff to deal sensitively and helpfully with divergent customer needs worldwide (see Box 9.5).

Box 9.5 Novotel: A Multinational Hotel Chain as a Learning Network

The first Novotel hotel was opened by two entrepreneurs near Lille airport in France in 1967. The first Novotel outside France was opened in 1973. By 1995 the chain had grown to 280 hotels in 46 countries around the world. The hotels provide 43 000 rooms and employ 33 000 people. Novotel is just one of the hotel chains belonging to the Accor Group of France, which operates more than 2000 hotels worldwide offering more than two million rooms at different ratings and service levels. Other chains in the group include Sofitel, Mercure, Ibis, Formule 1. These range from 4-star (Sofitel) to 1-star (Formule 1).

The fundamental characteristic of the Novotel hotel concept is international standardization of the offering in its positioning as a 3-star chain worldwide. For standardization, consistency is required of the offering in every location worldwide. This means putting in place a system that is robust enough to generate consistent service standards to satisfy customer expectations, irrespective of local conditions or infrastructure. Some of the physical elements of standardization are easily realizable. The design, style and layouts of the hotels are reproduced to precise specifications. For example, bedroom size is standard throughout Europe at 24 square metres although this does differ for Novotel Asia. Certain types of bedroom furniture, fixtures and fittings, or outside amenities such as swimming pools and amounts of free car parking space, are standard.

However, the more interesting elements of the Novotel offering for the purposes of this discussion are the management processes which enable standard service levels to be delivered at all locations worldwide. Since hotel design and guest bedrooms are standardized, basic housekeeping and maintenance functions can in turn be standardized. That means that the training of staff in all basic functions may be simplified and training procedures themselves standardized. Indeed, one of the features of Novotel's parent company the Accor Group, is the 'Acadèmie Accor', set up in 1985 as the centre for all staff training within the group. Its 'campus' is located on the site of

••▶

cont.

group corporate headquarters just outside Paris. From there, all training is designed and delivered. Standardized procedures and centrally designed training programmes are one of the core mechanisms for achieving consistency.

However, maintaining universal quality standards as the chain grew rapidly over a 25-year period became more and more problematic, especially when many new staff were recruited from other hotel groups with different working practices. A system to monitor standard procedures was introduced in 1987. It regulated the 13 main points of staff/customer interaction. These were: reservation, arrival/access, parking, check-in, hall, bedroom, bathroom/WC, evening meal, breakfast, shops, bar, outdoor games/swimming-pool and check-out. Each of these key interaction points was divided into a series of compulsory directives for staff, e.g. how to set out a bedroom, lay a place setting in the restaurant or welcome a guest. A booklet containing all 95 of these compulsory directives was issued to all staff and was a mainstay in the induction of new staff. The booklet became known as the '95 bolts'. An internal team of inspectors visited each hotel approximately twice each year to monitor standards. They functioned in the same way as 'mystery shoppers' in that they made reservations, arrived, stayed and departed incognito. On completion of their stay they would make themselves known to the General Manager (GM) for review and discussion. Percentage grades were awarded and recommendations made. This system, while helping Novotel to control and consolidate after a period of rapid growth, gradually became over-rigid and procedural in orientation.

At a meeting in 1992 for Novotel managers, the relationship of hotel GMs and their staff teams was redefined from hierarchical to enabling. A new corporate slogan 'Back to the Future' ('Retour vers le futur') was adopted to reflect the outlawing of the bureaucratic style of standardization and a return to Novotel's entrepreneurial roots. Inter-functional groups were set up across hotels and countries. GM groups were established which clustered together special interests across countries, to share ideas, innovations or best practice. These GM interest groups were constructed around common hotel types within the Novotel chain, e.g. all GMs of motorway locations, or airport locations, or city centre locations. The 95 directives were abolished as too rigid and replaced by three simplified general measures of performance – clients, management and people. One and a half layers of management were eliminated, leaving only one direct reporting layer between GMs and the (then) two co-presidents of

••▶

cont.

Novotel. (One of these, Gilles Pellison, a son of one of the founders of Accor, left in 1995 to take on the challenge of vice-president at EuroDisney in Paris.)

After 1992, the role of the GM was rethought and redefined as capturing the spirit of 'maitre de maison', much closer to the social role of a ship's captain. This led to a need for redevelopment of all GMs, who were required to go through an assessment activity incorporating role-play in such situations as conflict resolution with subordinates or guests. Not all GMs were reappointed.

It is also worth noting the continuous active involvement in the redevelopment process of the two original founders of Novotel (by then, co-presidents of the Accor Group), as well as the visible public involvement of the two current co-presidents of Novotel.

Source: Adapted from Segal-Horn (1995); Hunt, Baden-Fuller and Calori (1995). ■

In summarizing the outcomes of the process change described in Box 9.5 both the structure and operations of Novotel's corporate headquarters, as well as operations and routines in every hotel in the chain, were transformed, although in differing degrees and over different timescales. The transformations reflect the new roles and tasks of management in complex international organization structures as described in Table 9.2. International strategy benefits for Novotel arising from these changes included aspects of flexibility, responsiveness and the management of organizational learning:

- Information flows throughout the company were changed. Flattening the hierarchy enabled more relevant information to be conveyed faster.
- The role of headquarters was changed. It now acts as an information coordinator, collator and channel, rather than the instigator of time-consuming demands for central performance statistics. For example, the headquarters filters useful information to all hotels which they store for shared reference or as suggested best practice.
- Lateral communication (i.e. collaboration across and between levels) has increased (remember the description of Figure 9.1). GMs organize self-help clusters; training sessions are shared across the group; 'reflective clubs' ('clubs de reflexion') have been created in some hotels – mixed informal groupings of staff of a variety of levels who meet to discuss innovations. Significantly, these 'clubs' contain staff from across all service areas in the hotels and discussion covers the hotel as a whole, not the specific responsibility of any individual staff (club) member.

- The role of the GM has changed to that of 'coach', optimizing the service and amenities available to guests by developing the competencies of his team.
- Ways of working have changed for all staff. The horizons of staff have been broadened, giving greater awareness of the business as a whole as well as more responsibility, encouraging cross-functional links and increased autonomy, which adds value for staff and guests alike.

Novotel management see their competitive advantage as residing in their concept of 'hospitality'. The company's international strategy dilemma is making that happen across all their locations worldwide through the uncertain channel of their internationally-recruited clusters of hotel staff. It has to be achieved through clarity of positioning, clear understanding by all staff of corporate objectives and values, and consistent reinforcement of these objectives and values through the human resource management systems of the group (a close approximation to our three 'C's mentioned earlier): training, learning, sharing, discussing, transferring.

The Novotel chain is positioned as a 3-star chain worldwide. However, unlike the 1960s and 1970s when a 3-star international chain was an innovative concept, there are now many other 3-star chains (e.g. Marriott 'Courtyard') which have imitated Novotel's original concept and positioning. Whereas at inception, the 3-star concept and positioning was, of itself, a source of international advantage, now more dynamic processes and capabilities are required to stay ahead in the market.

Comparing the M-form and the N-form

> The N-form logic is one of multiplication and combination rather than of division. It also implies role assignments differing from those inherent in the M-form, at all levels of the firm. (Hedlund, 1994, p.74)

Both the multidivisional (M-form) and the network (N-form) are ways of managing large, diverse organizations, which MNCs always are. In earlier work (Hedlund, 1986) coined the term 'heterarchy' to describe what he saw as a new organizational paradigm emerging for MNCs. Heterarchies are heterodox, heterogeneous, non-uniform and uncomfortable. They operate in non-hierarchical ways because they have different organizational objectives and are trying to achieve different things. In comparing these two organizational forms at the heart of discussion in this chapter, it may be useful for us to follow Hedlund's (1994) six contrasting themes for hierarchies and heterarchies. He notes that differences between the two organizational forms may be made sense of by considering the following attributes:

1. Whether the organization focuses on *combining* things or *dividing* things in how it puts things together.

2. Whether the organization puts people together in *temporary* groupings (teams) or *permanent* structures (departments).
3. Whether the organization makes use of people at *lower levels* within the organization or always handles co-ordination through *'managers'*.
4. Whether the organization has more *lateral* dialogue or only *vertical* communication.
5. Whether the organization uses senior managers as technical, human and knowledge *catalysts* or as *monitors and resource allocators*.
6. Whether the organization *focuses* its development on combining rich areas of knowledge rather than *diversifying* into separate organizational units.

(Hedlund, 1994, p.82)

Summary

No organizational form is ever the last word in method of corporate governance. New forms emerge as needs and requirements for what the organization must accomplish, and the context in which it must operate, shift over time in accordance with industry and competitor dynamics. The assumption of earlier work on organization structure appeared to be that organizations would continue to be structured within some form of hierarchy, albeit steeper or flatter hierarchies, simply to 'get things done'. What appears to be happening at the end of the twentieth century is the beginnings of non-hierarchical organizational forms which are instead networks (N-forms).

We have introduced the idea of the transnational form as a non-prescriptive contingent form of organization, excellently suited to MNC objectives of optimal cross-border strategic flexibility, by breaking down internal structural barriers to movement of people or ideas within the organization. As such it is intended to be an asymmetrical organizational form, responsive to the MNC's central dilemma of having increasingly to be globally integrated but locally responsive at the same time. We have contrasted this network N-form of organization with the more traditional M-form.

These infant N-form organizations are all responding to the fact of geographic spread of resources and leadership roles; the need to work in richer partnership with other overseas subsidiaries; the necessity for cross-border communication and sharing; the imperative to utilize knowledge and experience from a multiplicity of diverse organizational units; the poverty and ineffectiveness of purely formal methods of organizational communication; and new emergent relationships between organizational centres and their subsidiary and related parts. However, all organizational forms have their own pathologies, and in the transnational it is the sheer practical difficulty of learning how to make such complexity work in a day-to-day way.

Although the concepts on which these organizational ideas are based have been around for a long time in organizational research (e.g. see Burns and Stalker, 1961), the current practical attempts at constructing these non-hierarchical transnationals have emerged in response to an increasingly resource-based view (Grant, 1991; Prahalad and Hamel, 1990; Teece, Pisano and Shuen, 1997) of international strategy. This had led to recognition that MNCs have to search for better ways of harnessing their scarcest resources within the firm. The scarcest resource is broadly now assumed to be knowledge, and that any MNC organization structure now must be such as to optimize knowledge creation, knowledge capture and knowledge distribution across the firm to ensure its future survival. It is this that the transnational form seems best fitted to do.

Part 3

New pathways

10

International strategy in services

Whilst service multinational corporations (MNCs) may follow any of the strategies or structures discussed in the preceding chapters, service industries and service firms have distinct characteristics which may add risk and delivery problems to the design and implementation of international service strategies. This chapter will present current research into service standardization and approaches to managing 'intangibles' across borders. It will cover potential sources of economies of scale and scope in services; and internal management processes for the effective implementation of international strategies in service firms.

Service industries are those whose output is not a physical good or product but an intangible 'experience'. This underpins an essential difference in the significance of internationalization or globalization in services as opposed to manufacturing. International service delivery is about controlling the quality of the offering at the point of sale to the customer. The expectation of the customer is for consistency and predictability of service levels in any location worldwide.

Growth in international services

Historically, the literature on global strategy (Bartlett and Ghoshal, 1989; Ghoshal, 1987; Ohmae, 1989; Porter, 1986; Prahalad and Doz, 1987; Yip, 1991, 1992) has taken its evidence overwhelmingly from manufacturing industry, although services now account for some two-thirds of GDP in developed economies (see Figure 10.1) and are significant in terms of output, jobs and trade balances (Enderwick, 1989; Riddle, 1986). Agreement on freeing trade in telecommunications was finally reached by the WTO in 1997 and a new round of talks in services trade is due to begin in 2000. Such deregulation allowing freer trade in services will help to clarify comparative advantage in services. It is already commonplace for systems and software engineers in

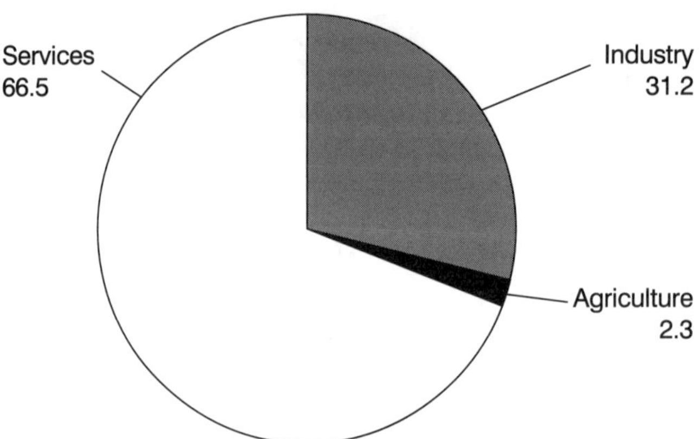

Figure 10.1 GDP in OECD countries, by sector, per cent, 1994. *Source:* OECD

developing countries to write computer programs for corporate customers in developed economies to process airline tickets or insurance claims. Any activity that can be conducted through a screen and a telephone can now be carried out anywhere in the world and linked to other offices or corporate centres anywhere in the world. This should both drive down prices to customers and create employment.

A prolonged process of concentration and cross-border restructuring has been occurring for the last 20 years in most service industries. Merger and acquisition have been commonplace. In services it is often the customer who internationalizes first, with the service company following to meet the needs of important clients. In the advertising industry worldwide, firms such as Omnicom, WPP or Interpublic needed to build international networks of agencies to service MNC clients, particularly those requiring the delivery of global campaigns. Similarly, between the late 1980s and the late 1990s, the 'Big 8' accounting and consulting firms became the 'Big 5', raising worries about lack of client choice for MNC accountancy services. Other professional services such as law are now following the same path of international merger and consolidation.

Service growth has partly come as a consequence of organizational trends towards delayering and outsourcing and downsizing. Specialist service suppliers are replacing service provision previously carried out in-house. Firms like EDS, the US technology and facilities management company, have grown rapidly, nationally and internationally, as external suppliers of information technology (IT) design and management for client companies. Large service firms can standardize and replicate facilities, methodologies and procedures across locations. Specialization and standardization are leading to high quality provision at lower cost to the client company or customer, whether in such different service businesses as car repair (e.g. exhaust, brake and tyre centres) or management consultancy. Building international brands for services has become an important guarantee of quality and consistency around the world.

Managing 'intangibles' across borders

Service industries have some important characteristics which distinguish them from manufacturing industries. Amongst the most widely recognized are those of 'intangibility' of the service offering and the simultaneous production and consumption of the service as a shared experience between the customer and the supplier of the service (Sasser *et al.*, 1978). Successful international service delivery is about being responsible for this quality of customer experience, often known as 'the moment of truth' (Carlzon, 1987; Lovelock and Yip, 1996; Normann, 1984) or 'the service encounter' (Bowen, Chase and Cummings, 1990).

For service industries, control of the offering at the transaction point with the customer or client is critical. When the service network is extended globally, the management of outcomes for the customer faces quality control problems in reproducing accurately the service concept in different cultural, political and economic environments and ensuring consistency of quality in the daily operational detail of face-to-face service delivery. In an influential article, Carman and Langeard (1980) argued that international expansion is the most risky growth strategy for service firms, since the quality control problems are exacerbated when firms attempt to operate across national boundaries. Most large service firms have met these requirements for consistency through standardization of their offering (Campbell and Verbeke, 1994). All the international hotel chains (Hilton, Sheraton, Inter-continental) undertake to make the traveller's experience of Tokyo, Cape Town, Manila or Sydney, as similar as possible. However, issues like staff training are critical in international service firms, since it is these front-line staff that are responsible for the quality of the customer's experience.

Erramilli (1990) distinguishes between 'hard' and 'soft' services. Many modern service businesses contain a shifting mixture of 'hard' and 'soft' elements. The 'hard' elements are increasingly amenable to management by means identical to a manufacturing business. The 'soft' (i.e. the service encounter) elements retain the distinctive needs of service management and service delivery. Thus, the role of management in services is particularly demanding, especially for complex services with a high intangibility content. What Heskett (1986) called 'the service triangle' (see Figure 10.2) describes the iterative relationship between the service organization, its employees and its customers. Often the strongest relationship in a service business is between the employee and the customer. It is balance in the triangle that

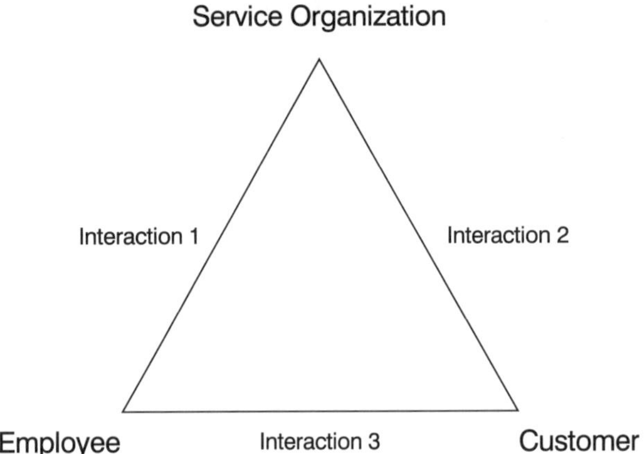

Figure 10.2 The service triangle. *Source:* Adapted from Heskett (1986)

enables the company to carry out the effective management of 'intangibles' across borders.

The management task for service MNCs is to develop a mix of hard and soft resources, and the internal competencies to combine these into consistency of cross-border 'service encounters'. In terms of the hotel industry (for example, see Novotel hotels, Chapter 9, Box 9.5) 'hardware' such as beds or televisions are relatively more straightforward to co-ordinate and deliver across borders than 'software', such as the style and atmosphere of a hotel or how staff conduct themselves in their dealings with guests (and each other). The firm infrastructure and procurement management policy and processes which support the selection and supply of beds or televisions to hotels around the world involve many levels of task and resource. However, the shared values and tacit understandings underpinning the delivery of service encounter 'software' is far more problematic in terms of management processes.

Consider how these issues have been addressed in a rather different international service business: contract cleaning (see Box 10.1).

Box 10.1 Cleaning as Knowledge Management – ISS of Denmark

In an industry characterized by perceptions of low status, low-skilled workers and high staff turnover, ISS invests heavily and continuously

cont.

in training its staff and attempting to retain their loyalty. Although a commonplace in most other industries, it may appear unusual to emphasize knowledge, skills and staff expertise in relation to office cleaners. Yet this is a service business and customer satisfaction depends ultimately on how front line staff (in this case, cleaners) carry out their jobs. Commercial cleaning requires high levels of efficiency in timeliness, use of cleaning supplies, avoiding accidents and dealing with idiosyncratic customers. In many hospitals and factories, conditions are often complex and hazardous.

In the commercial cleaning business there are now several international service providers such as Rentokil (UK), ServiceMaster (USA) and ISS (Denmark). These large service MNCs outbid local providers since they benefit from scale and investment in back-office systems to enable them to co-ordinate efficiently their purchasing, marketing and logistics to win national and international contracts with hospitals, offices, factories and government departments. However, to retain these contracts, service delivery by staff is what counts.

ISS itself operates throughout Europe and Asia, although it had to sell its USA business in 1997 because of an accounting scandal. It has a universal emphasis on training and an impressive staff retention record. ISS Denmark, for example, operates a six-month training programme for all employees covering things like safety and which chemicals to use on which stains. After a year with ISS employees may become team leaders. For this they need better overall knowledge of the business. So they are given prior training on the economics and finance of the business, so that they can understand where the profit in each contract is to come from and how to interpret each client contract. Team leaders have tight performance targets, measured on both profitability and customer retention. So they also receive training on how to deal with customers and how to coach less experienced members of their team.

ISS attempts to provide its employees with technical skills but also to motivate them as front-line staff and to keep the benefit of their expensive training inside the company. To do this the company has had to think creatively about how it organizes the work. ISS Denmark has grouped its cleaners into two or three-person 'hit squads' for its small office division. They work together travelling from site to site. This is in many ways less efficient and more costly than sending separate individuals to separate sites, but ISS believes that this system generates both higher motivation and makes possible more contact between ISS's supervisors and the client's site managers. To increase such customer

●●▶

cont.

contact, when crucial customer feedback may be obtained, ISS is rescheduling many of its accounts to provide overlap time between cleaning staff and office staff. As part of its focus on motivation, ISS also pays above the competitor average. So far it feels that it has not lost business as a result of its higher costs. Well-trained employees and good back-office systems have enabled it to bid for, and win, complex contracts, such as the hotel cleaning contract at Disneyland, Paris. Partly, ISS is helped by timing, since this industry has just emerged from a period of rapid concentration internationally, so that ISS faces only two or three major competitors in its market. Nevertheless profitability and productivity are major concerns, especially ISS's higher training and wage costs. It recently sold its ISS University which had co-ordinated training across regions. Instead, training is being decentralized in an attempt to tailor knowledge to local conditions.

Source: Adapted by authors from press articles and *The Economist* 25/4/98. ■

Let us compare Novotel (Chapter 9, Box 9.5) with ISS in how they each attempted to manage their service intangibles. Novotel first attempted to manage their cross-border 'service encounter' issues by what Levitt (1986) called the 'industrialization of service', in other words imposing rigid control processes (the 95 Bolts) on staff in order to ensure predictability of outcomes. After rethinking the business in 1992, they saw their competitive advantage as residing in their concept of 'hospitality', a classic 'intangible'. They returned to their entrepreneurial roots and replaced the hierarchical structure with an enabling culture of front-line discretion, supported by high levels of training. Whereas ISS could have defined itself as a business-to-business service and designed the timing of much of its operations to avoid any 'service encounter' contact, instead the company went out of its way to build it in. They wanted to utilize the service encounter both to motivate staff and to provide direct contact and feedback opportunities with customers/end users (even though these 'customers' did not themselves pay directly for the service). Each company also invested greatly in training both as a way of enhancing skill levels of staff but also as a way of ensuring a coherent and consistent worldwide knowledge base in the firm.

Scale and scope in services

Much of the historic pattern of competition in services occurred within domestic market boundaries as a result of the small-scale, fragmented structure of service industries, and their culture-specific patterns of demand and consumption. Under these conditions clearly scale and volume effects were limited. However, as has already been argued, in most service sectors restructuring has led to industry concentration replacing industry fragmentation. In addition, some homogenization of demand in services (as already discussed in Chapter 3) is also observable.

The important difference between 'back-office' and 'front-office' activities in services is extremely significant for the internationalization of services. 'Front-office' describes those activities which come into contact with the customer; 'back-office' are the operational activities which can be decoupled from the customer. The significance of this distinction in international strategy terms for service MNCs is that the larger the proportion of 'back-office' value chain activities in the service that can be decoupled from the location of the customer, the greater the potential for optimizing OLI advantages (Dunning, 1989), reconfiguring the organization's value chain (as discussed in relation to the configuration/co-ordination matrix in Chapter 6, Figure 6.1), and securing scale and scope advantages in the same way as manufacturing MNCs. If most activities of a service organization cannot be decoupled from the customer in this way, then strategic flexibility remains low and the costs and service delivery problems for an international strategy remain high.

The separation of back-office and front-office activities, combined with the standardization of many back-office processing functions, has created the opportunity for breaking out of the requirement for simultaneous consumption and production of a service. These developments, which are largely due to technological advances in IT, have had a huge impact on potential sources of economies of scale and scope in services. They allow for the reconfiguration of service value chains which can be desaggregated (just as for manufacturers) and parts of the activity may be located geographically for optimum scale, scope or cost advantage. For example, a company like VISA International has a geographically dispersed value chain whereby all its worldwide back-office data transactions (e.g. card clearances) are handled by just two global transaction centres in Japan and the USA. These types of international configurations for services are technology-dependent, rather than 'service encounter' dependent.

Under changed technical and structural conditions it becomes necessary to reconsider the definition of what constitutes a service and also to consider how firms actually design and deliver their services.

Figure 10.3 provides a simple illustration of some of these service design and reconfiguration possibilities. It reflects some of the differences in resources and service delivery between 'hard' and 'soft' services. It also reflects some of the rethinking of services that has occurred. For example, the location of retail banking in the top-left box, reflects the capital-intensive, volume-driven, transaction-processing part of retail banking operations.

	Resource emphasis	
	Back-office	Front-office
Standardization	Retail banking	Contract cleaning
Customization	Software	Professional service firms (PSF)

Figure 10.3 Standardization or customization of services. *Source:* Adapted from Segal-Horn (1993)

These activities are usually now centralized and regionalized. At the same time, the retail banks have been redesigning branch outlets to be more customer-friendly, in order to cross-sell other higher-margin financial services. Software houses may sometimes appear in the top-left box also if they are selling standardized rather than bespoke software packages.

However, the examples in Figure 10.3 are inevitably oversimplified (e.g. it ignores the search by PSF's for methodologies to increase productivity and margins via back-office standardization, an approach for which Andersen Consulting is well known). It is inevitable that continuous shifts such as those between standardization and customization, should result in firms continually seeking optimization of such features at the highest level of scale and cost position available to them. It is also to be expected that these positions of optimum efficiencies will be continually shifting.

We can now usefully return to the Ghoshal (1987) framework introduced in Chapter 6 (Table 6.1). Service firms seek to benefit from the same sources of potential advantage as manufacturing firms in their international expansion. The issue is whether such benefits from international expansion are as attainable for service firms as for manufacturing firms. Ghoshal (1987) summarized three potential objectives of international expansion to benefit from:

- *National differences* (e.g. to obtain beneficial factor costs, or offset country-specific government policies).
- *Scale economies* (e.g. to spread cost-reduction and experience effects across national boundaries, to expand or exploit scale in purchasing, distribution, capital costs, etc.).
- *Scope economies* (e.g. shared investments, knowledge and learning across products and markets).

A combination of structural, market, regulatory and technological changes has provided a shift in the balance of activities within service firms. Greater technological capability has led to the redesign of many services to enhance the back-office proportion of activities in the service value chain. This has lowered considerably the levels of perceived risk, and enhanced the potential benefits, attached to international expansion of service firms. In seeking a model to capture these developments in international services and also to look at their relative potential in different service industries, we have adapted Chandler's model (1977, 1986, 1990a,b) of manufacturing industry growth to explain the growth of service MNCs. We explore and develop this framework to show the potential of economies of scale and economies of scope within a variety of service industries. Scale and scope variables are particularly useful because they drive costs for a service firm; and one of the big issues in successful international expansion is that it must involve some efficiency advantages to justify the costs of integration of cross-border operations, compared to provision of the service by a domestic firm. These factors appear to be having some impact on the creation of international oligopolies in services.

The application of Chandler's model to services

Chandler's work (1977, 1986, 1990a, b) addresses the circumstances under which a firm will continue to grow to maintain a position of dominance. The economic basis of Chandler's model is 'the cost advantages that scale and scope provide in technologically advanced, capital-intensive industries' (1990a, p.132). It was a model of the managerial enterprise built on manufacturing industry data (e.g. oil, pharmaceuticals, agricultural machinery, steel). Chandler (1986) showed that in sectors where few large firms appeared, it was because neither technological nor organizational innovation substantially increased minimum efficient scale. Therefore, in those industries, large plants did not offer significant cost advantages over smaller ones and 'opportunities for cost-reduction through more efficient co-ordination of high-volume throughput by managerial teams remained limited' (1986, p.417). Hierarchies (Chandler's 'visible hand' (1977)) emerged and spread 'only in those industries or sectors whose technology and markets permitted administrative co-ordination to be more profitable than market co-ordination' (p.11).

The structure of service industries lay outside Chandler's study. Historically, despite considerable variance across sectors, service industries had been neither so technologically advanced nor so capital-intensive as manufacturing. They had exhibited minimum efficient scale at low levels, with significant diseconomies of scale reached at modest levels of growth. The special characteristics of service businesses had dominated thinking about the design and delivery of services. Received wisdom has been that services are 'different'. Thus the growth paths of service firms have indicated a different 'logic' to manufacturing firms. For Chandler's model of growth now to be applicable to service industries, would indicate similarity between manufacturing and service firms and that the special characteristics of services have diminished in significance.

More capital-intensive asset structures and high fixed costs in services, largely IT-related, have been influential in creating extra-national economies of scale which have encouraged the high levels of merger and acquisition activity in many service sectors already mentioned (e.g. hotel chains, accountants and management consultancy firms, airlines, software, information services, telecommunications, financial services, etc.). Service industries are no longer fragmented, but increasingly concentrated. In many sectors they resemble oligopolies (as in international contract cleaning), although a 'tail' of small local firms co-exist as local providers in most markets. We will now assess the significance of greater potential for economies of scale and economies of scope on the growth strategies of service firms. Some of the sources of scale economies and scope economies now commonplace in service MNCs are listed in Table 10.1

Any asset which yields scale economies can also be the basis for scope economies if it provides input into two or more processes, i.e. when the cost of producing two outputs jointly is less than the cost of producing each output separately (Teece, 1980, 1982). An obvious example of the interaction

Table 10.1 Some sources of economies of scale and scope in services

Economies of scale	Economies of scope
Geographic networks	IT/IS and shared information networks
Physical buildings or equipment	Shared knowledge and know-how effects
Purchasing/supply	Product or process innovation
Marketing	Shared R&D
Logistics and distribution	Shared channels for multiple offerings
Technology/IT/IS	Shared investments and costs
Operational support	Reproduction formula for service system
	Range of services and service development
	Branding
	Training
	Goodwill and corporate identity
	Culture
	Priviliged access to parent services

Source: Adapted from Segal-Horn (1993)

between scale and scope is the central role now played by computer reservation systems (CRS) in the activities of airlines, hotel chains, car rental firms, cinemas, etc. These not only support the geographic spread of the business and the rapid processing of volumes of transactions, but also provide customer databases for cross-marketing of services and the capability to design and deliver completely new services.

IT-based scale and scope benefits in different service businesses take many different forms. American Express can use its information systems to set and monitor service standards for fast response times for card enquiries, or to provide additional services such as 'free' travel arrangement or theatre bookings for cardholders. Benetton has become renowned for replacing inventory with information in the management of supplies to its worldwide outlets and in using real-time information from point-of-sale systems to tailor seasonal production to demand. Most large airlines have developed sophisticated software to maximize yield from higher-revenue seats on all flights, a major contribution to profitability in a service business with high fixed costs. Advertising MNCs such as Interpublic or WPP derive economies of scale from bulk purchasing of media time and space, as well as the internal transfer of market and design data in the management of global campaigns for clients.

Knowledge is a powerful scope economy in services (Nayyar, 1990; Vandermerwe, 1993) since many services are based on the capability to acquire, process and analyze information. Additionally, it has a shelf life, during which time it may be repeatedly used at little or no cost (e.g. an advertisement, a software programme). Many services comprise a firm-specific pool of both explicit and tacit knowledge (Grant, 1991; Nonaka and Takeuchi, 1995). Service firms (e.g. management consultancies and other PSFs, fast food chains, hotel chains) are increasingly attempting to codify this knowledge as the basis of standardization of their products, to achieve cost-reduction and increased productivity, as well as reliability of international service standards. Some of the strongest brands in services are based on perceived accumulated know-how, e.g. McKinsey, Reuters, McDonald's. Information-intensive resources are absorbing heavier investment in fixed costs which in itself exerts pressure to lower unit costs by spreading output over larger markets (for scale economies) and a wider variety of products (for scope economies).

Individual and organizational knowledge represent a generalizable capability or core competence (Prahalad and Hamel, 1990). This implies that where diversification is based on scope economies it makes sense for service firms to manage their international expansion by means of internalization (i.e. the internal control and co-ordination of assets and activities) rather than by market transactions. Internalization (part of OLI, discussed in Chapter 2: Dunning, 1985) means that firms retain control of their internal capabilities (rather than, say, outsourcing) which should give greater control over their use. Internalization is especially important in the growth of service firms in regard not just to efficiency, but to the management of the 'moments of truth' in which the quality of service firms is experienced by their customers.

The changed international potential of services

Chandler explains the growth of firms to a position of dominance in their sector, through the early pursuit of cost advantages derived from volume. Scale and scope are fundamentally volume and cost-driven. Chandler shows that companies which create and sustain dominant positions in their industries do so by making pre-emptive investments in scale and scope which enable the firm to strongly influence the evolving structure of the industry, and the bases of competition within the industry.

As denoted in Figure 10.4, phase 1 of the 'logic' of MNC growth (Chandler, 1986, 1990a,b) consists of four sets of core investments: in volume, to achieve cost advantages of scale; in scope, to achieve consistent capacity utilization; in

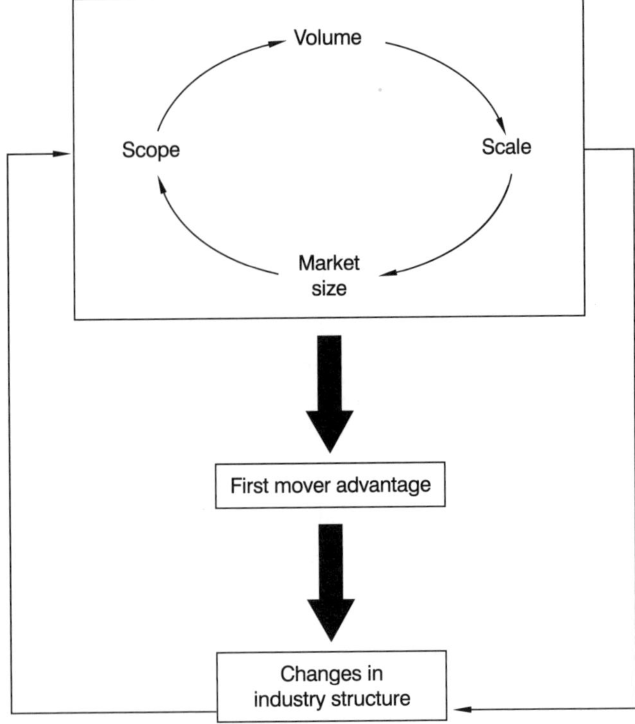

Figure 10.4 The dynamic of MNC growth, Phase 1. *Source:* Adapted from Chandler (1986, 1990a,b)

national, and then international, marketing and distribution networks; and in a management hierarchy to co-ordinate and allocate current and future resource utilization. Firms which moved first to make these co-ordinated sets of large investments could dominate their industries and influence its path of development, both in the short term and longer term. This is because challengers would have to match the first-mover advantages in comparable costs, build distribution and reputation to a point where the dominant incumbent could be effectively challenged, recruit teams of experienced managers and match specialized experience curve effects. (See Box 10.2).

Box 10.2 American Express: the Dynamic of MNC growth – Phase 1

The financial services company American Express is an organization in which scale and scope operate in a massive way. Over time it has successively made the investments in marketing, distribution, volume, product and process outlined in Figure 10.4. In so doing it created a world-scale service industry, which it dominated for more than a century after its first international expansion moves.

The development of American Express involved a series of 'phase 1'-style investments. The company was founded in New York, USA, in 1850 by Wells and Fargo, progressing rapidly from the express carriage of cash and parcels, to bonded carrier of freight and finance. It handled European imports to all US Customs interior ports-of-clearance. Investment in its distribution network proceeded beyond national US coverage to the beginnings of its European network in freight forwarding. From an initial office in Liverpool, UK, in 1881, to 300 European agency offices in 1890. Beyond scale expansion of the network, these also provided considerable expansion in scope, through the increased range of services offered, utilizing additional capacity in the same network of outlets. The company was already benefiting from a virtuous cycle of scale, volume and scope effects which enabled it to advertise in brochures in Europe at this time that American Express could:

> pay money on Telegraphic Order, at a moment's notice, between points thousands of miles apart and sell small Drafts or Money Orders which … can be cashed at 15,000 places.
>
> (Amex Company documents)

It began extending its management hierarchy in Europe by beginning its own directly owned chain of offices in Europe in 1895. The freight

••▶

cont.

express business encompassed many developing financial service activities e.g. paying foreign money order remittances from emigrants, or commercial credit transactions begun in Rotterdam in 1907. There were major new product development initiatives:

- Amex Express Money Order (1882)
- Amex Travellers Cheque (1891)
- Amex Charge Card (1958)

These provide illustrations of Chandler's proposition that incumbent first-mover advantages determine the future structure of an industry. Sale of travellers cheques unleashed demand to provide additional services to tourists, such as itineraries and tickets. A European, and eventually worldwide, travel network was established, uniquely combined with the Amex portfolio of financial products and services to create a new set of asset structures for a specialized segment of the financial services industry. By the 1960s 38 000 outlets worldwide sold American Express 'travel-related financial services' (TRS), which is still the source of 70 per cent of the American Express Company's revenues in the 1990s.

Source: Compiled by authors from Amex company documents. ■

The potential for scale and scope economies in different types of service businesses

Moving from a specific illustration of one service company, some more general observations may be made concerning scale and scope in services.

The grid in Figure 10.5 gives a customary historical representation of the spread of availability of scale and scope economies in different types of service industries. The top right corner of the grid is illustrated by financial services companies such as American Express; by the major international airlines; by travel firms such as Club Med; by information or news services such as Reuters or CNN. The top left corner is illustrated by food retailers where high-scale effects have arisen from electronic-point-of-sale equipment (EPOS) and concentration of retailer buying power, combined with limited scope opportunities, although some large food multiples also trade in clothing, homewares and financial services such as in-house credit cards. Bottom right of the grid is illustrated by management consultancies or other professional service firms (PSFs) such as accountants, surveyors, civil engineers, headhunters. PSFs may be high on potential scope economies from, e.g. shared client and project databases or shared teams of expertise across national or

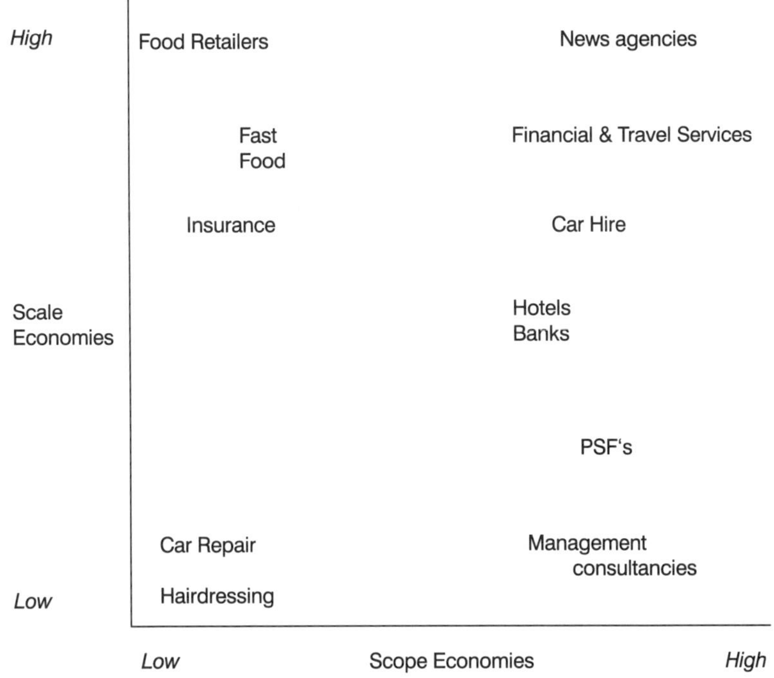

Figure 10.5 A historical view of scale and scope economies in various service industries. *Source:* Adapted from Segal-Horn (1993)

regional offices, but with low potential economies of scale, since these services are frequently customized, often within different national regulatory frameworks. Bottom left are typically small-scale service businesses, highly location-specific.

Although Figure 10.5 represents the historical view of these varying types of service industries, what is interesting from our point of view is the drift towards top right on the grid for many firms in these different sectors. The creation via mergers of very large international accounting and consultancy firms, which is mirrored in other PSF sectors, is part of the search for greater efficiencies in capacity utilization of scarce resources (expensive professional staff) and for productivity gains from implementation of standardized methodologies. Equally, food (e.g. Aldi) and non-food (e.g. IKEA, Toys'R'Us) retailers have begun to operate beyond domestic boundaries seeking scale benefit from volume purchasing and scope benefits from investments in information technology, logistics networks and branding. Retailers are also moving heavily into related services such as financial services and banking, now sold by many supermarkets and providing huge economies of scope in use of customer databases and intensive use of expensive sites. Insurance companies in Europe (e.g. Allianz of Germany, Generali of Italy, Prudential of the UK) are building cross-border operations, as regulatory differences become less extreme and varieties of distribution channels develop (Katrishen and Scordis, 1998). Finally, many erstwhile small service businesses are moving upward on the grid, for volume benefits in purchasing and operations arising from specialization and standardization (e.g. Kwik-Fit Euro specializing in repair of car exhausts or brakes only and international hairdressing chains such as Toni and Guy with centralized training and purchasing). What this shows is the ever-greater potential and intensity of the use of scale and scope advantage in international service operations.

Clearly also, none of these shifts would be possible without at least some perceived shift on the demand side in consumer buying behaviour. Economies of scope in services can lower transaction costs for customers. Common examples include the effect of retailer buying power on quality and price in multiple retail chains, worldwide reservation systems of hotel chains and airlines, cheaper products in banking and insurance, and in all brokerage services such as travel agents or investment analysts. Indeed, Nayyar (1990) discusses the potential benefit to diversified service firms from leveraging customer relationships across service businesses (cross-selling). He argues that buyers of services will attempt to economize on information acquisition costs, and their own time and risk, by transferring reputation effects to other services offered by a firm. This contributes to our understanding of the growing importance of the branding of services and reinforces, for services, two of the main propositions regarding the competitive advantages of MNCs. First, the ability of MNCs to create and sustain a successful brand image and its concomitant goodwill; second, the MNC's ability to monitor quality and reduce buyer transaction costs by offering services from multiple locations (Caves, 1982).

The dynamic of MNC growth – phase 2, shifts from national to international growth and competition. Fundamental shifts having occurred in the character of service businesses, international chains now exist in virtually all types of service businesses, even highly 'local', regulated and culture-specific services such as education or medical services, (e.g. AMI health care group, EF language schools, international campuses trading on well-known university brand names, even the funeral industry). Underlying these trends is what Levitt (1986) called 'the industrialization of service'.

Services can be industrialized in a variety of ways. First, by automation, substituting machines for labour, e.g. automatic car-wash, automatic toll collection, ATM cash machines, etc. Second, by systems planning, substituting organization or methodologies for labour, e.g. self-service shops, fast food restaurants, packaged holidays, unit trust investment schemes, mass-market insurance packages. Third, by a combination of the two (e.g. extending scope in food retailing via centralized warehousing and transportation/distribution networks for chilled, fresh or frozen foods in technically advanced temperature – and humidity-controlled trucks). Such industrialization of service is based on large-scale substitution of capital for labour in services, together with a redefinition of the technology-intensiveness and sophistication of service businesses. It also assumes a market size sufficient to sustain the push for volume and associated increased costs. This is the point at which a firm is likely to shift to international operations since the domestic market provides insufficient volume to support minimum efficient scale. This may come earlier for service firms than for manufacturing firms since for many types of services the option of exporting is not available.

Building on these changes in the concentration and industrialization of services, phase 2 of our model of dynamic MNC growth, relating to growth via the international expansion of scale and scope, may now be discussed.

Figure 10.6 shows how investments in scale, scope, distribution and management, allow large firms to build dominant positions, sufficient to influence the basis of competition in that industry in terms of structure, key resources and capabilities relevant to competing in their industry. Advantages of scale and scope lead to national and international concentration, so that competition rapidly becomes oligopolistic. Such oligopolistic competition is

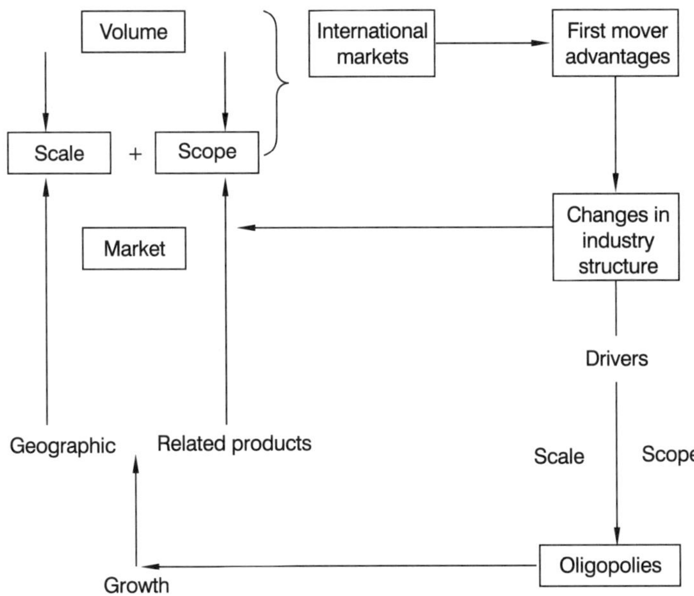

Figure 10.6 The dynamic of MNC growth, Phase 2. *Source:* Adapted from Chandler (1986, 1990a,b)

based more on innovation than price, although firmly rooted in continuously enhanced cost structures. Growth thus becomes a continuous search for improved quality, sourcing, distribution and marketing (especially branding and advertising), as well as new markets and lower costs. Some growth comes from acquisition, but the main emphasis for long-term growth is two-fold: first, geographic expansion into international markets in the continuous drive for increments in scale and cost advantages; second, related product markets in the pursuit of enhanced scope economies. Together these form a dynamic spiral of volume, scale, scope and cost curves, reinforced by organizational capabilities developed to cope with fierce oligopolistic competition. Chandler (1990a,b) emphasizes repeatedly that the opportunity to create such first-mover investments is short-lived. The logic of sustainable international competition is to make long-term scale investments to create organizational capabilities, and then to continue to reinvest in them. We will continue with our example of American Express to illustrate phase 2 of this process of international expansion (see Box 10.3).

Box 10.3 American Express – Phase 2

Many of the innovations made by American Express in new products, new markets, branding, advertising and distribution, have already been referred to above. Amex followed closely the twin routes for long-term growth, geographic expansion into international markets and the development of related product markets in the pursuit of enhanced scope economies. Amex had the earliest branded products in financial services and advertised these branded products heavily from the 1880s onwards. It invested heavily and continuously in distribution and marketing and in the extension of its network of outlets for its products and services worldwide. There was some growth via acquisition, as in the purchase of Fireman's Fund in 1968 to consolidate its move from a travel company across into financial services. Its related product markets now cover the express business, the travel business, financial services, movement of goods, movement of people, and the flow of money. These related businesses provide scale and volume, supported by company-wide global communications, data and information systems networks, which in turn support volume, worldwide geographic coverage and the monitoring of service quality in all outlets. Following Chandler, Amex attempts not to compete on price but on product innovation, market development and levels of service. Whether its scale, scope and cost advantages are still sufficient to fight off the cur-

••▶

rent new efficient competitors in its main markets (e.g. VISA, and many other 'free' gold card offerings) remains to be seen. It is facing very tough competition and increasing pressure on price and margins from both trade and retail customers.

Source: Compiled by authors from Amex company documents. ■

Rethinking services

The model we have been exploring (adapted from Chandler) is of international growth and competition based on firm-specific assets and resources. It is interesting to note that such resource-based theories of the firm have dominated competitive strategy in the 1990s (Amit and Schoemaker, 1993; Grant, 1991; Rumelt, 1991), balancing the industry structure-driven emphasis of strategic thinking of the 1980s. Since such assets may erode over time and must be continually upgraded to sustain their advantage (as we discussed in Chapter 4), it is important to review the implications of this approach to the changing nature of competition in services.

Enderwick (1989) provides insight into firm-specific advantages (FSA) and location-specific advantages (LSA) available to the service MNC. He builds on the work of Dunning (1985, 1989), and the eclectic paradigm of international production based on ownership, location and internalization (OLI) advantages introduced in Chapter 2. (Enderwick uses the term LSAs, where Dunning uses CSAs for the same factor). Ownership incorporates competitive advantages; location incorporates configuration advantages; and internalization incorporates co-ordination advantages. (You will recognize the similarity to the configuration/co-ordination matrix (Figure 6.1, Chapter 6) in international strategy terms, since both are concerned with the organization of value chain activities by the MNC.

Enderwick includes under FSA, factors familiar from the earlier scale and scope debate in services: privileged access to assets such as goodwill and brand name, particularly important in consumer buying processes for services; scale economies obtainable from high fixed costs and low variable costs of operation; other economies of common governance available from single hierarchical management of complementary assets; and scope economies which enable incumbent firms to offer innovatory or complementary services which reinforce their competitive position. Under LSA factors, most significant is the differential between services which are location-specific because production and consumption are inseparable and therefore where physical presence is mandatory (e.g. fast food chains), compared to those services which are tradable and therefore choice of international location would result from considerations of comparative advantage (e.g. software houses). Lastly, the internalization issue is of exceptional importance for service MNCs , since they will wish to retain internal control over anything affecting their management of the 'service encounter'.

The continual search for optimization of OLI advantages in services, using the same models and criteria as for manufacturing firms, makes simple distinctions between product and service obsolete.

The future for international services

Many services (e.g. credit cards, automated teller machines, airline seats, software, automatic carwash) have emerged relatively recently in human society. Therefore, in international terms, they have the advantage of no prior patterns of usage or acculturation, thereby making them more easily acceptable across national boundaries. However, alongside social, cultural and technological changes affecting demand for services, there are additional economic and political pressures on governments to create, or remove, regulatory barriers as the WTO has been attempting. Current difficulties affecting international trade in services still include issues such as intellectual copyright protection.

Restructuring and concentration in most service sectors in recent years has meant that many service industries (such as travel, fast food, some financial services, information services) now meet Kobrin's (1991, p.18) definition of a global industry, defined in terms of 'the significance of the competitive advantages of international operations' arising mainly from the structural characteristics of scale economies and technological intensity. Strong international segments exist for many types of services; we have already discussed many of these local adaptations around a global standard core such as Benetton's leisurewear, Pizza Hut's food or Sheraton's hotel rooms. Therefore both demand for, and efficient supply of, global services exists (Lovelock and Yip, 1996).

However, service industry growth has often been across traditional industry boundaries (e.g. retail/financial services; retail/leisure; leisure/travel; travel/hospitality; accounting/management consultancy; advertising/public relations, etc). This leads to the notion of increasingly 'fuzzy' industry boundaries in services, with industries not viewed discretely but as fuzzy sets. The example of American Express used above is of service firm growth within a fuzzy industry set of leisure/travel/financial services. It also demonstrates how it is precisely because Amex operates across this fuzzy set that it is able to sustain such strong branding across its portfolio of related services. This may suggest that 'growth' for service firms may not involve a deepening of asset structure as in manufacturing companies, but a horizontal accretion of assets across different markets and different industries – i.e. scope.

Nevertheless, the concepts of economies of scale and economies of scope explored in this chapter and the dynamic MNC model of growth used here, is a resource-based explanation of successful international competition, driven by sustained investment in the development of firm-specific resources. Therefore, while the issue of change in service industry structure is central to any discussion of the growth of international competition in services, it may be that the most important factors determining successful international expansion in services should be understood at the level of the firm, as in the Novotel, Benetton and ISS examples already given. This is particularly important with regard to the managerial and organizational capabilities of the firm. The point has been made with regard to MNC activity in general (Dunning, 1989), and service MNC activity in particular (Enderwick, 1989), that the way in which firms organize their international activities may itself be a crucial competitive advantage. This is strongly reinforced in recent work by Rumelt (1991), concluding that the most important sources of long-term business rents 'are not associated with industry, but with the unique endowments, positions and strategies of individual businesses' (p.168). These points may go some way towards explaining both the successes and the failures in international expansion undertaken by individual service firms.

Summary

The special characteristics of services have been diluted in significance. Many services contain 'hard' tangible components which are capital-intensive, amenable to separation from the point of service delivery, and responsive to standardization. In addition, core knowledge and information-based assets of service firms are codifiable and transferable across national boundaries, as is the consumer franchise from strongly branded international services. These issues can be simply summarized in Box 10.4.

Box 10.4 Service Characteristics – Historic and Current

Then: services were time dependent and could not be inventoried.

Now: because of technology, information is the one part of a solution which can be stored, retrieved and transported.

Then: services always had to have local presence with service providers physically on the scene.

Now: many services can come from far away via remote linkups.

cont.

Then: services were culturally bound and were difficult to transplant from one country to another.

Now: technology has created many new types of services which have no prior cultural associations.

Then: services were considered to be a domestic business.

Now: many services are global, customers neither know nor care where they originate.

Then: most services were accessible only at certain times in clearly defined places.

Now: it's possible to deliver a growing proportion of services anyplace and anytime.

Source: Adapted from Vandermerwe (1993) p.208. ■

As a result of this combination of factors, service industry dynamics are beginning to parallel those of manufacturing. Manufacturing businesses and service businesses appear to be following similar development paths, creating similar types of organization structures, and competing in similar ways. Even the most distinctive characteristic of services, the criticality of the interface with the customer, is increasingly a hygiene factor for all types of businesses. The emphasis is on customer service in manufacturing, and on efficient deployment of back-office assets in services. Each is trying to capture the advantages the other has traditionally utilized. This once again illustrates the 'dynamics' of strategy-making.

11

Co-operation in international strategy

In recent years the growing globalization and regionalization of markets, with the steady reduction of trade barriers, has led to the dramatic growth of cross-border co-operation between companies, particularly from the mid-1980s to the present time. This has been accompanied by considerable economic turbulence and uncertainty in world markets, and the spread of a high degree of trade liberalization in most countries of the world. That is in complete contrast to the period of economic history immediately preceding this, when many of the world's economies were still centrally planned, especially those remaining within the socialist and communist blocs. The removal of the Berlin Wall in 1989 was probably the historical event which most obviously symbolized the shift from one economic period to the other.

According to Chandler (1986) the process of economic and industrial change in the West since the end of World War Two can be characterized by a number of phases. First there was the immediate post-war phase of inherited rigidities from the inter-war period, and the protection of ravaged economies. Then from the 1950s onward came the dramatic growth of the major multinationals, and of the multi-divisional M-form of organization. However, this led in due course to significant administrative and bureaucratic diseconomies. These had to be weighed against the opportunities available for clear scale and scope economies obtainable within large-scale operations which, if achieved, led to a continuing cycle of reducing unit costs from increasing volume of operations.

The third phase came in the late 1970s and the 1980s when the system 'began to unravel to a degree' (Jorde and Teece, 1989). This period saw the growth of the entrepreneurial firm funded by venture capital, with substantial outsourcing of non-key processes. Thus, previously internalized value chain activities were returned to the external marketplace through outsourcing. Of course, if poorly managed or enacted on inappropriate criteria, this led in many cases to the disadvantage of fragmentation, and the limitations of inadequate resources, particularly in the face of the concurrent movement towards the increasing globalization of markets.

Some compensation for this came from a simultaneous gradual movement towards relational contracting, the first of a number of types of more co-operative, rather than competitive, approaches to strategy. This was an attempt to gain some of the perceived advantages of the Japanese keiretsu system, in which a brand name company would subcontract many activities to tried and tested subcontractors, who in exchange for the reliability of regular orders would submit to quality inspections, and the requirement to hold stock to be called for 'just in time' use.

A different response to these same forces was the dramatic growth of strategic alliances and other forms of co-operative strategy between companies, particularly in technology and marketing. For Porter and Fuller (1986) the basic motivation for an alliance is that:

> Coalitions arise when performing a value chain activity with a partner is superior to any other way.... Coalitions can be a valuable tool in many aspects of global strategy, and the ability to exploit them will be an important source of international advantage.

These latter forms are sometimes characterized as N-form organizations, i.e. based on the development of active networks as discussed in Chapter 9. A more complete theoretical basis for the development of co-operative strategy is needed, however, that accepts the possibility that co-operation may take a number of different organizational forms. Each of these forms may be equally potentially viable as an integrated company. Notwithstanding, all co-operative forms are in some ways less superficially attractive than either markets (governed by the price mechanism) or organizational hierarchies (governed by clear internal organizational requirements), because they lack the quality of simplicity of these other two approaches. In his discussion of corporate governance structures, Williamson (1975) distinguishes between 'markets', where activities are externally bought and sold, and 'hierarchies', the term he uses for the business corporation which integrates its activities internally. It is clearly not necessarily true to claim that activities must all be carried out either in organizational hierarchies or in markets. As Richardson (1972) pointed out long ago, most business activities have some elements of both market and stable organizational hierarchy in them. The factors leading to an organizational form's viability must be not the position on the continuum between markets and hierarchies, but the nature and volatility of the internal and external environmental influences, and the behaviour of those managing the organization.

Types of co-operative strategy

Much of business activity is co-operative. As Figure 11.1 shows, the most elementary form of co-operation is that of distributor and supplier networks.

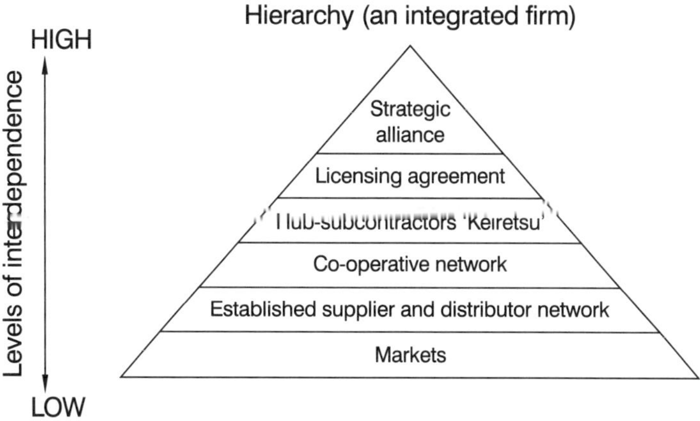

Figure 11.1 Levels of co-operation. *Source:* Authors

This grows in terms of interdependency until a strategic alliance is reached. A strategic alliance is where two or more firms pool part of their activities in order to strengthen their market offering whilst still retaining their separate corporate identities. The firms involved then become relatively dependent upon each other, at least in that sphere of their activities. The only form more interdependent than that is the integrated hierarchy as Williamson (1975) calls it, i.e. in our terms, the MNC.

Different forms of co-operation have different purposes. There are, however, two basic purposes behind co-operating with other companies, that of *organizational learning* and that of *skill substitution*. As is shown in Figure 11.2 skill substitution co-operation comes about when one company realizes that another can carry out a particular activity better and cheaper than it can. Traditional distributor and supplier agreements belong to this category of co-operation, but so does the more modern virtual corporation or the Japanese keiretsu. The currently fashionable outsourcing movement is built on the skill substitution rationale. Little risk attaches to skill substitution co-operation, since if one co-operator withdraws, it can be replaced by another. There need be little exchange of proprietary information between the companies of the kind that would make the erstwhile allies subsequently vulnerable.

The learning co-operations are quite different. They come about because the allies wish to learn from each other, and improve their skills and competencies in areas strategically important to them. Joint ventures, collaborations without a separate venture company and consortia are the most common forms of learning alliances. Such relationships are more strategic than the skill substitution type, as they do involve the exchange of proprietary information between the partners. Thus if they fail, both partners have to balance

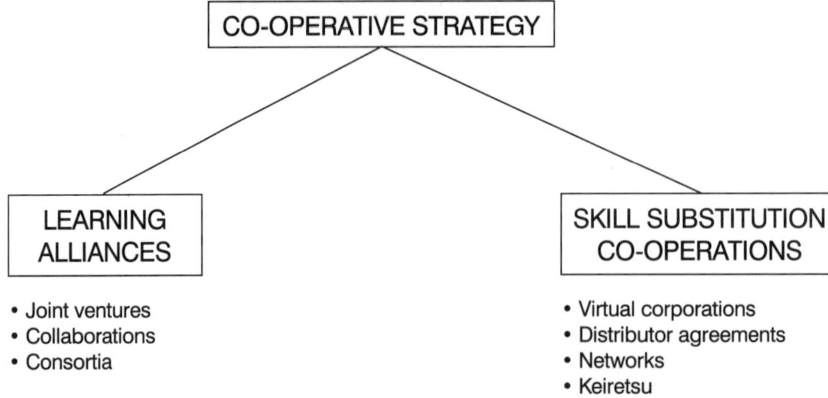

Figure 11.2 Co-operative strategies fall into two distinct types. *Source:* Adapted from Faulkner (1995a)

their learning against their information loss in assessing the cost/benefit of the alliance. It is these forms of co-operation that are the genuine strategic alliances that are currently so popular.

Such alliances may be advantageous to a company, but they are also risky. They may be advantageous if the partner is carefully chosen to have complementary assets capable of realizing synergies with your own organization. However, they may also be risky because all business activity is potentially and simultaneously both competitive and co-operative. Therefore the outcome from an alliance depends upon the relative strength of each of these characteristics. As can be seen from Figure 11.3, if the co-operative element in the relationship is strong and the competitive element relatively weak, an ongoing alliance can

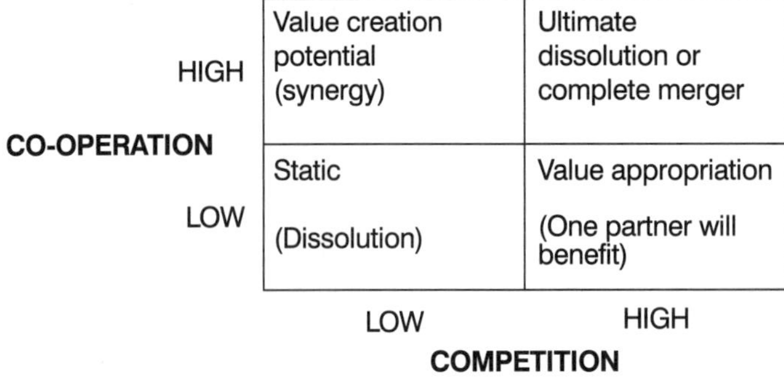

Figure 11.3 Alliances involve both co-operation and competition. *Source:* Adapted from Faulkner (1995a)

be maintained in a stable way. As in a sports contest between friends, the rules attending the competition do not damage the co-operative relationship. The strategic alliance between two automobile companies Rover (UK) and Honda (Japan) fell into this box. They co-operated closely in teaching each other respectively about European styling and operational quality control, and although they sold cars competitively under different marques, they were careful to limit their competition as far as possible to different markets.

Where both competition and co-operation are weak, it means of course that you have ill-assorted partners. There is little synergy in an alliance that falls in this box, and it will soon fall to the bottom of the agenda in board meetings for both partners.

The box representing strong competition and weak co-operation is a dangerous one to find oneself in. This is where two companies come together to gain each other's secrets but with little intention of honouring the co-operative side of the bargain. Hamel, Doz and Prahalad (1989) in an article interestingly entitled 'Collaborate with your competitors and win', suggested explicitly that the primary aim of alliances is to gain your competitors' secrets and skills before they can gain yours. An alliance falling into this box of the matrix is likely to dissolve in recrimination with one partner appropriating the key skills of the other. Although these types of problem alliances do frequently still occur, understanding of the potential of co-operative strategic behaviour has moved on from this rather acrimonious short-term view.

The fourth box is equally dangerous, but need not have such a negative outcome. An inevitable powerful tension will develop when both partners have a great need to co-operate but an equally great need to compete. Such a relationship is inherently unstable and is unlikely to endure over the longer term. Once the respective skills have been acquired the outcome is likely to be an end to the relationship, or a complete merger between the companies. The strongly competitive element in the relationship is likely to inhibit the development and preservation of trust and transparency of behaviour.

Clearly an alliance may move from one box to another during its life. The best that initial negotiations can do therefore, is probably to ensure that at least they start in an acceptable box, ideally top left, but if top right then the new partners should do it knowingly.

Why an alliance?

Of course there are other ways than alliances of dealing with the problem of not having the necessary competencies and resources to succeed in today's markets. One can 'make' your own, i.e. develop further competencies internally; 'acquire', i.e. outsource the area in which one is not excellent, or engage in a merger and acquisition process, high risk though it may be. Figure 11.4

Strategic importance of activity	Low	Medium	High
High	alliance	invest & make	make
Medium	alliance	alliance	make
Low	acquire	acquire	acquire

Company competence in activity

Figure 11.4 The make/acquire/ally matrix. *Source:* Adapted from Bowman and Faulkner (1997)

shows a matrix with company competence on one axis, and strategic importance of the activity on the other. It can give useful pointers to the best way to tackle this problem.

The matrix in Figure 11.4 suggests that where an activity is of low strategic significance the company should buy it, even though it could make it excellently itself. This idea lies behind the trend towards outsourcing. Since all companies have limited resources, they are not best used carrying out activities of little strategic significance. Thus, most companies outsource catering, security, maintenance and other such activities. At the other end of the scale, if an activity is of medium or high strategic significance and the company is the best in the industry, then the company must make it itself. If the activity is of high strategic significance and the company is only a moderate performer it needs to invest to improve its performance. This leaves an 'L' shape for alliances. Activities that are moderately or highly significant, and in which the company is a poor or moderate performer are candidates for an alliance, probably a learning alliance.

Of course both prospective allies need to have different activities in the alliance squares to be appropriate partners. Thus, in the Rover/Honda alliance, Rover's manufacturing quality expertise was in the top left-hand box of Figure 11.4 (i.e. high strategic importance/low competence), as was Honda's knowledge of European styling. Each had both a competence gap, as well as a high level competence, in the areas of importance to the other. The alliance enabled both companies through organizational learning to cause these competencies to migrate to their respective top right-hand boxes.

Particular motivations behind the formation of specific strategic alliances, or other co-operative strategies, are many and varied. Most may well fall within the basic motivation for joint ventures succinctly defined by Aiken and

Hage (1968): 'Organizations go into joint ventures because of the need for resources, notably, money, skill and manpower.'

However, the relationships that develop are generally far wider and deeper than this economic perspective would suggest, and involve significant sociological factors as well. Co-operative relationships become embedded in a structure of routines, involving such social factors as trust and commitment. These come to have at least as much importance for success as the normal 'rational' economic motives.

Thus, although the formation of alliances is presented as a unitary decision based on appropriate and sufficient information, mostly they are also made as a result of subjective viewpoints. Usually, a coalition of views develops in both partners, pointing to the possible advantages of such an alliance. This process always precedes the actual benefits and costs, which cannot be known until the alliance has been in operation some considerable time. They are therefore as much political as economic decisions, depending heavily on the internal corporate political power of their champions, and placed at risk if those champions should lose power in their home organizations (Tallman and Shenkar, 1994).

Although decisions to set up alliances may be strongly conditioned by political issues and the relative organizational strengths and positions of a number of stakeholders, economic arguments will almost certainly be advanced to justify those decisions, and these arguments are likely to be based on either the *transaction cost* body of theory (cf. Williamson, 1975), or the *resource dependency* perspective (Pfeffer and Salancik, 1978). Such an argument will urge that the alliance is the most likely solution to a competitive environmental challenge facing either or both organizations. The alliance will be proposed as the optimal solution on the grounds of its showing the best probable benefit relative to cost, since the joint value chains of the proposed partners give a higher probability of competitive advantage than either partner value chain on its own.

At a more specific level, the economic arguments for alliances are that they are formed generally as a result of an external stimulus or change in environmental conditions. Companies respond to this external change by recognizing and identifying the resource and competence gaps that they feel are best filled by seeking a relationship with another corporation. What might be called an eclectic theory of alliance motivation suggests that all alliances are sparked off by a change in external trading conditions, and that this change reveals an internal resource inadequacy that needs to be corrected if competitive advantage is to be maintained. An alliance will result from such an analysis if both the company, and its proposed partner, find themselves to have complementary resources and perceived inadequacies. The theory is termed eclectic since there exists a long list of both external and internal conditions; any one is sufficient to provide the underlying motivations for an alliance. For example, the external driver for one company might be the need to achieve scale economies to be able to compete on the world market, while the internal need might be to fill up underutilized factory capacity. For the other company the external driver might be shortened product lifecycles, and the internal driver an insufficiently innovative design team, or inadequate investment funds. Whatever the external and internal drivers, one of both is necessary for each potential partner to provide a strong enough motivation for a strategic alliance. Co-operation between the companies however might be motivated unilaterally by either.

DeFillippi and Reed (1991) distinguish here between unilateral arrangements and bilateral agreements (strategic alliances). Unilateral arrangements come about when one company perceives a resource deficiency need that can be satisfied by another company, but the feeling is not reciprocated by the other company. Thus, Rover might have needed Honda's technology skills, but Honda might need nothing from Rover. In this case Honda might license the technology, and provide technical consultancy for a royalty and a consultancy day rate. This is a unilateral arrangement. A resource is transferred in exchange for money. Such arrangements are regularly provided in outsourcing agreements, consultancy studies and externally provided training courses. These are still co-operative strategies but not strategic alliances. However, in fact Rover required Honda's technology, and Honda required Rover's European styling skills. This provided the conditions for a bi-lateral agreement, i.e. a strategic alliance.

There exist a whole variety of co-operative strategies ranging in levels of integration from single source subcontracting, through loose network associations, to keiretsu type configurations ultimately to strategic alliances. The different forms vary in their level of interdependence between the partners (as indicated in Figure 11.1): they also differ in the degree to which the partners have learning as a fundamental objective of the co-operation. In relational subcontracting functional substitution is the aim, rather than learning. At the other end of the spectrum a close strategic alliance typically has mutual learning and competence development as its primary objective. This chapter will deal mainly with such strategic alliances rather than the less integrated forms of co-operative strategy, since it is the strategic alliance in particular of all co-operative forms that is categorically different from other forms of doing business. The strategic alliance is uniquely based on the development of consensus arrived at between equals, and not on a set of orders given by a contractor to an order recipient.

External stimuli

Some of the key external driving forces for alliance formation are currently:

- turbulence in world markets;
- the existence of economies of scale and/or economies of scope as competitive cost-reduction agents;

- the globalization or regionalization of a growing number of industries;
- the globalization of technology;
- fast technological change leading to ever-increasing investment requirements;
- shortening product lifecycles;
- high economic uncertainty.

Of course the above conditions do not all have to be present to provide the external stimulus for alliance formation at any one time. Most, however, can readily be observed in the current economic and political world. Any single strong external factor impelling firms towards alliance formation is sufficient to set the alliance train in motion, without any one specific factor being necessary in itself.

The conjunction of certain conditions in the structure and nature of the external environment makes alliances more likely at some periods of economic and political history than at others. Periods of trade protectionism, and when anti-trust, anti-monopolist philosophies are strong, militate against alliance formation, and co-operative activity between companies tends to be denigrated as anti-competitive or as cartels. Correspondingly, during periods when the power of large MNCs is perceived as being excessive but world trade is nevertheless buoyant, the less threatening nature of the strategic alliance comes into favour, set up to combat the threat of the MNC and frequently giving a competitive chance to smaller more flexible companies.

The most common explanation of the rapid growth of alliances in recent years takes the following form. Technology change has become increasingly rapid, and global in nature; as a result of this the difference between markets in different parts of the world has become smaller (Levitt, 1983; Ohmae, 1985). Globalization of markets has given major opportunities for companies to realize economies of scale and scope. These factors have lowered unit costs for the firms large enough to take advantage of them. However, a side effect of technological change and globalization has been shortening product lifecycles, leading to ever increasing investment demands, both to install the new technology and to develop new products. Competitive advantage has therefore gone to the company able to adopt the new technologies, achieve economies of scale and scope, serve global markets, and change its product range regularly. Since few companies have the resources and competencies to meet these stringent requirements, there has been a widespread resort to strategic alliances to meet the needs of the new economic order.

So we would summarize the most common external forces behind international strategic alliance formation as: the globalization of markets and technologies; the shortening of product lifecycles; the consequent need for enterprises large enough to take advantage of scale and scope economies, and the need for enterprises large enough to afford access to adequate resources and competencies. Other factors do, however, exist in specific situations, and are less generalizable in nature. These, like the internal motivations, relate in the main to perceived resource or competency imbalances in the face of the external challenges. There is also no necessary association between the external factors impelling a firm to seek an alliance, and the business effectiveness of that alliance. Its effectiveness would depend upon whether the co-operative enterprise has any sources of competitive advantage in its market.

Types of internal stimuli

An external motivation is not sufficient by itself to drive a company into formation of an alliance. The external driver must resonate with an internal feeling of either vulnerability or challenge. Such internal stimuli are also eclectic, in that there are many of them and no one particular factor is necessary.

Companies are motivated to form alliances for a wide variety of specific reasons, but many come under the general heading of perceived resource deficiency. Alliances may be of the defensive variety, e.g. the partners collaborate in order to defend their domains in the face of an external threat from a common enemy. Or they may be aggressive, e.g. the globalization of their market affords opportunities for companies able jointly to operate on a global scale. In both cases the motivation for the alliance is resource based. Alone, the potential of each partner's value chains, financial and other resources, core competencies and skills, and networks of contacts are perceived to be inadequate to achieve the identified objectives, but together the potential synergies from co-operation are perceived as leading to competitive advantage jointly, which would not be available to them separately. So a key internal motivation for alliance formation is to gain skills or resources needed in response to an external challenge or opportunity of some sort.

Anand and Delios (1997) refer to the fact that technology is perhaps the most powerful foreign entry driver for MNCs intent on foreign direct investment (FDI), because it is fungible across borders and is therefore the most common firm-specific advantage (FSA). However, lack of local knowledge is the most common country specific *dis*advantage. Such lack of local knowledge inhibits FDI greenfield investment. It therefore encourages either alliances with a local partner, or a local acquisition, to remedy this resource deficiency. If local knowledge and local content are a significant part of an MNC subsidiary's operations, then a strategic alliance with a local partner will be relatively more attractive to the MNC than FDI.

One aspect of such alliance motivation normally stems from a feeling of internal organizational needs. Such needs will vary in nature, but all are usually able to be classified as specific resource, skills or competency inadequacy or imbalance. Such an imbalance may be exhibited in surplus production capacity or in skill deficiency. A key motivation for alliance formation then, is to gain skills or resources needed in response to external challenges or threats.

Each of the partners is likely to seek a different resource or skill compensation from the other. Unless both are able to match their resource or competency needs in a particular partner, then they do not have the right partner. Their options are then to seek a different partner, or alternatively to buy in the skill from the proposed partner, but without providing a complementary skill in return. In this case the deal will be a unilateral exchange and not an alliance.

Changing technology is an important factor in triggering resource needs. The reputation of the partner may be an internal motivation for an alliance, especially if this gives access to new and strong brand names. Local knowledge, marketing skills and distribution channels are other common resource needs which research has shown may act as motivating factors towards seeking alliances. Other possible attractive resource needs include: key labour skills of one type or another; seeking to learn from the partner's perceived managerial skills; and gaining access to markets. In general, for an alliance to be formed, it is clear that a mutual Resource Dependency Perspective (Pfeffer and Salancik, 1978) of some sort is a key internal motivator, and that both partners are likely to have different but complementary resource needs that they perceive their chosen partner can help them to meet. The specific nature of the resource dependencies will of course depend on the specific circumstances of the case.

There are more ways of dealing with a resource deficiency than just following the strategic alliance route: alternative actions might involve raising further capital in the market, recruiting key personnel in areas of perceived expertise weakness, a merger, or an acquisition, or the development of contractual arrangements to license technology in, or distribution out. Resource deficiency then, is one important condition for alliance formation, but not a sufficient one, since there are alternative ways of dealing with that deficiency.

The need to limit risk is a further factor in favour of alliance formation, as opposed to the alternatives of merger/acquisition or organic development. The spreading of financial risk is frequently quoted in the literature as a fundamental motivation for the formation of strategic alliances (Mariti and Smiley, 1983; Porter and Fuller, 1986). It also seems intuitively reasonable that a company with only moderate financial resources may deal with either an opportunity or a defensive challenge by seeking an alliance with a partner who can help spread the financial risk.

Even if the company has sufficient funds to approach an opportunity by means of organic (internal) development and eradicate a resource deficiency, for example by recruitment, 'greenfield' business unit development, or training, such organic development may not occur fast enough to take successful advantage of the opportunity. Alliances are formed when partners need to strengthen market presence faster than could be done by other means. Internal development would take much longer. Acquisition, the other fast alternative route to filling a resource deficiency, has the disadvantage of having to deal with the possible demotivating effect of the relationship with the acquired company, and the higher level of prior investment required.

In the decision to pursue the formation of an alliance to meet a need, the question of the cost is a further factor that companies should consider, when deciding whether or not to pursue the alliance route. This economic efficiency criterion is central to transaction cost theory. Thus, it is held that companies will only form alliances, rather than adopt other strategic options, if the transaction costs involved in so doing are perceived to be lower than those for the other options. Transaction costs, of course, are in many aspects highly judgemental entities, since they involve such basically unquantifiable 'costs', like the costs of loss of proprietary expertise to a partner who subsequently becomes a competitor. Although these costs may well be important, they cannot be computed as easily as can the costs of production, and it is questionable whether they are considered in detail before deciding to set up an alliance. Despite such provisos, the overall question of costs is undoubtedly a major consideration in most decisions to form alliances.

Risk is also a major factor cited as an internal driver for alliance formation. Thus, the risk of attempting to carry out a project with a partner is perceived in many ways as less than doing it alone. The route of internal development takes longer and involves a much higher initial investment. The alternative route of acquisition involves the high risk of buying a company, which may turn out to be less attractive after purchase than it did before. Of course the alliance route involves working with new partners which involves risk, but the cost of unravelling a failed alliance is generally seen as less than disposing of an unwise acquisition or writing off a failed internally conducted project.

Partner selection

Having been stimulated both internally and externally to seek an alliance, the next major question facing a firm is to identify an appropriate partner. What happens in the real world is that companies seek partners with whom they perceive good strategic fit in that they have a complementary set of assets and competencies, and they can recognize clear opportunities for realizing operational synergies. They also often conduct an analysis to assure themselves that both they and their prospective partner bring something to the party that will be valued, i.e. learning opportunities exist between the two partners as well as strengthening of their joint value chain in the face of those of rivals.

However, what is generally ignored, and is frequently the cause of alliance breakdown, is the question of corporate cultures, and, in the case of international strategic alliances, national cultures also. Cultures are made up of many social and behavioural constructs as discussed at length in Chapter 5. These subtle factors are often difficult to analyze but as Johnson (1990) has shown, are critical to the successful management of changing relationships and implementing strategies. This applies strongly to the management of partnerships between organizations in an alliance. If the organizational cultures of the respective alliance partners conflict, and considerable flexibility is not shown in moving towards a workable integration, then an alliance with strong *strategic* fit can founder for lack of *cultural* fit or at the very least, cultural sensitivity.

Figure 11.5 illustrates at a general level the potential problem facing prospective alliance partners. Clearly if there is no strategic fit then the alliance makes no sense anyway, even if the companies get on well in terms of similarities of cultures.

If the companies have high strategic and high cultural fit then this should augur well for an alliance. However, even companies with low cultural fit can have successful alliances if they are aware of that fact and take positive steps to improve their cultural compatibility. Western and Asian partners almost inevitably face this problem, but so also do seemingly less contrasting Western/Western cultures such as Italian/Swedish or USA/UK. Since there is a proliferation of partnerships between Japanese or Chinese partners and Western MNCs, often as a result of regulatory requirements stipulating a 'local' partner for FDI purposes to access these markets, these issues must be understood and positively addressed. That is by no means insuperable given insight and cultural sensitivity on both sides. Some of the ways of improving such cross-cultural awareness have been discussed in Chapter 5.

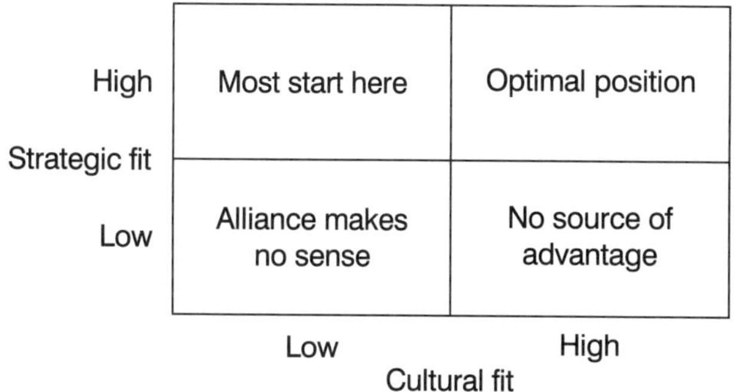

Figure 11.5 Partner selection. *Source:* Adapted from Faulkner (1995a)

Choice of alliance form

Different circumstances prescribe different alliance forms although not all companies entering alliances seem to realize this. There are many ways of categorizing alliances. Two will be noted here which, in the authors' views, are the most helpful. Garrette and Dussauge (1995) talk of 'scale' and 'link' alliances. 'Scale' alliances are those in which two sub-critical mass companies combine to achieve economies of scale that enables them to compete with their larger rivals in unit cost terms. These alliances may well be inherently unstable, since they are by definition between erstwhile competitors, and the ever present possibility of defection is likely to be in the minds of both partners at all times, even if they are currently working well together. 'Link' alliances are between partners at different points in the value chain. Thus, a firm may ally with its major supplier or distributor. Such alliances reduce uncertainty from transactions and should be stable, since the partners are not competitors. Of course the categories are not mutually exclusive. The Rover/Honda alliance contains elements of both types. It is 'scale' in that both Rover and Honda vehicles are manufactured in the same plant. It is 'link' in that Honda provides the engines for some Rover cars. However, the distinction can be very useful in analyzing alliances.

The other taxonomy is that between joint ventures, collaborations and consortia. Joint ventures are new companies formed by the partners. They are generally run like any other company with a board of directors and a management hierarchy. The partners sit on the board, appoint the chief executive, provide resources of a variety of types and may second staff to work in the joint venture. Joint ventures are the most common type of alliance and are most appropriately created when the domain of the venture is distinct from the core business of the partners, either in product/market terms or geographically. Where separate resources can be allocated to the venture, management can be set targets and assessed and the partners can set boundaries to their level of financial commitment.

Box 11.1 The Royal Bank of Scotland/Banco Santander Alliance

The 'collaboration' alliance between Royal Bank of Scotland and Banco Santander of Spain set up in 1988, is a partial union of two medium-sized national banks in the face of the expected Europeanization, and hence regionalization, of the banking industry across Europe. The partners own a small minority of each other's

••▶

cont.

shares. The alliance operates on many fronts, including joint ventures in Germany and Gibraltar, and a consortium for money transfer covering a number of European countries. This consortium, named IBOS, is to date the most successful part of the alliance, and was not foreseen as a significant project at the outset of the alliance, demonstrating the importance of allowing evolutionary forces to develop in successful alliances. The alliance partners have learnt that, through the extension of IBOS they can achieve all they wish to achieve on the European scene without the added expenditure and risk of acquisition.

The basic external motivation for the alliance was prospective regionalization of the European financial services industry. The internal motivation was a combination of lack of size, limited geographical reach by both banks individually, and the perceived need for speed and to economize on costs. The partners selected each other because of their perceived similar profile – large banks in small territories but small banks in Europe – and because they felt their cultures would blend well together.

Over the six years of the alliance's life there has been considerable evolution of the relationship. Most of the activity areas set out at the beginning are now well under way. The IBOS system is developing in a far greater fashion than had been envisaged. Staff are being exchanged on secondment to the other partner. The appropriate alliance attitudes of commitment, trust and bonding are well developed between the personnel directly involved in the alliance, and organizational learning is evident on both sides.

The alliance is a very successful venture from the co-operation viewpoint, representing a considerable increase in the Royal Bank's and Santander's European standing, and as a byproduct has considerably strengthened RBS's ability to serve its customers in Central and South America. However, customers flow only one way at present. The propensity of UK investors to go into Spain is not matched by those of Spanish investors to invest in the UK, so Santander tends to gain from increased sales more than RBS.

Only the future will tell whether the mature development of the EU Single Market in financial services will leave the alliance partners strong enough to compete with the major European 'supermarket' banks, or whether adequate niches will develop to avoid the need for head-on competition. Furthermore, both banks are domestic banks in essence, and to put two domestic banks together does not create an

●● ▶

cont.

international bank, as this requires different types of teams, possibly a wider range of services, and perhaps a different culture. The alliance always envisaged the partners staying as individual banks rather than creating a unified bank. So it must remain an open question over the next few years at least, whether even a successful alliance could possibly still fall between the two stools of being not sufficiently specialist for a niche bank, or sufficiently large for a major Eurobank.

Source: Authors. ■

Rover/Honda is the second type of alliance, namely a collaboration in which a new company was not formed. Executives from both partners merely worked together on designated projects. There was no 'Rover/Honda plc' partly because this would have involved a direct conflict of interest with the partners' existing businesses, but also because, since the scope of the alliance covered most of the major functions of both partners, other than sales and marketing, resources and management could not easily be allocated to the alliance in a measurable fashion. Such alliances are necessarily more flexible than joint ventures need to be. They can also accommodate varying levels of commitment from the partners without showing strain. It is not possible to attach a profit and loss account to a collaboration in the way in which it is to a joint venture. Collaborations are then selected as the best alliance form when the partners are primarily intent on learning from each other; when they are uncertain of the appropriate boundaries to the relationship; and when the scope of the alliance involves the core activities of the partners.

The third principal form of alliance is the consortium. This is normally created in situations where large size and resources are vital to credibility. Thus Europe's Airbus Industrie needed a consortium form to be able to compete credibly with its American competitors Boeing/McDonnell Douglas in the international commercial aircraft market. Expensive R&D activities are often tackled by consortia since this limits the risk of the participating companies. Consortia normally have a joint venture legal structure in order to provide clear boundaries but this need not be the case. In fact Airbus Industrie only began the politically difficult process of reconstituting itself legally as a one corporate entity after more than 10 years of operation without such a legal framework.

Summary

Stimuli for creating partnerships may be both external and internal. The increasing globalization of international business in large numbers of sectors, coupled with competitive pressures, create a need for partners to ameliorate resource shortfalls, to gain time, and to improve competitive position. Higher needs for 'systemic' solutions involving several types of competencies, and product/service offerings bundled into packages to suit customer requirements, creates a need to bring together distinctive competencies from several partners. Rapid technological developments leading to shorter product life-cycles and calling for considerable responsiveness create a need to have joint R&D, a sufficient technical resource base, and to put together scarce competencies so as to leverage the outputs for broad commercial application. These reasons may be summarized as:

- faster penetration and exploitation of key markets and other opportunities in which there is a substantial probability that organic (internal) growth will be too slow;
- where alliances are broadly structured, such partnerships create options to develop in major new strategic directions which otherwise might not be possible for one partner alone;
- the potential payoffs to collaboration are felt to offset the costs and risks of collaboration;
- immediate access to markets, to resources, to funds, to skills and technologies, to rights;
- cost-reduction through increased economies of scale;
- synergies via blending of complementary strengths or assets;
- safety by spreading financial risk, sharing novelty risks, reducing political risk, reducing market volatility, rationalizing standards, influencing new industry developments;
- as a way of building defences.

So runs the economic argument for the establishment of alliances. However, such explanations need to be supplemented by the identification of motivations that stem from intra-corporate political agendas. The economic arguments may be necessary but they are by no means sufficient. Ultimately neither transactions costs, the extent of risk, nor future economic benefits can be known at the time the decision is taken to set up an alliance. There must therefore also be a political motive for the alliance, and a commitment to the alliance, perceived by a coalition of the company's key decision-makers. Since political agendas within a corporation are many and varied, there is usually also a need for a corporate champion or champions, to steer the company's key decision-makers towards thinking in terms of an alliance. In the absence of such alliance champions, the motives for the formation of strategic alliances may be insufficient to lead to their creation.

12

The management of international strategic alliances

Despite the increasing popularity of international co-operative enterprises, the record of managing these arrangements is somewhat mixed. Porter (1987) found that no more than half the alliances he identified were successful by any reasonable criteria. The management consultants Coopers & Lybrand, and McKinsey in separate studies came to similar conclusions. As Niederkofler (1991) explained:

> ... a major cause for co-operative failure is managerial behaviour. In nature, co-operation differs fundamentally from competition. Whereas competitive processes are well understood and practiced daily, the key success factors in co-operative processes are widely ignored.

This highlights the fact that the success of an alliance lies more in its management than in the circumstances of its initial creation. Harrigan (1986) emphatically stated: 'Alliances fail because operating managers do not make them work, not because contracts are poorly written'. The reason for this is not hard to find. Most managers, especially those raised within the traditions of the Western world, have been trained to operate within an organizational hierarchy. Such hierarchies are typically captured by organization charts, sets of job descriptions and various reporting relationships within a formal power structure. Managers know the scope of their responsibilities, the level of their decision-making authority, whom they must obey and whom they can command. Even though modern management styles require that such commands be couched in courteous and motivational language, e.g. 'I wonder if it would be possible for' rather than 'Do this today!', employees understand who their bosses are, and what they can be required to do. Also they are used to operating in a competitive environment where competitor firms are viewed as rivals. Relationships with these competitors and also often with suppliers and distributors, are frequently somewhat adversarial.

Co-operative enterprises display virtually none of these characteristics. To get action, each firm needs to develop consensus with their alliance partner. Relationships with colleagues in the partner company are typically those between equals, rather than superior to subordinate, and often reliable operational routines do not yet exist by which managers can get operational matters carried out efficiently. Systems that apply in one partner company may well clash with practice in the other. Ways of getting things done usually need to be devised as projects develop. Furthermore, the underlying adversarial assumption on which competition is based, with its clear depiction of rival firms as 'the enemy', no longer exists. The erstwhile 'enemy' may now well be a partner in some activities, although still remaining a competitor in others. Suppliers and distributors are often renamed 'complementors', to reflect the actual degree of their joint involvement in the success of the firm, rather than identified as contractors with whom tough negotiations must to be conducted. Co-operative enterprises therefore need to be managed quite differently from integrated companies, and normally in ways for which managers have not been adequately prepared.

Managers from partner companies come from different company cultures, and have difficulty in understanding or approving of their new allies' ways of operating. The Prisoners' Dilemma game (see discussion in Kay, 1993) also suggests that in the short term the strategy of defection is a dominant one, i.e. stealing secrets or customers from your partners and then absconding. Thus, newly wedded partners are all too aware of the tension existing between them in terms of whether to trust each other, or make off with each other's proprietary information.

Axelrod (1984) discovered that in a somewhat stylized computer game between co-operators and competitors, the best long-term strategy for games with an unspecified number of 'rounds' is to co-operate in the first round, and then apply a tit-for-tat approach in subsequent rounds, i.e. mirroring the action taken by the other player each time. Thus, a player would behave with absolute integrity in the first round, and if the other player (partner) reciprocated with similar behaviour, then the alliance would prosper. If, however, the partner defected, then the initial actor would punish him, but subsequently revert to a co-operative form of behaviour if the punished partner did so too. This strategy was recommended since it was perceived as fair, forgiving but ultimately tough.

Although this strategy worked best in the computer simulations carried out by Axelrod, it is questionable whether it would work so well in real life. In a living alliance the new partners may be too nervous to apply tit-for-tat effectively, and one 'defection' action would probably destroy the alliance. The best management approach to improve possibilities of success in an alliance may be to:

- act sequentially so you know what your partner has done before you act, and can avoid misunderstandings;

- make commitments that are irreversible to create confidence;
- in terms of management systems:
  - create regular reports on soft as well as hard aspects;
  - have regular meetings;
  - carry out a regular but not too frequent total review of the alliance with the aim of adjusting any arrangements that need to be adjusted;
  - emphasize the need for regular formal and informal dissemination of information between the partners;
  - recognize the probability of changed strategic imperatives and consequently the need to be flexible.

This chapter discusses some of the key factors involved in the successful management of international strategic alliances when compared with unitary companies. Specifically, it argues that long-term success, whilst obviously reliant to some extent upon the economic benefits the partners receive from the alliance, is also particularly strongly dependent upon the attitudes of the partners towards each other, how they manage their joint enterprise, and the degree to which they adopt a positive learning philosophy, thus enabling the alliance to evolve.

The nature of general management

A general manager has a number of roles (Kotter, 1979). He/she has responsibility for an organizational unit that extends across several specialist functions, such as finance, sales and production. Over the long term the general manager must: establish goals; set the direction for the unit; decide which businesses to focus on and possibly divest others; develop product/market strategies; and ensure the unit has adequate resources to carry out its mission. The task in the medium term is to determine the appropriate allocation of resources; and in the short term to ensure that human, financial and material resources are used efficiently. In unitary companies the nature, scope and tools for carrying out these responsibilities are generally clear-cut. In alliances this is less the case, although the mission should still be the same.

Ring (1996) identified three formal processes and three informal processes necessary for the successful management of an alliance. The formal processes are negotiational, transactional and administrative; and the informal processes sensemaking, understanding and committing.

Negotiational processes are particularly important during the formation stage of an alliance, but they are also required whenever any change becomes necessary to the evolving arrangement, or when an increase in resources is needed from the partners. In alliances, negotiating skills may also come into play in decision-making arenas which, in unitary companies, would probably be unilateral executive decisions. *Transactional* processes, in Ring's terms, involve the partners in making commitments to action and in settling the terms on which the alliance will operate. *Administrative* processes are concerned with managing the partners' commitments in an efficient and effective manner, and therefore involves the setting up of jointly agreed routines and systems.

For these formal processes to bed down effectively in an alliance, requires a further level of informal process development by individuals and groups. The manager needs to be able to *make sense* of the arrangement from his viewpoint. This involves successfully aligning his preferences and motivations with those of his alliance partners and accepting some necessary limitations on individual action. *Understanding* is a process whereby the partners reach a shared view of the context, scope and nature of the enterprise in which they are involved. If such an understanding fails to come about, inevitable conflict will ensue. *Committing* is a psychological process in which individuals come to accept unwritten expectations, assumptions and obligations about each other's rights and duties in relation to the alliance.

Ring discovered that the time it took for these processes to develop in an alliance depended strongly on how 'embedded' the partners already were in a shared social context, and also more particularly how well they know each other already. Thus, USA/Japanese alliances might well be successful, but they would generally take longer to mature than USA/USA or Japanese/Japanese ones. This also emphasizes that alliance managers should be selected, if at all possible, from those who had already taken part in the early stages of the alliance formation, since they would have trodden some way along the path of sensemaking and understanding. The early processes of negotiation themselves, if successful, would have made some contribution towards incremental adjustments and growing commitment.

General managers of alliances need to wear several different hats for many different roles, often simultaneously. Particularly important roles and skills in alliances include: decision-maker, in order to implement strategy, allocate resources and clarify for subordinates what they are expected and empowered to do; internal integrator, appropriately managing relationships with superiors, subordinates and peers; motivator and supervisor of subordinates; manager of agendas in the interests of superiors in both or several partner organizations; identification of areas of mutual interest to peers/colleagues for positive action, even without formal authority over those involved.

Another important role for the general manager in an alliance is that of external integrator between the organization and its immediate business environment. The requirement here is to be a networker overseeing the boundaries of the organization, developing new opportunities and preserving the importance of the alliance.

Finally there is the role of information manager. How information is obtained and selected, what is disseminated and to whom, play an important part in establishing the style and effectiveness of the alliance organization. At the extremes, companies exist where information is freely disseminated with few secrets retained by top management, and others in which the 'need to know' principle rules and individual managers regard the possession of particular bits of information as a key part of their personal power base. In alliances, what information to share with your partner is always a key issue.

In joint venture alliances, additional requirements arise for general managers, since they are responsible to two or more partners or bosses, and they will often have to create conditions for effective co-operation between staff from each different organization with their different cultures and different agendas.

All these role requirements are summarized in Table 12.1 which illustrates some of the key differences between the manager in an integrated company and one in a strategic alliance.

It is evident from Table 12.1 that there are two aspects of alliance general management which add significantly to its difficulty. The first stems from the presence of more then one principal, in the form of the two or more partner companies. If there are just two partners in the alliance, their demands may well be potentially conflicting, unless one clearly dominates. Either way there lies the potential for power struggles. When there are more partners, each with a smaller stake, the pressure that each can exercise over the alliance general manager will be reduced, but the demands they place on the alliance will tend to be more diverse. A high level of political and negotiating skills is therefore mandatory.

In addition to the partners, the general managers of alliances may find themselves having to take account of the expectations of multiple groups, such as governmental agencies and community organizations, in the country where the venture is located. The expectations of these local groups do not necessarily coincide with those of either or all partners, and this sets up further potentially conflicting pressures on an alliance general manager. In an international alliance, these conflicting pressures will typically extend to the partners, the host company government, home company colleagues (some senior to the manager), and local staff and pressure groups with diverse customs.

The second source of difficulty arises from the almost inevitable cultural problems that have to be managed within the alliance. These are a product of the parents' different corporate cultures, and are likely to be greater in the case of international alliances when a mix of national cultures is also present. The more that the alliance partners have different structures, modes of operation, and divergent cultural attitudes, the more challenging is the situation facing the general manager, although some alliance managers claim that dealing with very different cultures, e.g. USA and Japan, is less difficult than dealing with superficially similar ones, e.g. USA and UK.

Table 12.1 General manager roles in strategic alliances

GM of unitary company	GM of strategic alliance
Decision maker	
Innovator	
Initiates change	Tries to develop support from partner
Resource allocator	
Decides on how and where to allocate resources	Role overlaps here with negotiator
Negotiator	
Aims to maximize company's interest	Seeks 'win-win' situation with partner
People problem-solver	
Takes charge in a crisis	Has to act delicately because of multiple constituencies
Internal integrator	
Leader	
Motivates and supervises subordinates	A role to be played with extreme discretion
Teambuilder	
Acts as motivator and co-ordinator	Has to overcome cultural and agenda barriers in pursuing the same objectives
External integrator	
Figurehead	
Personifies the firm on formal occasions	May play a lesser or greater role here
Networker	
Interacts with outside bodies	Difficult role as he may not always be seen to be representing the alliance
Information manager	
Receives key information through the usual channels	Usual channels may not exist. Needs to be a very active role as a result
Disseminator	
Ensures information is conveyed to members of the firm	Decisions as to what information to share are key to success

Source: Adapted from Child and Faulkner (1998)

Shenkar and Zeira (1992) analyze these two problems in terms of role conflict and role ambiguity. Role conflict arises when the priorities of one alliance partner conflict with those of another, which means that the alliance manager faces at the same time conflicting demands from each partner. Cultural differences within the alliance adds to role conflict, because it presents the general manager with conflicting expectations about the values which should inform the alliance and how they should be handled. Role ambiguity arises when the senior management of an alliance is unclear about the expectations which various key groups have of it – the partners, the various employee groups in the alliance, and institutions of the country where the alliance's operations are located. Role ambiguity for alliance general management therefore arises from the lack of clarity about what is expected of it, whereas role conflict arises from differences in the expectations that are placed upon it.

This analysis implies that the general managers of an alliance will experience higher levels of role conflict when there are a few but active alliance partners, who differ markedly in the objectives they have for the alliance and in their defining corporate characteristics such as size and ownership. One would similarly expect that having a larger number of partners, especially if they were culturally diverse, would increase the role ambiguity experienced by alliance general managers. In the main study of the subject conducted so far, Shenkar and Zeira (1992) found among international joint ventures in Israel that having fewer parent companies was associated with greater role conflict, while divergence between the parent companies' national cultures gave rise to role ambiguity.

The factors we have identified as predictors of role conflict and ambiguity are all normal and predictable aspects of the situation in which alliance general managers find themselves working. This leaves open the important possibility that managers with more experience of handling such situations will find the conflict and ambiguity inherent in them to be less of a problem. They may even be able to turn situations of this kind to their advantage by negotiating between the parents to secure greater autonomy for the venture under their charge, and perhaps to encourage competition among the parents in their provision of resources to it. Shenkar and Zeira did indeed find that joint venture general managers with longer tenure in their jobs suffered less from role conflict and ambiguity, while better educated general managers also tended to report less ambiguity in their roles. Those who were permitted, or had negotiated, greater autonomy for themselves, also experienced less ambiguity about their roles.

Nevertheless, these conditions, which create role conflict and ambiguity, are ones which if not handled with subtlety could threaten the breakdown of an alliance. Role conflict often reflects the presence of a competitive undertone to a partnership, and this clearly contributes to the high failure rate of alliances emphasized in Chapter 11. Both role conflict and role ambiguity can generate stress, dissatisfaction and difficulties in decision-making for alliance general managers. Severe role conflict, due to incompatible demands from the partners, could make the role an impossible one to fulfil. Evidence from the company delineated in Box 12.1 describes some of these processes occurring in EVC, the joint venture between ICI of the UK and Enichem of Italy. Role ambiguity may even present opportunities for general managers to formulate their own policies for the alliance. That is more likely if the ambiguity arises either from the partners' lack of clear policy or from their disinterest. In such situations if the general manager has the requisite skills, experience and standing to chart his or her own course, he may find himself free to do so.

Box 12.1 Eurovynil Chloride Corporation Joint Venture

EVC is a joint venture set up in 1986 by ICI of the UK and Enichem of Italy to rationalize the production and sales of PVC in Europe. In order to do this it was judged necessary to take up to 1 million tonnes of capacity out of the joint capacity of the two partners. EVC is a 50:50 owned joint venture company based in Belgium. Its remit is to sell PVC and allied products based largely on ICI and Enichem raw material, and manufactured in plants still run by ICI and Enichem separately.

This joint venture has to be regarded as relatively successful, since it achieved its primary objective of returning this area of activity to profit for both partners, in normal non-recessionary times. This was accomplished largely through capacity rationalization and efficiency improvement. However, the fact that EVC was forced to buy 90 per cent of its raw materials at above market prices from the shareholders, and that production took place in factories owned by the partners and not by EVC, has considerably constrained its developmental potential.

Basic organizational arrangements have been appropriate, i.e. a joint venture, but culture differences between the partners have made life somewhat difficult for the EVC personnel. There is little commitment or bonding evident, beyond that required for getting out of the over-capacity problem with as little financial burden as possible. There is little evidence that the partners have developed strong trust for each other, and the first managing director claimed that both partners complained that he was favouring the other partner. This, he said, was how he felt certain that he was actually being fair and even-handed.

●● ▶

cont.

No obvious learning philosophy has been adopted by either partner. Due to the limited appreciation by the shareholders of the most appropriate principles to follow if a joint venture company is to thrive and evolve over time, and the somewhat bleak prospects for PVC in the medium-term future, a prognosis for the longer-term future would suggest that the best solution for all parties would be a third party sale, as was apparently in prospect in the early 1990s. EVC cannot realistically expect to achieve this until it has ownership of its manufacturing, and possibly raw material producing plants, so that the joint venture can present itself as a stand-alone business.

Source: Authors. ■

There are in effect two main aspects to managing an alliance successfully. The first requires that the differing expectations of the partners are reconciled and incorporated into the strategy for the alliance. The more that their expectations are met, the less onerous is likely to be the control that the partners place upon alliance management. Meeting the expectations of alliance partners therefore involves a combination of securing consensus on the alliance's strategic objectives as well as maintaining the partners' continuing support in achieving them.

In a joint venture, the board of directors should, in principle, establish its strategic objectives, leaving the general manager free to achieve them so long as he or she is supported with adequate capital and other resources. By contrast, in an alliance with a number of partners such as a consortium, parent support mainly takes the form of non-contractual resourcing. This may lead to a more direct form of parental intervention in the alliance. The management of relationships between the alliance and its partners will always form an important part of alliance general management, as will attention to its strategic direction and viability, but the autonomy that general managers are granted to lead the alliance is likely to vary according to how that alliance is constituted.

In collaborations without a joint venture form to focus managerial attention, the running of the alliance is carried out through high level decisions to embark upon joint projects. The principles of project management then hold, but with the additional difficulty that the designated project manager has the problem of managing personnel from different home companies over whom he does not have ultimate authority. Thus, the management of such projects has to be carried out with extra sensitivity.

The circumstances which generate role conflict and other special difficulties for alliance general management are ones which lend a certain delicacy, even fragility, to the process of co-operation between organizations. This means that alliance general managers need to have a special concern for the conditions required to nurture and develop the co-operative relationship in which they play a pivotal part.

The other aspect to managing alliances successfully is located within the framework of co-operation between partners. While the ease with which it can be performed adequately is conditional on the quality of that co-operation, it is in principle similar to the general management of all companies. It concerns measures to promote the alliance's internal effectiveness as an ongoing operation. These include establishing appropriate organizational arrangements, providing leadership to achieve co-operation and motivation among employees, and ensuring appropriate information flows within the alliance.

Alliance management success factors

Certain principles have been proposed to underpin organizational arrangements in alliances if potential frictions and other problems are to be avoided. Collins and Doorley (1991) emphasized the establishment of a clear dispute resolution mechanism; Lorange and Probst (1987) stressed the importance of giving a joint venture managing director clear authority; Taucher (1988) argued that partners will feel much more comfortable with each other if they have an agreed divorce formula if things go wrong; and Kanter (1989) mentioned the importance of a good information dissemination system with the partner companies and the alliance itself.

Niederkofler (1991) has argued that:

> By limiting the actual amount of co-operation, by a careful selection of appropriate boundary spanners, and by stepping up the involvement with the partner as the firms get to know each other, the effects of organizational incompatibilities may be moderated. (p.251)

Thus, boundary spanning is a critical aspect of alliances, particularly collaborations, and the skill with which it is carried out seems to have considerable impact on the success of the alliance.

It is widely agreed that a fundamental attribute for effective international managers is to possess the broader strategic awareness which is necessary for operating on a global scale, or within an international network. The parallel for alliance managers, even those with responsibility for purely domestic alliances, is that they have to understand and accept the strategic rationale for the alliance and the business objectives the partners place upon it. Yoshino and Rangan (1995) comment that if the managers representing each partner are to be successful in carrying out their company's mission they need to be senior enough in their own company hierarchy to affect the nature of the implementation of their mission. In that way they can make concessions to their partner without losing sight of the ultimate objective. Some alliance companies find assistant director level to be of appropriate seniority for their interface managers.

International and alliance managers must also be willing to work towards a set of objectives which is both defined by, and attained through, meaningful relationships with others. Hence further requirements for success in both roles are the ability to communicate effectively and to be flexible in relating to others. These requirements point to relevant personal skills and sensitivities. They imply that, whatever training is offered, certain kinds of people are better suited to the demands of the job than are others. In the case of international managers, the relevant personal skills which have been identified include: adaptability; the ability to function in uncertain conditions; the ability to cope with ambiguity and personal stress; the capacity to work in and manage teams with diverse memberships; personal self-reliance; relationship and negotiating skills; and the capacity to communicate in more than one language. All of these are also necessary for an alliance general manager, perhaps in even greater measure. Several sensitivities have been identified as requisites for international managers: sensitivity to different cultures; awareness of their own cultural background; openness to learning from new situations and diverse points of view. Again, these requirements apply equally strongly to alliance general managers, although for them the cultural diversity is organizational as well as national.

Alliance managers have to work with large numbers of people over whom they have no direct authority, especially when the alliance takes the form of a collaboration or consortium. They have to possess a capacity to build trust among people, many of whom may be on secondment and will therefore tend to retain their identification with their own parent organizations and career paths (Child and Rodrigues, 1996). This clearly places a premium on personal flexibility and finely tuned interpersonal skills.

Four factors are key in the successful management of alliances (Faulkner, 1995a) in addition of course to having chosen a partner with good strategic fit. These are:

- positive attitudes between the partners;
- clear organizational arrangements for the alliances;
- a philosophy of organizational learning;
- congruent long-term goals.

We will discuss each of these in turn in greater detail.

Positive partner attitudes

For the alliance to be effective the partners must have positive attitudes towards the alliance, notably:

- a sensitive attitude to national and corporate cultural differences;
- strong commitment by top and lower level management in the partner companies;
- mutual trust.

Kanter (1989) identifies the critical nature of corporate and national cultural sensitivity between the partners; Anderson and Narus (1990) point to strong top and middle management commitment as a key factor for alliance success; and Lynch (1990) emphasizes the need for mutual trust. Inkpen and Crossan (1995) found that when top managers in partner companies did not understand or commit themselves to their alliances, their companies failed to realize the potential learning benefits that co-operation offered.

It may be argued with some justification that these factors are important in any enterprise involving people working together; but they are particularly important when the normal sanctions present in a unitary company are absent and the presence of people from different cultural backgrounds in joint teams is the norm rather than the exception.

True trust does not come immediately and has to be earned: it is sometimes useful to think of it in three phases. Calculative trust is that which exists at the outset when the partners calculate that they could be of benefit to each other, and are likely to make good partners. It is, of course, fragile. Predictive trust develops when the partners have worked together for a while and found each other to be reliable and to have integrity. The third kind of trust, affective trust, comes about sometimes when the partners develop a friendship with each other. It is not reached in all alliances but when it is, the alliance is considerably more robust and able to withstand the occasional setback and disappointment without falling apart.

Yoshino and Rangan (1995) were able from their case studies of global strategic alliances to identify a number of 'critical tasks' for alliance management, several of which amplify the considerations of co-operation between partners which have already been raised. One task they call 'establishing the right tone'. This is largely concerned with building trust between the partners through encouraging personal relationships between their staff who have to work together for the alliance to succeed. This includes all levels: senior managers, functional managers, engineers and technical staff. A second key activity which a general manager can perform is to monitor the contributions that the partners are making to the alliance and to initiate appropriate corrective action if these are found to be insufficient or unsatisfactory. These contributions can range from the tangible and relatively easy to monitor, such as supplies of components, to more difficult cases such as the quality of staff and information offered by a partner. A third task is to be aware of strategic reassessments by the partners and their implication for the alliance. They may offer opportunities for alliance general management to propose new activities for the alliance which will contribute to its long-term development.

Clear organizational arrangements

Success is most likely if certain principles underpin the organizational arrangements for the alliance, notably:

- the establishment of clear dispute resolution mechanisms;
- in a joint venture alliance, clear authority vested in the chief executive;
- an appropriate legal form;
- a divorce mechanism agreed at the outset, and;
- processes for wide dissemination of information within the alliance.

Mohr and Spekman (1994) found from a study of 140 personal computer manufacturers and dealers that the successful management of alliances depends on processes which are comparable to those mentioned above, and to those identified by Ring (1996). With regard to negotiation between partners, Mohr and Spekman draw attention to the benefits of constructive conflict resolution processes such as joint problem-solving rather than attempts either to dominate or smooth over problems. They also recommend the creation of commitment, interdependence and trust, which is promoted by participation, information sharing and a high quality of communications. They conclude that all these processes serve to better align partners' expectations, goals and objectives. The processes emphasized by Mohr and Spekman have a clear affinity with the sensemaking, understanding and committing processes identified by Ring (1996) as necessary conditions for co-operation to develop and thrive.

These factors go some way to reducing the uncertainties, tensions and ambiguities present in all alliances. However, if mistakes are made in working out these arrangements, the existence of good positive attitudes makes flexible adjustment more possible and more likely.

A learning philosophy

For the greatest hope of successful evolution and success of an alliance, a philosophy of constant learning should be adopted by the partners. Alliances that are set up with the prime purpose of substituting for skills or products in which a partner is deficient tend to have limited scope for development. Where both or all partners have the prime objective of learning from each other, the prognosis for the future is much brighter. It is interesting to observe how, in the early days of the Rover/Honda alliance, Rover merely sought a model to market as a mid-range saloon. It was not until much later, when learning became Rover's primary objective, that the company experienced dramatic benefit from the alliance. (See Box 13.1, Chapter 13).

For the alliance to succeed long term it needs to evolve by means of the partners constantly seeking new things to do together. In essence it is a learning arrangement between companies with different things to teach and learn. If the partners enter the alliance understanding this, the success of the alliance is highly probable. A capacity to learn might be indicated by setting up explicit systems to disseminate learning, and explicit reviews of current learning and expected learning. Therefore for the greatest prognosis of success, a philosophy of constant learning should be adopted by the partners.

Congruent long-term goals

A further condition for continuing success in an alliance is that the long-term goals and objectives of the partners do not conflict. It is not necessary that the objectives dovetail. Clearly those of Rover and Honda did not, but the objectives must not actually conflict, otherwise the alliance will have difficulty in developing consensus for any particular course of action.

Many alliances are set up for short-term gains in order to deal with temporary situations. These obscure the nature of the true strategic alliance, in which the intent is a learning one, in the cause of joint sustainable competitive advantage, the extension of individual and joint core competencies, and in which long-term mutual benefit is supported by trust, commitment and a willingness to be flexible and robust in dealing with the tensions inherent in the alliance genre.

In terms of the possibilities presented by an alliance, there are a number of different types of learning, e.g. technological learning, process learning, opportunity learning and the development of a learning philosophy (Faulkner, 1995b), each with different implications . The ease with which learning takes place within an alliance depends firstly, upon the type of learning and secondly, the relationship between the nature of the learning and the condition of the would-be learning company.

Summary

We have considered various managerial skills, attitudes and processes significantly associated with the success of international strategic alliances. Positive partner attitudes, especially regarding trust and commitment, have been seen to be the dominant management factors. Also necessary are clear organizational arrangements, including dispute resolution procedures and a possible divorce mechanism, as well as processes for the dissemination of information. Organizational learning has also been shown to be of central importance in the success of an alliance, and the establishment and maintenance of congruent goals between the partners. Of the factors identified above, by far and away the most important seem to be the commitment, mutual trust and flexibility in the relationship between the partners. Given such positive attitudes, any frictional problems can be resolved. However, in the absence of flexible and trusting relationships any problem encountered places the relationship in jeopardy. Relationship management skills and attitudes thus seem to be the key to a successful alliance.

13

International strategy and learning

Successful strategies are those which develop a fit between the competencies of organizations and the opportunities presented by their environments. This applies as much to international as to domestic strategies and generally involves 'organizational learning'. The term has come to be used to emphasize that organizations, just as individuals, can acquire new knowledge and skills with the intention of improving their future performance. It has indeed been argued that the only sustainable competitive advantage the company of the future will have is its managers' ability to learn faster than its rivals (De Geus, 1988, p.740). These contentions are never more relevant than when developing and implementing international strategies.

The nature of organizational learning

Organizational learning has both cognitive and behavioural aspects. While learning is clearly a process, the concept of learning also incorporates the outcomes from such learning processes. Thus, an organization does not necessarily benefit from the acquisition of knowledge and understanding unless and until these are applied to improving organizational actions. Learning outcomes therefore include not just the potential for, but the actual realization of, improvements and changes.

There is a paradox at the heart of the idea of organizational learning which Argyris and Schon (1978) describe as follows: 'Organizational learning is not merely individual learning, yet organizations learn only through the experience and actions of individuals' (p.9).

As Nonaka and Takeuchi (1995) recognize, in a strict sense knowledge is created only by individuals. Therefore the role of an organization can be only to support creative individuals or to provide suitable contexts for them in which to create knowledge. Nonaka and Takeuchi's description of 'organizational knowledge creation' provides an indication of how this individual learning can become available, and retained, within the organization as a whole. In so far as this increased knowledge can be incorporated into improved systems and routines, the learning can be captured by the collectivity, and extended beyond the individual.

This touches on the very practical question of how learning by individuals, or groups of individuals, can become transformed into an organizational property. The challenge here is partly one of how to make explicit, codify, disseminate and store the knowledge possessed by the members of an organization in ways that convert it into a collective resource. This is a particular challenge for MNCs, which may encompass individuals of widely varying national cultures. It is also partly a problem of how to reduce the barriers which organizational structures, cultures and interests can place in the way of knowledge-sharing and learning. Of course the nature of learning achieved in an organization will vary according to its organizational form and culture. Organizational learning in a transnational for example is likely to exceed that in a global company.

The nature of the knowledge contributed by the members of an organization is of considerable significance for the process of learning. An important requirement for converting knowledge into an organizational property is to make it sufficiently explicit to be able to pass around the knowledge network. Polanyi (1966) distinguished between *tacit* knowledge and *explicit* knowledge. The former is usually regarded as personal, intuitive and context-specific. It is therefore difficult to verbalize, formalize and communicate to others. Explicit knowledge, by contrast, is specified and codified. It can therefore be transmitted in the formal systems and language of the organization. To make tacit knowledge available to the organization as a whole, in a form which permits its retention for future use, it has to be converted into a codified or programmable form. By definition, tacit knowledge is not amenable to such codification. Furthermore, where an organization makes efforts to better capture and codify the knowledge which exists within it, it may be extremely difficult to accomplish this, either for technical reasons or because the people with tacit knowledge do not wish to lose their control over it, or more frequently neither they nor the organization recognize either the existence of such tacit knowledge or their possession of it. If this is the case, then the only way to put tacit knowledge to organizational use may be to delegate responsibility for action to the persons concerned and/or to persuade them to share their knowledge with others on an informal basis.

Categories of learning

A distinction which has important implications for practice is that between the different categories of organizational learning. This distinguishes between *technical*, *systemic* and *strategic* types of organizational learning (Child and Faulkner, 1998). The technical level includes the acquisition of new, specific techniques, such as techniques for quality measurement or for undertaking systematic market research, or blue-prints for the application of new technologies. This type of learning may be thought of as routine learning. The systemic level refers to learning to introduce and work with new organizational systems and procedures. The focus here is on the restructuring of relationships and the creation of new roles and ways of doing things. The strategic level involves changes in the mindsets of senior managers, especially in their criteria for organizational success and their mental maps of the factors significant for achieving that success. The emphasis here is on vision, which is somewhat different to that on 'learning how to learn', but there is a parallel in the cognitive processes involved with a view to generating new insights and being proactive.

Learning is required at all three levels – technical, systemic and strategic. Technical learning is the easiest type to achieve. Given the complex nature of many modern technologies, and the necessity of deploying these technologies by harnessing human skills and the motivation of employees, a multi-disciplinary technical competence is required. The absence of certain technical skills can cause problems in international companies. An example of such an obvious and basic technical skill is that needed in languages. Hamel (1991) noted how the fact that employees in Western firms almost all lacked Japanese language skills and cultural experience in Japan limited their access to Japanese know-how. Their Japanese partners did not suffer from a lack of language competence to the same degree and benefited from the additional insight this gave them into the knowledge-base of Western partner firms and into their ways of doing and thinking about things.

There is a conceptual difference between what we learn, and how we learn. Therefore in addition to these different categories of learning, Andreu and Ciborra (1996) point to the different dynamic processes of learning which link these three categories of learning together. They describe these different learning processes by means of three 'loops': the routinization learning loop; the capability learning loop; and the strategic loop.

At the technical learning level is the routinization learning loop. This level of learning is aimed at mastering the use of standard resources and gives rise to efficient work practices. Andreu and Ciborra cite as an example 'mastering the usage of a spreadsheet by an individual or a team in a specific department, to solve a concrete problem'.

The category of systemic learning is required in order to make the most innovative use of new knowledge or technology which is acquired. For example, the introduction of mill-wide computerization in the paper and pulp industry opened up radical new possibilities for the constructive redesign of mill organization and the combined empowerment and enrichment of mill workers' jobs

(Child and David, 1987). This new technological development came about through close co-operation between paper manufacturers and system suppliers. The ability of UK paper manufacturers to take full advantage of the potential offered by the new systems depended on their organizational vision and competence, in terms of being able to envisage and accept radically changed roles and relationships. Such new work practices can be internalized by the firm in the form of routines, and in this way they become part of its capabilities. This gives rise to Andreu and Ciborra's second type of learning process, the capability learning loop, in which new work practices are combined with organizational routines. The learning process is systemic in character, because it involves generalizing work practices and techniques and placing them into a wider context. This defines not just what the practices do and how they work, but also the circumstances under which it becomes appropriate to use them, and who has the authority or competence to apply them.

In the strategic learning category, the ability of a senior executive to derive broad strategic lessons from a business experience rather than the more restricted perspective only of narrower issues, is a common problem. It often displays itself in international strategies based on historic industry 'recipes', rather than on new insights into the actual industry dynamics. General Motors (USA), for example, approached its NUMMI joint venture with Toyota (Japan) with the expectation that what it could learn from Toyota would be confined to production skills in the manufacturing of small cars. As a consequence, although the lessons to be learned were actually of general relevance, they were unfortunately not applied to General Motors as a whole (Inkpen, 1995a). Andreu and Ciborra's third type of learning process is the strategic loop. In this learning process, capabilities evolve into core capabilities that differentiate a firm strategically, and provide it with a competitive advantage. Capabilities can be identified as 'core' (i.e. central to the firms activities), or as 'key' (i.e. having strategic potential) by reference to the firm's mission as to what will give it a distinctive edge in its competitive environment (Bowman and Faulkner, 1997).

Multinational corporations (MNCs) and international alliances offer the potential for learning in all three categories and by all three processes. MNCs may provide direct and fast access to improved techniques and specific technologies. They can facilitate the transfer and internalization of new systems, such as lean production and total quality management (TQM), and they can utilize both to develop new strategic insights for the realization of new strategic opportunities.

Forms of organizational learning

Learning also takes different forms. Some forms of learning become far more embedded within the firm's evolving culture than others (Child and Faulkner,

1998). The first form is that of *forced* learning. Here there is no change of cognition, and hence understanding, but new behaviour is acquired under some pressure, perhaps from head office. A common example of forced learning might arise when MNC headquarters insists on the unilateral introduction of new organizational routines or systems without other parts of the firm either understanding the rationale for them, or indeed being offered adequate training in how to implement them. Although the term 'forced' refers here to how the acquisition of new behavioural practices is brought about, and not necessarily to how the process is perceived by those on the receiving end, it is likely to meet with some reluctance on their part. Forced learning can readily arise in a situation where there is strong centralization of power in the firm and a low motivation to learn by members outside head office.

A second possibility also results in the adoption of new practices (behavioural change) but without any appreciable learning of the rationale behind them (cognitive change). This is *imitative* learning. There is probably at least a moderate level of motivation to learn in this situation, but the fact that the learning takes the form of imitation might indicate some limitation in the quality of training offered to support the learning process. Markoczy and Child (1995) give an anecdotal description of an occasion in China when Child had to go in and out of one hotel in China several times in succession with various packages. He was greeted on each entry by the same commissionaire with 'welcome to our hotel' and on each exit with 'have a nice day, sir'!

The two situations mentioned so far are ones in which, at best, behaviour and practices have changed, but without any significant increase in know-how or understanding. However, the opposite can also occur, when the members of an organization undergo changes in cognition that are not reflected in their behaviour. This could be due to inadequacies of resourcing which prevents implementation, an over-general or theoretical formulation of the new knowledge, or existing strongly-held beliefs displacing the new knowledge. These factors cause the translation of new understanding into revised behaviour to be blocked. *Blocked* learning can arise when staff receive training, perhaps on a course, but are not accorded the resources or opportunities to put what they have acquired at the cognitive level into practice, or find that their boss has not had their training and is sceptical of their newly acquired ideas. Their motivation to learn may well be high, but the organization of the training may not be matched to that of the responsibilities and resources allocated. This may be one reason for a marked preference by MNCs that executive training and development programmes should more frequently involve groups of internal MNC staff undergoing the development programme together, rather than sending an individual manager on an outside programme, where no other representatives of the MNC would be present.

Another aspect of learning is that individuals learn both cognitively and behaviourally. This might take the form of a unilateral process of *received* learning when one executive willingly receives new insights from another. If both parties endeavour to express and share their knowledge and practices, a level of *integrative* learning may be attained. Integrative learning has the potential for organizational learning in its most advanced form, that in which innovative synergy is attained between the different contributions and approaches which the participants in a MNC bring to their interactions. Integrative learning involves a joint search for technical, system-building and strategic solutions for the needs of the MNC. It means that people are receptive to the concepts and practices brought in by others, and are willing to modify their own ways of thinking and behaviour in the light of these.

Two further forms exist. The first is *segmented* learning (Child and Faulkner, 1998). This is a situation in which, at best, very restricted learning can take place because the firm is organized such that separate responsibilities are allocated very clearly. That would be typical of the multidomestic MNC organizational form. The final possibility is that of *non-learning*, in which no learning takes place at all. This is likely to arise when the motivation to learn is low and/or because there is low transparency of knowledge between the parts of the firm. For example, in the case of a Chinese–European joint venture, reported by Child and Markoczy (1993), a negative learning priority was illustrated. The Chinese partner attempted to resist the reconfiguration of production and support functions along more effective lines because it saw this as reinforcing the power of the European management over the running of the venture's facilities and over the labour force.

Learning and organizational form

Different types of MNCs, as well as different international alliances, naturally lend themselves to organizational learning of a different degrees and types. The three levels of learning (technical, systemic and strategic), and the three positive, non-pathological forms of learning (received, segmented and integrated, from the seven forms discussed in the previous section) are likely to display themselves differentially in MNC organizations of different types as shown in Table 13.1.

Thus, *global* MNCs are strongly directed from head office and show only limited feedback or response to local conditions. Received learning is therefore the most characteristic in the technical and systemic categories, with a low level of strategic learning. *International exporter* companies are an avowedly transitional MNC form and are likely to display forced learning from the centre at best, in all three categories, technical, systemic and strategic. *Multidomestic* MNCs of the traditional type are characterized by largely autonomous subsidiaries, and are therefore likely to display segmented learning, with the rest of the group and the other subsidiaries learning little from

Table 13.1 Types of learning in different MNC forms

Organizational form	Categories of learning		
	Technical	**Systemic**	**Strategic**
Global	high/received	high/received	low/forced
International	low/forced	low/forced	low/forced
Multidomestic	high/segmented	low/segmented	high/segmented
Transnational	high/integrated	medium/integrated	high/integrated
Alliance	high/received or integrated	medium/received or integrated	low/received or integrated

Source: Authors

one another's experiences. Learning in *transnationals* is likely to be high, especially in the technical and strategic categories and of the highest integrated variety, since the major purpose of setting up an MNC in a transnational configuration is to maximize flexibility, sensitivity of response and integrated learning. Systemic learning in the essentially flexible, and sometimes fluidly organized transnationals may, however, be less strong than in other categories, as transnational frequently have diffuse control systems. In strategic *alliances* the level of learning will of course vary with the success of the alliance. It may be of the received variety in all three categories where one partner 'milks' the other as much as it can, but in the best alliances it will be of the integrated variety where both partners learn together and embed that learning in their partner companies.

Of course there is no inevitability that a particular organizational form will necessarily display the particular categories of learning set out above, or indeed any of the non-pathological learning forms. Indeed some will display pathological forms like blocked learning, forced learning or even non-learning. However, we do propose that the different MNC and alliance forms each have a tendency to achieve predominantly certain types of organizational learning, by virtue of their underlying organizational characteristics.

Requirements for learning

Even when a corporation undertakes to adopt a learning philosophy, there are certain requirements for learning to take place. The first is that the intent to promote learning is high on the personal and corporate agendas of senior executives, so that learning objectives are automatically included in the formulation of objectives and outcomes at all levels in the organization. As part of this philosophy, managers must also be able to identify and attach value to those learning opportunities which do arise. Second, the corporation must have the necessary capacity to learn. Most importantly, it needs to be able to convert the knowledge into a collective property so it can be disseminated to the appropriate persons or units within its organization, understood by them, and retained for future use. These factors are not easy to achieve in practice.

Learning intent

In a detailed study of nine Western/Asian MNC international strategic alliances, Hamel (1991) found that the partners varied considerably in how far they viewed the collaboration as a learning opportunity, and that this attitude in itself was an important determinant of the learning which they actually achieved. For instance, several of the Western firms had not intended to absorb knowledge and skills from their Japanese partners when they first entered alliances with them. They appeared, initially, to be satisfied with substituting their partner's competitive superiority in a particular area for their own lack of it. In every case where this skill substitution intent was maintained, the partners failed to learn much from their collaboration.

Other companies, especially the Japanese partners in any of the alliances, entered into the alliance regarding it as a transitional device in which their primary objective was a learning objective. They therefore had an explicit strategic intent to understand, capture and transfer their partner's skills. In several cases, partners undertook co-operative strategies for the purpose of learning the business, especially to meet international requirements, mastering a technology and establishing a presence in new markets. These are illustrations of a company's intention to use the learning opportunities provided by collaboration to enhance its competitive position and internalize its partners' skills, as opposed to collaborating over the long term and being content merely to gain access to a particular partner skill, without attempting to acquire such skills itself. Where one partner has a learning objective and the other merely a skill substitution objective, the threat posed to an unwitting partner is obvious. Such an imbalance does not provide the basis for an enduring long-term co-operative relationship. In fact, when learning from a partner is the sole aim, the termination of a co-operation agreement cannot necessarily be seen as a failure, nor can its stability and longevity be seen as evidence of success. Hamel noted that a partner's ability to outstrip the learning of the other contributes to an enhancement of that partner's bargaining power within the co-operative relationship, reducing its dependence on the other partner, and hence providing a gateway to the next stage of internalizing those partners' knowledge and skills. For these reasons, Hamel concludes that, in order to realize the learning opportunities offered by an alliance, a partner must both give priority to learning and consciously consider how to go about it.

OFF
RST SPORT
MBER STREET, NOTTINGHAM
d in any other store.
rther discounts on sale prices.
s Act 1964)
ST SPORT
BER STREET, NOTTINGHAM

NIKE
20% O
ALL FULL PRICED PRODUCT AT
FIR
Valid until 31st October 2001.
16 CLU

This conclusion, derived from evidence from international alliances, applies just as powerfully to internal attitudes and processes for facilitating intra-unit, cross-border learning in MNCs.

Learning capacity

A company's capacity to learn will be determined by a combination of factors: the transferability of the knowledge, the receptivity of its members to new knowledge, whether they have the necessary competencies to understand and absorb the knowledge, and the extent to which the company incorporates the lessons of experience into the way it approaches the process of learning.

Transferability indicates the ease with which the type of knowledge can be transferred from one party to another. Explicit knowledge, such as technical product specifications, is relatively easy to transfer and to be absorbed. Tacit knowledge is, by definition, far more difficult.

The more receptive people are to new knowledge, the more likely they are to learn. When the members of an organization in different parts of the world adopt the attitude of students towards their teachers, they are being more receptive to insights than if they assume that they already possess superior techniques, organizing abilities and strategic judgement. For example, some Chinese partners in joint ventures with foreign companies make the mistake of assuming that they cannot learn useful motivational practices from their foreign collaborators because they already have a superior specific knowledge of Chinese workers (cited in Child and Faulkner, 1998). Equally, some foreign partners unwisely overlook or ignore advice from their Chinese collaborators on the best ways to relate to external governmental authorities, which in China wield an unusual degree of influence over the conditions for doing business.

Hamel (1991) found several influences on a partner organization's receptivity to learning new knowledge. Firms which had entered an alliance as competitive 'laggards' in their sector, in order to provide an easy way out of a deteriorating competitive situation, tended to possess both little enthusiasm for learning from the other partner and little confidence that they could achieve such learning. They tended to be trapped within deeply embedded organizational cultures and behaviours which made the task of opening up to new knowledge all the more difficult. In clinging to the past in such a way, they were not capable of the 'unlearning' which is a necessary prerequisite to receptivity to learning (Hedberg, 1981). Receptivity also depended on the availability of some time and resource to engage in the processes of gathering knowledge, and embedding it within its own routines through staff training and investment in new facilities. The organizational learning paradox thus emerges for poorly performing organizations. Deteriorating competitiveness creates a great pressure to learn and need to learn for the poorly-performing organization; yet this pressure itself constitutes the largest constraint on being able to achieve learning and move forward. Sometimes this may be resolved by additional cash and other resource forthcoming from MNC headquarters, or injected by the other partner in an alliance. If an organization has slipped very far in the skills and competencies necessary for it to absorb new knowledge in its sector, or a collaborator has slipped too far behind its partner in an alliance, it may find it extremely difficult to close the gap. Similarly a low technology company may not be sufficiently receptive to new knowledge for it to be able to transform itself into a high technology company even when such an opportunity arises, simply due to the limited educational level of its key employees (Faulkner, 1995b)

Cohen and Levinthal (1990) argue that a firm's 'absorptive capacity' is a crucial competence for its learning and innovative capabilities. Absorptive competence is a firm's ability to recognize the value of new, external information, assimilate it and apply it to commercial ends. This competence is largely a function of the firm's level of prior, related knowledge. Hence existing competence favours the acquisition of new competence. That implies that a partner entering an alliance with learning objectives should ensure that it does so not only with a positive attitude towards learning but also with at least some appropriate level of skills. If those skills are not available, the training of staff to acquire them should be an immediate priority.

Experience can be both an enabler and an inhibitor. Previous experience of the learning process will normally enhance one's capacity to learn because it gives greater knowledge of how to learn: how to manage, monitor and extract value from new information. However, prior knowledge which has been converted into existing organizational routines can become a barrier to further learning, especially that of a discontinuous rather than merely incremental nature. Being good at single-loop learning may therefore become a handicap for double-loop learning (Argyris and Schon, 1978).

The learning process experienced by Rover in its international alliance with Honda (Faulkner, 1995a) provides a practical illustration of this interplay of learning conditions between the two organizations, the nature and level of their respective knowledge-base , and the learning intent and learning experience of each partner (see Box 13.1).

Box 13.1 The Rover/Honda Alliance: Learning by Rover

In the alliance between Rover and Honda, Rover had a high intent to acquire technology and this technical learning was relatively easy to

cont.

achieve. Well into the later stages of the alliance, Rover was receptive and remained keen to undergo technical learning. The nature of the technology transfer was clear and Honda was willing to provide the information in joint learning working teams.

Process learning, however, involving knowledge about Honda's organizing systems, was more difficult, since by its nature it involved a lot of tacit knowledge as well as features related to Japanese cultural paradigms. This kind of knowledge was less transparent and less easily transferred, but as Rover's learning intention and receptivity grew throughout the lifespan of the alliance, it became one of the success stories of the alliance from the Rover viewpoint. Processes such as 'just-in-time' were adopted and adapted to Rover's situation, and organizational innovations such as multifunctional teams and a flattening of the management hierarchy were introduced.

Once the co-operation had deepened by the mid-1980s to embrace the joint development of new automobile models, Rover's intent and receptivity to learning from Honda increased dramatically. The whole nature of Rover's attitude to itself, its personnel and its way of working underwent a transformation, so that a learning philosophy came to be established and underpinned greater organizational openness and rising self-confidence. By this stage, Rover's senior management had fully accepted the strategic value of the alliance. Unfortunately though, Rover's parent company British Aerospace, as part of its review of its own corporate strategy and business portfolio, decided to focus on its aerospace businesses and divest its automobile business (Rover Cars), since the expected R&D synergies between the two divisions had not been forthcoming. British Aerospace then sold off its Rover division to another automobile company, BMW of Germany. As this meant that BMW/Rover was now in direct competition with Honda, this sale led to the gradual unwinding and termination of the co-operative alliance.

Source: Adapted from Faulkner (1995a). ■

Making knowledge collective

Drawing largely upon cases of successful Japanese innovation, Nonaka and Takeuchi (1995) stressed that the creation of knowledge for organizational use is a 'continuous and dynamic interaction between tacit and explicit knowledge'. For this process to succeed, in their view, the possibility must exist for four different modes of knowledge conversion:

1. *Socialization (tacit knowledge/tacit knowledge):*

   A process of sharing experiences and thereby creating tacit knowledge such as shared mental models and technical skills. (p.65)

2. *Externalization (tacit knowledge/explicit knowledge):*

   A process of articulating tacit knowledge into explicit concepts

This form of knowledge conversion is typically seen in the creation of concepts which offer wider access to the knowledge and also links it directly to applications

3. *Combination (explicit knowledge/explicit knowledge):*

   A process of systematizing concepts into a knowledge system. This mode of knowledge conversion involves combining different bodies of explicit knowledge ... through media such as documents, meetings, telephone conversations, or computerized communication networks

Typical examples are: training manuals, e.g. how to submit a proposal, for new management consultants; or how to lay out a slide to improve presentation skills; or how to answer the telephone and take messages properly.

4. *Internalization (explicit knowledge/tacit knowledge):*

   This process is closely related to 'learning by doing'; knowledge acquired by practice. It involves the embodiment of explicit knowledge into individuals' tacit knowledge bases in the form of shared mental models of personal technical know-how. For example, putting a student teacher into a classroom with a more experienced teacher to see how the more experienced professional handles given situations.

Nonaka and Takeuchi (1995) emphasize that organizational learning depends upon the tacit knowledge of individuals, and upon the ability first to combine tacit knowledge sources constructively, and then to convert these into more explicit forms which are subsequently, in turn, combined. Tacit knowledge itself is enhanced by explicit knowledge, taking the form for example of training inputs. Theirs is an insightful framework for understanding the processes which must be in place for new knowledge to become a property available to the whole organization, and hence to constitute organizational learning.

Barriers to organizational learning

There are often obstacles to the smooth operation of organizational learning which derive from the nature of an organization and its culture. When a company is international, such barriers are almost inevitably increased by the variety of different national identities in the employee group. Such barriers reduce what Hamel (1991) terms transparency, namely the openness of one person to the other, and the willingness to transfer knowledge between different parts of an organization, or between different national partners in a cross-border alliance. Hamel found that some degree of openness was accepted as a necessary condition for carrying out joint tasks, but that in international alliances in particular, managers were often concerned about unintended and unanticipated transfers of knowledge – transparency by default rather than by design. Obstacles to the necessary transference of knowledge identified by Nonaka and Takeuchi (1995) are liable to arise because of divergent approaches to sense-making and are associated with the social identities of the different participants which make up an MNC.

When the members of a worldwide MNC organization come together to collaborate, they bring their own social identities with them. These social identities are sets of substantive meanings which arise from a person's interaction with different reference groups during his or her life and career. They derive therefore from belonging to particular families, communities and work groups within the context of given nationalities and organizations (Tajfel, 1982).

The receptivity of the members to knowledge transfer from other parts of the MNC or from their alliance partners, and their ability to learn collaboratively from their knowledge resources, are bound up then with their social identities. Social identities are likely to create the greatest difficulties for learning in relationships which consist of MNC firm members who are distinct culturally, nationally and in terms of the economic development level of the society from which they come. Learning in these circumstances is not a socially-neutral process. Just as with the transfer within the MNC of specialist technical knowledge, so knowledge and practice transferred from one firm member impinges on the other members' mental constructs and norms of conduct. Their social identity derives from a sense both of sharing such ways of thinking and behaving, and of how these contrast with those of other groups with whom they are brought into contact within the MNC. The process of transferring practical knowledge between different managerial groups will be interdependent with the degree of social distance that is perceived between the parties involved. So, if initially this distance is high, the transfer is likely to be difficult. If the transfer is conducted in a hostile manner or in threatening circumstances, then the receiving group is likely to distance itself from those initiating the transfer. There is a clear possibility of virtuous and vicious circles emerging in this interaction, and thus contributing to positive and negative learning outcomes.

MNCs present a particular challenge for organizational learning, since MNC learning is intended to draw upon knowledge transferred between the firm members and to build upon the potential synergies between their complementary competencies (Child and Rodrigues, 1996). Although international organizational networks are an extremely important means for international knowledge transfer and synergistic learning, they do introduce special sensitivities into the process. It is often difficult to accommodate the interests of their constituent groups and to manage the cultural contrasts between them. These differences contribute to a sense of separate social identity, rather than social cohesion, between staff.

Some types of internationally transferred knowledge have more impact on group social identity than others. This is particularly true of knowledge relating to new systems and strategic understanding. Resistance to the transfer of such knowledge is likely to heighten the separate identities of groups, including those doing the knowledge transfer for whom persuading their recalcitrant colleagues may take on the nature of a crusade. The relationship between social identity and international knowledge transfer is a dynamic one, in which contextual factors such as performance also play a part through inducing changes in factors which condition the process. By contrast, the sharing and transfer of technical knowledge is normally less socially sensitive. Indeed, technical knowledge transfer is likely to benefit from the common engineering or other common technical, professional or managerial occupational identity shared by the staff directly involved.

Members of an organization will be reluctant to give up the beliefs and myths which constitute important supports for their social identity. Jonsson and Lundin (1977) write of the 'prevailing myth' as one which guides the behaviour of individuals in organizations, at the same time as it justifies their behaviour to themselves and hence sustains their identity. Beliefs and myths also form an important conceptual part of the 'cultural web' (Johnson, 1990) by sustaining an existing paradigm (such as 'we are the biggest firm in our market', irrespective of continuously declining profitability) and an existing set of practices, against the possibilities of their replacement through organizational learning. The social identities of those involved in an MNC are likely to be tied up in this way with their distinctive and separate beliefs and an adherence to these myths and organizational beliefs.

The management of organizational learning

Cognitive barriers

Organizational learning needs to be managed to achieve its optimal level in a firm. This involves recognizing and overcoming a number of common barriers.

A lack of intent to learn can be an important cognitive barrier in the way of realizing the learning potential within, or between, organizations. This can arise because an MNC is focusing on objectives other than learning, such as spreading the costs and risks of R&D across its different businesses, or achieving production economies of scale. Often in international alliances, one partner may not even appreciate that it has something valuable to learn from its alliance partner, not simply because it has other primary objectives for the alliance than learning, but because it takes time to become more familiar with that partner's capabilities and the possibilities for learning and knowledge transfer that they offer. Inkpen (1995b) found several examples of American firms which did not have a learning intent when entering a collaboration with a Japanese partner, and only developed this when they became aware of their inferior levels of skill. Ways of reducing lack of intent to learn, due to inadequate prior knowledge, include programmes of visits and secondments to prospective partner organizations, and close examination of their products and services.

Emotional barriers

Emotional barriers to learning often boil down to a problem of mistrust. Genuine trust cannot be instantly established. It is, nevertheless, possible to identify conditions which promote trust and therefore to derive practical guidelines to further the building of trust within the MNC across its various divisions and businesses or between alliance partners. Commitment to the relationship, and a degree of direct personal involvement by the partners' senior managers, are again important here. Personal contact enhances and reinforces trust-building. If the principals take the time and trouble to establish a close personal relationship, this gives confidence and a signal for other staff to regard one another in a positive light. The opposite is also the case, as when inter-departmental or inter-divisional rivalry generate deterioration of trust and increasing suspicion and lack of co-operation or effective integration. The conditions for reducing emotional barriers to learning within MNCs and alliances, require a long-term view and sufficient visible managerial commitment, especially from the top (Faulkner, 1995a). These points apply particularly in the integration of cross-border MNC acquisitions.

Organizational barriers

Serious organizational barriers are created if the senior managers do not know how to benefit from the opportunity to learn. Inkpen (1995b) found that a major problem arose where American and Japanese managers and staff had to work together, because of the arrogance of the American staff as to the superiority of their knowledge, systems and procedures. Clearly under such circumstances, both the recognition of potential learning opportunities and the potential exploitation of such opportunities will be missing. No organizational mechanisms were established to assist potential exploitation. In some cases they resisted even the idea that there was something to learn from the

Japanese. In American/Japanese alliances this attitude often contributed to a situation of blocked learning where joint venture managers could not get their improved understanding carried over into practical actions (Inkpen and Crossan, 1995).

Managers and staff will take their cue from senior levels. Senior management is in a position to establish organizational procedures and provisions which foster the learning process. Inkpen and Crossan (1995) identified ways in which such provisions can be designed, or practices encouraged, by senior managers which facilitate links across boundaries within the organization and which promote the learning process These included (p.609):

1. The rotation of managers from the businesses or the divisions back to the parent headquarters; regular meetings between divisional and headquarters management, or for joint ventures (JV) and parent management.
2. Plant visits and tours by groups of managers from different parts of the organization or different international partners.
3. Senior management involvement in cross-border divisional or JV activities.
4. The sharing of information between the businesses or international divisions and the MNC headquarters.

A further organizational feature which facilitated learning in Inkpen's experience was *control*. There are two main aspects to this:

- establishing limits to the actions of participants in the learning process;
- assessing outcomes.

Control is not usually regarded as a facilitator of learning. Indeed, learning is normally associated with autonomy and creativity which are considered almost the opposite to control. However, control seems to be a very important condition for a learning intention to be given clear direction. Also, the systematic assessment of outcomes should ensure that these are recorded and so entered into the organization's memory. In addition, systematic assessment provides feedback on the effectiveness of the learning process and therefore should enable MNC or international alliance members to improve their capacity to promote learning.

This focus on the facilitation of learning by senior and middle managers derives from their pivotal position in the middle of the vertical communication and decision-making hierarchy of most organizations (although not of the transnational form). It echoes the conclusion reached by Nonaka and Takeuchi (1995) that what they term the 'middle-up-down' style of management can make a crucial contribution to fostering knowledge creation. Managers in the middle can reduce the gap that often otherwise exists between the broad strategic vision coming down from top management, and the hard operational reality experienced by employees in their day-to-day functioning. The manager in the middle has the additional responsibility for articulating the objectives for learning and providing the practical means to facilitate it.

The aim of organizational provisions is to promote the conditions for integrated learning. Another requirement, which the techniques of organizational behaviour can facilitate, is to break down the hostile stereotypes which may exist within a firm, and which if allowed to persist will militate against the development of trust and bonding. Many of the techniques first developed by practitioners of 'Organization Development' can be used to advantage in this situation, though one must remain sensitive to the cultural mix when deciding on specific methods. The 'confrontation meeting' approach which often works well with North American personnel could, for instance, cause grave offence if tried with staff from East Asia. Once the problems inherent within such stereotypes are recognized, various techniques for team-building are available to promote a collaborative approach to learning between members of the firm.

Open communication and information circulation

A climate of openness can also facilitate organizational learning. It involves the accessibility of information, the sharing of errors and problems, and acceptance of conflicting views. The idea of 'information redundancy' expresses an approach to information availability which is positive for organizational learning. Redundancy is 'the existence of information that goes beyond the immediate operational requirements of organizational members. In business organizations, redundancy refers to intentional overlapping of information about business activities, management responsibilities, and the company as a whole' (Nonaka and Takeuchi, 1995, p.80). This adds flexibility to the organization, as in a changing environment it ensures a pool of knowledge available to draw on to implement new strategies.

For learning to take place, information, data, ideas, or concepts available to one person or group, need to be shared by others who may not need the concepts immediately. It may, for example, be information on how a particular problem was tackled creatively in another part of the MNC. If that information is circulated, it is accessible to others should a comparable problem arise. Redundancy also helps to build unusual communication channels, and it is indeed fostered by the combining of horizontal, with the more usual vertical, channels for reporting information. In this way it is associated with the interchange between hierarchy and non-hierarchy, or heterarchy (Hedlund, 1986). Non-hierarchical interchange, including Nonaka and Takeuchi's 'middle-up-down' process, helps to promote learning on the basis of procedures which are different from those already formally specified by the organization, and hence based on the existing solutions to old problems, rather than new solutions to problems (Nonaka and Takeuchi, 1995).

Modern information technology makes a very significant contribution to the promotion of information redundancy, through its capacity for information storage and, more importantly, through its ability to transmit that information to virtually all points within an organization. Electronic mail (e-mail) in particular offers access to information and the facility to communicate in ways which are not constrained by boundaries of time, geography or formality. So long as firm members link up their e-mail systems, these provide an excellent vehicle to circulate non-confidential information and to encourage immediate, creative, cross-border, cross-divisional commentary around it.

The case of PepsiCo, summarized in Box 13.2, illustrates how information redundancy and modern information technology are used to promote learning within that company. Open and fast communication is coupled with an encouragement of local managers to act upon the information circulated to them, including initiatives to contact others within the company worldwide from whom they might usefully learn.

Box 13.2 PepsiCo's Approach to Creating Information Redundancy

PepsiCo is one of the world's largest global food and beverage corporations, ranked 19th among USA companies by market capitalization in 1996. It operates through many local alliances, and stresses the value of open communication both within its corporate systems, and with its partners. An illustration of open communication with its partners is the fact that, in PepsiCo's joint ventures in China, all the general managers speak Mandarin Chinese, and its Asia-Pacific budget meetings are conducted entirely in Mandarin.

Despite its size and scope, PepsiCo does not operate with organization charts or many formal procedures, but instead prefers to encourage informal communication flows and to promote the empowerment of its constituent units. As one corporate officer recently said, 'At the end of the day, the most relevant information for me and the job I have to do, is going to come from the people who are closest to the project ... so the lines of communication are open at all levels'. Senior officers of the corporation stress the benefits of this approach for encouraging learning.

PepsiCo circulates information within its corporate network to the point of redundancy. Its internal e-mail system is an important vehicle for this information circulation. It overcomes international time differences, permits simultaneous communication with several people, is very fast, and encourages an open, informal expression of views. Consolidated reports for different countries and regions are

••▶

cont.

also widely circulated. If, as a result, managers wish to learn more about developments elsewhere in PepsiCo's worldwide operations, they have access to all the company's telephone numbers and are encouraged to make direct contacts and to decide whether to travel to the location, subject only to their travel and entertainment budgets. Many examples are told of how this rich circulation of information, and the ability to act upon it, have promoted learning and the transfer of beneficial practices throughout the corporation. For instance, it facilitated the transfer from their Hungarian operation to their JVs in China, of knowledge about ways of curbing theft on distribution runs.

Source: Personal interviews by John Child, cited in Child and Faulkner (1998).■

Summary

In this chapter, organizational learning has been analyzed in three basic categories: technical, systemic and strategic. These categories do not come about automatically but need to be facilitated by organizational and cultural factors. Different MNC forms (multidomestic, global, international exporter, transnational, international alliance) lend themselves to learning to a varying degree, within these three learning categories. For learning to take place in an MNC or in an international alliance, there are several requirements. There must be an intention to learn; there must be the necessary capacity to learn; and there must also be the capacity within the organization to transform individual knowledge into a usable organizational resource.

We have also emphasized the various forms of learning within MNCs: forced learning, imitation, blocked learning, received learning, integrative learning, segmented learning and of course non-learning. As would be expected, each of these is associated with different degrees of organizational and interpersonal change in understanding and in behaviour. They are also more or less likely within the different MNC organizational forms we have discussed in earlier chapters. The successful promotion of organizational learning within MNCs, and within international alliances, requires a number of important organizational and interpersonal conditions. These include the surmounting of cognitive and emotional barriers to learning and the reduction of organizational barriers to learning. Finally, organizational learning needs openness of communication and effectiveness in dissemination of information throughout the organization so that actual, and not just potential, learning outcomes may be realized.

14

Conclusion: Looking forward

This book takes a deliberately idiosyncratic view of international strategy. We have emphasized throughout certain characteristics of international strategy: its nature as dynamic, contingent and aggressive. This has coloured the perspective with which we have presented theories, frameworks and issues that we considered of relevance and also, hopefully, of interest to the mindset of the international strategist.

In this concluding section, rather than summarizing the topics already presented within the book, we will instead highlight some areas of critical thinking which, in our view, are those which are emerging as of great importance for the next generation of managers of multinational corporations (MNCs). Having read the preceding chapters, none of these areas should surprise you: they are embedded in our earlier discussions. However, they are the thoughts that we would like to leave in your minds.

Living with industry dynamics

A sense of dynamics is critical in strategy because strategies are always being developed and refined, reviewed and implemented against a set of moving targets which combine every aspect of industry conditions. Industries change, markets change, competitors change or may become partners in certain activities. How these changed industry dynamics and competitive dynamics affect current and future resources and capabilities has already been illustrated in Chapter 4 in relation to the international dynamics of the European food processing industry.

Similarly in the Novotel hotel minicase (in Chapter 9) you have seen an example of how a company had to adjust itself not once, but again and again, to changes in its business context. Each time it had to review what it was doing, why it was doing it that way and how effective its strategy was relative to what its customers wanted and what its competitors were doing. Novotel's top management had continually to review and monitor its positioning, its hotels, its internal procedures and processes. What at one point in the development of the business had been considered excellent, gradually became average or even substandard as the market developed and customer expectations continued to rise. Costs were rising too, and competition was getting ever tougher. It was not that the company was doing anything particularly bad, it was just that the context was shifting all around them all the time. Capabilities which have been developed and work well under one set of conditions can become inappropriate or downright inadequate when those conditions change, as they undoubtedly will.

The comparative advantage of nations and the competitive advantage of firms

In the earlier part of this book, considerable discussion was devoted to explaining the concept of comparative advantage, both from its original roots in economic theory and its relevance to the design of international strategies. Most importantly we wanted to make clear two things. First, that comparative advantage occurred within countries and had only an *indirect* relationship with international competitive advantage for a particular firm. In other words, comparative advantage at the level of the country did not automatically translate into competitive advantage for the firm located within that country. Such competitive advantage for the firm depended on the capabilities of the firm to utilize the potential source of advantage effectively. This should be clear from our lengthy discussion of the competition between Caterpillar and Komatsu in the 1970s, 1980s and 1990s, or indeed from many of the minicase discussions we have used in the book. Secondly, many types of comparative advantage may be relatively short-lived. The example of cheap wage rates rising over time as living standards and welfare expectations rise has already been mentioned. One may add to this other examples such as the potential erosion of many infrastructure advantages like transportation or education, either because governments do not invest adequately in them or because others have invested heavily over a period and 'caught up'.

There is also a third aspect of comparative advantage that was discussed earlier and to which we wish to return now. That is the type of comparative advantage that is at the heart of the Porter 'diamond' framework discussed in Chapter 2. With his introduction of the 'diamond' framework into international strategy thinking in 1990, Porter has put the idea of 'country-specific advantage' (CSA) (Buckley and Casson, 1998b; Dunning, 1989; Enderwick, 1989; Rugman *et al.*, 1985) back at the heart of international strategy, whilst at the same time changing the emphasis of the debate. His research, covering 10 countries and more than 100 industries, suggested that the conditions at a company's 'home-base' are crucial to its competitiveness abroad. He introduced the concept of national 'clusters' which might be strong or weak for different industries in a given country. So we should not be surprised at their being so many strong consumer electronics firms all based in Japan; or so many strong financial services firms all based in the UK; or so many strong movie-related firms all based in West Coast USA.

The implication of what Porter said is that the strength of individual MNCs is not 'home-base' country-neutral. It will vary according to the specific CSA conditions in the 'home' domestic market in which the company is based and in which it has its roots. If we refer back once more to our example of Benetton from Chapter 2, we might ask whether the fact that it is an Italian company is relevant to the international success of Benetton as a global retailer? Porter's 'diamond' would lead us to affirm resoundingly that the answer to that question must be yes. Porter stresses that firms located within very competitive industries with high levels of *national* rivalry (like the intense rivalry and overcrowded domestic consumer marketplace of the Italian fashion industry) are likely to do well in international markets, compared to those with few or no national rivals. These may survive or grow within a relatively protected domestic marketplace, but are unlikely to perform strongly internationally. Benetton is located in an overcrowded domestic fashion market, which has strengthened it for competing internationally. However, not all international strategy thinkers agree with Porter's (1990, 1998) view that national roots matter. Amongst those who disagree totally with that view is Ohmae.

Ohmae (1989) coined the term 'borderless world' to describe his view that nations have become less important to companies, whether as home bases or as sources of identity. The old 1960s model of the MNC, with a dominant parent company and stand-alone subsidiaries in each overseas market, has been replaced by one in which firms locate activities wherever the costs are lowest and organize on a more global scale. As they attempt to turn themselves into 'truly international' or 'truly global' corporations, firms are responding to the need to compete in a world market rather than in national ones. Although Ohmae accepts (as Porter suggests) that companies emerge from national origins which determine their competitiveness, he argues for a borderless world economy and market in which governments should cease building obstacles to a prosperous borderless world by their policies of protectionism. Ohmae has advocated that global companies are becoming, and indeed should become, 'stateless' world citizens with an internal culture which is independent of their original nationalities.

For a successful global strategy, a company should ensure that it is not dominated by its parent 'home-based' headquarters, where strategy will remain dominated by its domestic customers requirements. If markets are worldwide, then managers must act equally responsively to all their customers. Ohmae stresses that this does not mean that products should become standardized: rather it means that in each main market the firm must seek to act as an 'insider', tailoring products to local customers. But to do that effectively requires that local and regional managers must be able to act independently. The centre may be divided into several regional headquarters with control of different functions (production, marketing, etc.) dispersed to differing degrees at different locations. All senior management positions within the MNC must be filled on a culture-free basis, to enable the firm to draw in and benefit from ability and expertise derived anywhere within its spread of operations.

In some respects Porter and Ohmae agree with each other. Both are concerned with the global/local 'central dilemma' for MNCs raised in Chapter 9. Both are observers of the progressive globalization of industries and the cross-border integration of firms. What they disagree about is the shape that integration should take: not in structural terms (i.e. M-form or N-form) but in terms of the cultural identity and management style behind the shape of the firm. Porter discusses the 'paradox of location' in a global economy – that:

> What happens *inside* companies is important, but clusters reveal that the immediate business environment *outside* companies plays a vital role as well. This role of locations has long been overlooked, despite striking evidence that innovation and competitive success in so many fields are geographically concentrated – whether its entertainment in Hollywood, finance on Wall Street, or consumer electronics in Japan. (1998, p.78)

In the importance they each attach respectively to 'home-base' or 'borderless' organizations in international strategy, Ohmae argues that MNCs should shake off their origins, whilst Porter thinks they must preserve them. Ohmae's vision sees global companies operating as what he calls 'true insiders'. These are both at home in, and perceived as direct investors ('honorary citizens') in, each 'home' market in which they operate. Porter sees the continuous enhancements of comparative factor endowments as the basis of distinctive capabilities and the source of dynamic (i.e. sustainable) long-term advantage of any MNC.

So, Porter welcomes the fact that markets and businesses are becoming more global, since it introduces greater competition in each country. But he thinks that, far from making nations less important, globalization makes them more so. The homogenizing forces of a shrinking world, with computer and communications technology available to all, makes it ever more important for firms to remain different from their rivals. Such differences, especially in their capability to innovate, appear (according to Porter's 1990, 1998 research) to be established at home. Porter notes that some countries are wealthier than others and that some industries take successful root in some places, and some in others. Porter thinks that these clusters of excellence are most usefully defined by nation. Nations remain the most important area for determining demand conditions (affected by a government's macro-economic policy); the dynamism of competition (affected by a government's antitrust/monopoly and trade policies); the level and type of skills (affected by a government's approach to the education system); and attitudes of managers, workers and consumers (affected by each national culture).

Firms such as Philips, IBM, ABB, Proton, Sony or Nestlé clearly all have global reach. However, although they all attempt to benefit and learn from their presence in, and understanding of, these various national markets, each firm's style of competition probably still remains recognizably, Dutch, American, Swedish, Malaysian, Japanese and Swiss. The extent to which this is holding back their strength as international competitors, or is their abiding source of advantage in their sectors, is at the heart of what this debate is about.

Let us also note once again Rugman and D'Cruz's (1993) argument for the existence of a 'double diamond' effect: that the strength of a domestic diamond is not restricted to national firms of that country. Indeed their research has shown that Canadian firms frequently take advantage of the strength of the USA diamond in transforming themselves into MNCs. Such Canadian firms have their own primary diamond in Canada, but also a stronger USA one across the border. This principle can, of course, be applied universally, for example to Japanese or German transplants in the USA. Mexico may also derive a 'double diamond' effect from its membership of NAFTA.

Knowledge competition in MNCs

The term 'Red Queen' has been introduced into strategic thinking (Barnett and Hansen, 1996). It has been taken from the field of evolutionary biology where it is used to denote a self-reinforcing system of evolution in response to a continuous cycle of external pressures on the survival of a given species. In the field of strategy it has been applied to explaining competitive success or failure over time and how exposure to competition affects organizational survival. Successful organizations (in terms of survival) were found to be those facing a competitive environment in which they were required continually to search for ways of adapting and improving. Thus the consequence of an organization being exposed to competition is that it is likely to learn. This learning and the resultant adaptation by the firm is likely to make it a stronger competitor. This response by the firm, in turn, triggers a similar adaptive learning response in its competitors, and so on. Although each adjustment may be minor, over time they add up to a formidable amount of change.

However, competitiveness within a dynamic marketplace is a property of *organizations* rather than markets. Organizational innovation within a dynamic marketplace involves interaction between competitors and these interactions are not static; they themselves contribute to the next stages of development or 'evolution'. Nevertheless, there are limits to this type of evolutionary learning. Sometimes learning which has happened in the past teaches organizations outdated lessons. Levitt and March (1988) have called this the 'competency trap'. The timing of organizational learning is therefore crucial. Barnett and Hansen's (1996) work led to the conclusion that learning from recent experience is likely to increase competitiveness and probable survival; whereas learning from experience in the distant past is likely to decrease competitiveness and probable survival, since the wrong things are likely to be learned (hence the 'competency trap' of past competencies). It appears then that organizations benefit if they have strong competition, even though their competitors also learn and thus competition is endlessly intensified.

This analysis reinforces the two themes discussed so far in this conclusion: the continuously dynamic nature of competition and the beneficial effect of industry clusters on the ability of organizations to compete. We will now discuss further the third area of critical thinking in international strategy which you need to carry forward with you: knowledge management and organizational learning in MNCs.

It should not have escaped your attention as you read various parts of this book that 'knowledge' and 'learning' have featured sometimes explicitly (as in Chapter 13) and at other times implicitly (as in the minicases on ISS, Hewlett-Packard or Novotel) in our discussion of international strategic thinking. This is not an accident. We wish at the end of this book to bring out its importance as a key resource (some might argue it is the *only* truly differentiating resource for long-term advantage – for example see Nonaka and Takeuchi, 1995; Quinn, 1992) for MNCs in the future. Quinn (1992) has used the term 'knowledge-based intangibles' to capture his view that the value of most modern products and services lies in how the creative and intellectual capabilities of a firm are managed (advanced factors of production), rather than on traditional factors of production such as capital or equipment (as we discussed in Chapters 1 and 2). He further argues that the capacity to manage 'knowledge-based intellect' is the most important managerial skill for advanced corporations. In Chapter 13 we discussed types of organizational learning and examples of how such learning may be managed in MNCs of various types, and some of the huge literature in that area was considered. Learning both within an organization and also between organizations, as with strategic alliances, was presented. Here, our purpose is different. As part of the need to look forward, we want to review some of the problems that have been associated with knowledge management and the transference of learning within organizations, and that still remain to be resolved. We shall look at three: knowledge myopias; knowledge 'stickiness'; and knowledge protection.

Knowledge myopias

It may be useful to explain why there is such unanimity on the importance of this subject in the strategy literature. Learning is perceived both to increase average performance as well as to increase reliability within an organization. It achieves this because more experienced and better trained individuals usually perform better than inexperienced or poorly trained ones. And since experience and learning is cumulative, organizational routines may be established that convert individual experience into better average performance. Levinthal and March (1993) call this 'processes of experiential learning as instruments of organizational intelligence'. It is through this process that organizational learning may contribute to potential competitive advantage.

Levinthal and March (1993, p.109) see strategic management as having to deal with three major decision-making problems: first, the problem of ignorance (uncertainty about the past and the future); second, the problem of conflict (between inconsistent attitudes, preferences and time periods); and third, the problem of ambiguity (lack of clarity in cause and effect). Despite these endemic problems, managers still have to make strategic decisions. Each of these limitations on decision-making also applies to managerial ability to design organizations capable of learning from experience and exploiting its own (and others') embedded knowledge. Levinthal and March (1993) further suggest specific sources of organizational 'myopia' which limit the ability of organizations to become intelligent learning organizations. As distinctive competencies are developed and learned, this in itself reduces learning from outside these competencies. This they call 'temporal myopia' which echoes Levitt and March's (1988) 'competency trap'. They also identify 'failure myopia' which emphasizes learning from successes rather than learning from failures. Clearly both are needed if organizational learning is to maintain a balance between learning as *exploitation* of existing knowledge, and learning as further *exploration* of areas of new knowledge.

Knowledge 'stickiness'

In order to benefit from organizational knowledge resources, some form of knowledge transfer must take place within the organization. This is often referred to as the ability of the firm to transfer best practices internally. As a practical issue for organizations its importance cannot be overemphasized. It is a key stage in the process by which a firm can build a potential source of advantage from its own internal knowledge base (what economists would call securing the appropriation of rents from scarce internal knowledge) as shown in Figure 14.1.

Internal 'stickiness' of knowledge refers to internal impediments to the transfer of best practice within a firm. Internal transfers should be straightforward. Logically, internal transfers are not impeded by the legal restrictions or the issues of confidentiality which might be expected to affect (and

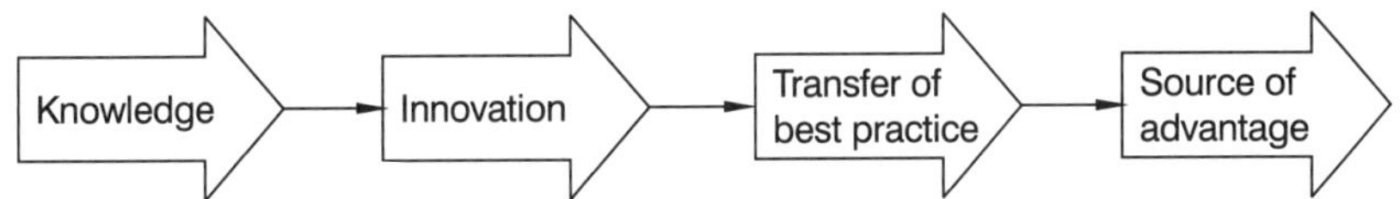

Figure 14.1 Stages in the transformation of knowledge into competitive advantage. *Source:* Authors

sometimes to deliberately block) ease of transfer of knowledge from one organization to another, or perhaps between alliance partners. Still, major barriers to internal knowledge transfer are common and the transfer process highly complex. Since this is of great practical importance to organizations it would be useful to understand why that should be so. The transfer of best practice within a firm has an unambiguous meaning defined by Szulanski (1996) as:

> ... the firm's replication of an internal practice that is performed in a superior way in some part of the organization and is deemed superior to internal alternate practices and known alternatives outside the company. (p.28)

Transfers of best practice within a firm thus involve the exchange of organizational knowledge. Szulanski (1996) observed 122 best practice transfers in eight companies – AMP, AT&T Paradyne, BP, Burmah Castrol, EDS, Chevron Corporation, Kaiser Permanente and Rank Xerox. The transfers covered both technical and administrative practices. Szulanski provides an interesting discussion and an even more interesting set of conclusions, with high relevance for our concerns as international strategists.

Managers' conventional wisdom usually ascribes stickiness problems in internal knowledge transfers to what Szulanski (1996) calls 'motivational' factors. He cites the following typically quoted as barriers: interdivisional jealousy; lack of incentives; lack of confidence; low priority; lack of buy-in; an inclination to reinvent the wheel; employees' refusal to do exactly as they are told; resistance to change; lack of commitment; turf protection; and NIH ('not invented here') syndrome. Some academics have supported these views. Porter (1985, p.368) blamed both the lack of motivation of the knowledge recipient and also the knowledge source within the firm, saying they '.... will have little incentive to transfer [know-how], particularly if it involves the time of some of their best people or involves proprietary knowledge that might leak out'. Szulanski's (1996) findings tell quite a different story, however. His findings suggest that it is knowledge-related barriers and not these motivation-related barriers which are the dominant causes of stickiness in internal transfers. He calls these knowledge-related barriers:

- lack of absorptive capacity: i.e. inability to assimilate or apply the new knowledge;

- causal ambiguity: i.e. inability to clearly separate out, and therefore replicate, the interactions between different knowledge elements;
- and the arduousness of the relationship: i.e. lack of ease of communication between the knowledge source and the recipient.

Similar points are developed by Hamel (1991) and by Faulkner (1995a), who also emphasize in their research findings that knowledge is only transferred successfully in circumstances where: there is motivation by both partners to effect the transfer; the partner transferring is 'transparent' about his knowledge; and the recipient of the knowledge has the ability to absorb and assimilate the knowledge. Larsson *et al.* (1998) reinforce these same points in their 'receptivity/ transparency' matrix, which they explain as follows: 'Interorganizational learning is therefore a joint outcome of the interacting organizations' choices and abilities to be more, or less, transparent and receptive' (p.289).

Szulanski's (1996) work is therefore well supported. In the light of his findings Szulanski suggests that using only incentive schemes to ease internal transfer of knowledge is at best inadequate and at worst misguided. Instead he recommends that organizations 'devote scarce resources and managerial attention to develop the learning capacities of organizational units, foster closer relationships between organizational units and systematically understand and communicate practices' (p.37).

This is important work which is useful in its wider implications for international strategy and reflects many issues raised earlier in this book. Barriers to the transfer of skills and capabilities reduce organizational flexibility (Kogut, 1985); the chances of success of strategic alliances, technology partnerships or joint ventures (Hamel, Doz and Prahalad, 1989; Ring, 1996; Tallman and Shenkar, 1994); and the ability of an MNC to leverage current knowledge (Bartlett and Ghoshal, 1989; Nonaka and Takeuchi, 1995). It goes a long way to better explaining why organizations do not seem to know what they know. It may be less because they do not want to learn than that they do not know how to.

Knowledge protection

If organizational knowledge is as important as we have suggested in the previous sections, then just as important as learning how to share knowledge internally is the ability to protect it from expropriation or imitation externally. Sometimes, as in attempting to share learning with an alliance partner, organizations wish to share with another organization. Even here, however, limits to sharing and control over knowledge flows is important. In contrast to the problem of internal stickiness, where the organization seeks to enhance openness and remove blockages to shared learning, the problem of knowledge protection is to construct appropriate protective barriers. Most MNCs will face both requirements simultaneously.

Traditional discussions about the boundaries of the firm have been largely derived from transaction-cost economics and have focused mainly on identifying the boundaries of the firm between markets and hierarchies (Williamson, 1975). Transaction-cost theory has paid little attention to knowledge, although Teece (1980) did discuss tacit knowledge. As knowledge has become of greater importance as an economic asset and organizational resource, the role of the firm in protecting knowledge has started to become more prominent.

> Foreign direct investment (FDI) offers better opportunities for information capture than either licensing or exporting, since ownership of assets confers ownership of information too. (Buckley and Casson, 1998a, pp.39/40)

Buckley and Casson may be assuming that ownership of knowledge also means control of that knowledge. In considering how the firm can ensure that that is so, the arena of transaction-cost theory is being extended to understanding where knowledge can be better protected: by the market or by the firm. Social protection (security measures) and market protection (unambiguous ownership or property rights can be asserted) can be given relatively easily to tangible assets such as buildings or equipment. For intangible assets such as knowledge, legal protection by means of copyrights and patents are narrowly defined, costly to enforce and of limited use. For example, patents and copyrights have a limited life, have to be published and therefore reveal their contents publicly, are costly to enforce and can be expensively challenged. Many areas of copyrights such as software designs, technical drawings, artwork, music are notoriously difficult to protect. These issues are of great moment to MNCs, who are often fighting copyright and patent infringement or outright piracy of their products and innovations. The nascent CD industry in China exists almost entirely as a pirate industry and while China remains outside the WTO there is little MNCs can do to enforce international copyright or patent law.

Since, as we have repeatedly emphasized, competitive advantage is increasingly determined by knowledge rather than by raw materials or cheap labour, global expansion has actually increased the exposure of many firms to loss of proprietary knowledge through expropriation or (unlicensed) imitation. Liebeskind (1996) has instead been exploring internal institutional capabilities for the protection of knowledge, rather than the traditionally market-reliant forms discussed so far. She argues that:

> ... firms can both extend the scope of knowledge protection and/or reduce the costs of such protection, relative to legal protections. Thus firms are able to replace the limited and costly property rights in knowledge with far more extensive possession rights. (p.104)

Such a deepening of a firm's possession rights, as opposed to its property rights, would consist of a careful alignment of all internal incentive systems, job design and employee rules of behaviour with maximum knowledge protection benefits to the firm. For example, attention to possession rights in job design would look at disaggregation of tasks and their co-ordination to ensure maximum protection without loss of effectiveness. Or incentives would extend control over transactions to include residual rights and their associated rewards. These are early suggestions in what will undoubtedly become an area of growing sophistication in how MNCs operate to protect their knowledge-base.

What works over time: the sustainability of strategies

We have stressed our view of the dynamic, contingent and aggressive nature of international strategy. Competition is profoundly dynamic in character. There is no stable state: no equilibrium. Every chapter in this book, and every section in this concluding chapter, has addressed the reasons why this is so. Managers in every type of organization and context agree with the assertion that their jobs and their organizations are subject to continuous change. The notion of 'turbulence' has become a cliché. Some of the causes may be industry-specific or sector-specific: most (technological change; financial shifts) are not. Sometimes, turbulence overwhelms us all, as in the global financial crises that hit the world economies at the end of the 1990s. In more usual times it may be less overt, but still continuous and rapid, and just as dramatic in its cumulative effects. International organizations are in the eye of all these storms and international strategies have to try to steer clearly and creatively through it all.

Firms gain advantage initially, nationally and then internationally, by changing the basis of competition. In the vocabulary of strategic management this has become called the basis of 'competitive advantage' (Henderson, 1989; Porter, 1985). Historically, international firms have used a combination of scale advantages, scope advantages (cf. Ghoshal's framework in Chapter 6), new product development and new market development to build, and then to sustain, their international positions. We can think back to our example (in Chapter 10) of the way American Express used a combination of all these things to consolidate its international presence over time. Strategy became perceived as a search, by firms and increasingly also by non-commercial organizations such as international charities, pressure groups and aid organizations, for sources of defensible and sustainable competitive advantage. To this end was directed their efforts to secure, retain and build resources and capabilities. Sustainable competitive advantage was reliant upon improvement, upgrading and further innovation in these sources of advantage. However, sometimes an innovation was a total step change and came from a rival or a firm outside the existing industry boundaries (retailers competing with banks), or from a part of the world not previously identified as strong in that sector (Indian software). Changing the basis of competition in an industry is not a controllable process.

Firms that gain advantage in an industry are those that not only perceive a new market development, or the potential of a new technology, but that move early and aggressively to exploit it (FMA – 'first-mover advantage'). If the timing and the product/service are right, FMA allows a market leadership position to be established. For an MNC, the opportunity exists for market leadership to be established across many international markets either simultaneously or within a relatively rapid period of time. Where firms have failed to do this, to benefit from their presence in a number of national markets, often they have been unable to recapture the ground lost to a faster local competitor in a particular national market. Sometimes FMA is something that has to be carried out over a very long time period, as with the current investments by foreign MNCs in China. Although returns on these investments in the short term are mostly negative, the strategic thrust of these investments is clear: to establish trust, commitment and market knowledge to benefit from future opportunities. Many firms use aggressive strategies in a 'second-strike' way: aggressive in time-to-market; aggressive in pricing; aggressive in rapid incremental improvements on a market innovation. These firms may beat the more innovative firm to market with their new idea; reverse engineer a product or service and then undercut the price of the original whilst enhancing value further by means of small changes to specifications or service levels.

Again and again, such situations return us to our first principles of flexibility and responsiveness as the basis for competitiveness for MNCs. It is not size and the advantages of scale and scope, or distinctive market or technological knowledge *per se* that determine MNC performance. Instead it is the ability of the particular MNC to harness the combined potential of all these attributes through the medium of its people and its processes.

Summary

Thus, the international strategy agenda has changed. Figure 14.2 summarizes our view of these changes. In this book we have discussed both the causes and the nature of these changes, so that MNC managers may understand them and respond to them appropriately.

Perhaps we should leave the last word to Lewis Carroll and the phenomenon of the Red Queen, which Ridley (1994) explains as follows:

> The concept that all progress is relative has come to be known by the name of Red Queen, after a chess piece that Alice meets in *Through the Looking Glass*, who perpetually runs without getting very far because the landscape moves with her.

Then	Now
firm-specific and country-specific sources of advantage	building capabilities and sharing knowledge within continous uncertainty
Then	**Now**
international location and configuration issues	international flexibility and responsiveness issues
Then	**Now**
decisions about the boundaries of the firm and its business scope	international co-operative strategies and N-form organizations

Figure 14.2 The changed international strategy agenda. *Source:* Authors

When Alice asks the Red Queen about this phenomenon, the Red Queen replies that Alice must be from a slow world, since in a fast world we all have to run just to stand still. Given environmental turbulence and industry dynamics, the faster you run, the more the world moves with you, so the least we can do is try is to ensure that we are running in the right direction.

References

Aiken, M. and Hage, J. (1968) 'Organizational interdependence and intra-organizational structure', *American Sociological Review* 33(6):912–30.
Alden, V.R. (1987) 'Who says you can't crack Japanese markets?', *Harvard Business Review* Jan-Feb:52–6.
Amit, R. and Schoemaker, P.J.H. (1993) 'Strategic assets and organisational rent', *Strategic Management Journal* 14:33–46.
Anand, J. and Delios, A. (1997) 'Location specificity and the transferability of downstream assets to foreign subsidiaries', *Journal of International Business Studies*, 28(3):579–625.
Anderson, J. and Narus, J. (1990) 'A model of distribution firm and manufacturing firm working partnership', *Journal of Marketing* 54:42–58.
Andersson, T. and Fredriksson, T. (1996) 'International organization of production and variation in exports from affiliates', *Journal of International Business Studies*, 27(2):249–63.
Andreu, R. and Ciborra, C. (1996) 'Core capabilities and information technology: an organizational learning approach', in B. Moingeon and A. Edmondson (eds) *Organizational Learning and Competitive Advantage,* London: Sage.
Ansoff, H.T. (1984) *Implementing Strategic Management*, 2nd edn. Hemel Hempstead: Prentice-Hall.
Argyris, C. and Schon, D. (1978) *Organizational Learning: A Theory of Action Perspective.* Reading, MA: Addison–Wesley.
Axelrod, R. (1984) *The Evolution of Cooperation*. New York, HarperCollins.
Barnett, W.P. and Hansen, M.T. (1996) 'The Red Queen in organisational evolution', *Strategic Management Journal* 17:139–57, Special Issue, Summer.
Bartlett, C.A. (1986) 'Building and managing the transnational: the new organizational challenge', in M. Porter, *Competition in Global Industries,* Boston, MA: Harvard Business School Press.
Bartlett, C.A. and Ghoshal, S. (1989) *Managing Across Borders*, London: Hutchinson.
Bartlett, C.A. and Ghoshal, S. (1990) 'Matrix management: not a structure, a frame of mind', *Harvard Business Review* July-August:138–45.

Bartlett, C.A. and Ghoshal, S. (1993) 'Beyond the M-form: toward a managerial theory of the firm', *Strategic Management Journal* 14:23–46, Special Issue, Winter.

Barwise, P. and Robertson, T. (1992) 'Brand portfolios,' *European Management Journal* 10(3):277–85.

Baumol, W.J., Panzer, J.C. and Willig, R.D. (1982) *Contestable Markets and the Theory of Industrial Structure*, New York: Harcourt Brace Jovanowitch.

Begg, D., Fischer, S. and Dornbusch, R. (1994) *Economics*, 4th edn, Maidenhead: McGraw-Hill.

Birkinshaw, J. (1996) 'How multinational subsidiary mandates are gained and lost', *Journal of International Business Studies*, 27(3)467–95.

Birkinshaw, J., Morrison, A. and Hulland, J. (1995) 'Structural and competitive determinants of a global integration strategy' *Strategic Management Journal* 16:637–55.

Bjorkman, I. (1990) 'Foreign direct investments: an organizational learning perspective,' working paper given at The Swedish School of Economics and Business Administration, Helsinki.

Black, J.S. and Mendenhall, M. (1990) 'Cross-cultural training effectiveness: a review and a theoretical framework for future research. *Academy of Management Review* 15:113–36.

Bowen, D.E., Chase, R.B. and Cummings, T.G. (1990) *Service Management Effectiveness*, San Francisco: Jossey-Bass Inc.

Bowman, C. and Faulkner, D. (1997) *Competitive and Corporate Strategy,* London: Irwin Books.

Brown, A. (1995) *Organizational Culture,* London: Pitman.

Buckley, P.J. and Casson, M.C. (1998a) 'Models of the multinational enterprise', *Journal of International Business Studies* 29(1):21–44.

Buckley, P.J. and Casson, M.C. (1998b) 'Analysing foreign market entry strategies: extending the internationalization approach', *Journal of International Business Studies*, 29(3):21–43.

Burns, T. and Stalker, G.M. (1961) *The Management of Innovation,* London: Tavistock.

Campbell, A. and Verbeke, A. (1994) 'The globalisation of service multinationals', *Long Range Planning* 27(2):95–102.

Carlzon, J. (1987) *Moments of Truth* , Cambridge, MA; Ballinger.

Carman, J. and Langeard, E. (1980) 'Growth strategies for service firms', *Strategic Management Journal* 1:7–22.

Casson, M. (1995) *The Organization of International Business: Studies in the Economics of Trust* Vol. 2, Aldershot: Edward Elgar.

Casson, M., Pearce, R.D. and Singh, S. (1991) 'A review of recent trends,' in M. Casson (ed.) *Global Research Strategy and International Competitiveness*, Oxford: Blackwell.

Caves, R.E. (1996) *Multinational Enterprise and Economic Analysis*, 2nd edn, Cambridge, Cambridge University Press.

Caves, R.E. (1998) 'Research on international business: problems and prospects', *Journal of International Business Studies*, 29(1):5–19.

Caves, R.E. and Porter, M.E. (1977) 'From entry barriers to mobility barriers', *Quarterly Journal of Economics*, 91:242–61.

Chamberlain, E. (1939) *The Theory of Monopolistic Competition*, Cambridge, MA: Harvard University Press.

Chandler, A.D. (1962) *Strategy and Structure,* Cambridge, MA: MIT Press.

Chandler, A.D. (1977) *The Visible Hand*, Cambridge, MA: Harvard University Press.

Chandler, A.D. (1986) 'The evolution of modern global competition', in M. Porter (ed.) *Competition in Global Industries*, Boston, MA: Harvard Business School Press.

Chandler, A.D. (1990a) 'The enduring logic of industrial success', *Harvard Business Review* March-April: 130–40.

Chandler, A.D. (1990b) *Scale and Scope: The Dynamics of Industrial Capitalism*, Boston, MA: Harvard University Press.

Child, J. and David, P. (1987) *Technology and the Organization of Work,* London: National Economic Development Office.

Child, J. and Faulkner, D. (1998) *Strategies of Cooperation,* Oxford: Oxford University Press.

Child, J., Faulkner, D. and Pitkethly, R. (2000) 'Foreign direct investment in the UK 1985–1994: the impact on domestic management practice', *Journal of Management Studies* (forthcoming, January).

Child, J. and Markoczy, L. (1993) 'Host-country managerial behaviour and learning in Chinese and Hungarian joint ventures' *Journal of Management Studies*, 30:611–31.

Child, J. and Rodrigues, S. (1996) 'The role of social identity in the international transfer of knowledge through joint ventures,' in S. Clegg and G. Palmer (eds) *The Politics of Management Knowledge*, London: Sage.

Choi, J.J. and Rajan, M. (1997) 'A joint test of market segmentation and exchange risk factors in international capital markets', *Journal of International Business Studies*, 28(1):29–49.

Cohen, W.M. and Levinthal, D.A. (1990) 'Absorptive capacity: a new perspective on learning and innovation' *Administrative Science Quarterly*, 35:128–52.

Collins, T. and Doorley, T. (1991) *Teaming Up for the 90's*. Homewood, Illinois: Irwin.

Contractor, F.J. and Lorange, P. eds. (1988) 'Why should firms cooperate?: The strategy and economic basis for cooperative ventures', in *Cooperative Strategies in International Business*, Boston, MA: Lexington Books.

Deal, T.E. and Kennedy, A.A. (1982) *Corporate Cultures: The Rites and Rituals of Corporate Life,* Reading, MA: Addison-Wesley.

DeFillipi, R. and Reed,R. (1991) 'Three Perspectives on Appropriation Hazard in Cooperative Agreement', paper presented at the Strategic Management Society Conference, October, Toronto.

De Geus, A. (1988) 'Planning as learning'. *Harvard Business Review* 66(2):70–4.

De Koning, A., Verdin, P. and Williamson, P. (1997) 'So you want to integrate Europe: How do you manage the process?' *European Management Journal* 15(3):252–65.

De la Torre, J. and Neckar, D.H. (1988) 'Forecasting political risks for international operations', *International Journal of Forecasting*, 4:221–41.

Douglas, S. and Wind, Y. (1987) 'The myth of globalisation', *Columbia Journal of World Business*, XXII(4) Winter.

Dunning, J.H. (1974) *Economic Analysis and the Multinational Enterprise*. London: Allen & Unwin.

Dunning, J.H. (ed.) (1985) *Multinational Enterprises, Economic Structure and International Competitiveness*, Chichester: Wiley/IRM.

Dunning, J.H. (1989) 'Multinational enterprises and the growth of services: some conceptual and theoretical issues', *Service Industries Journal*, 9(1):5–39.

Dunning, J.H. (1998) 'Location and the MNE: A neglected factor?' *Journal of International Business Studies*, 29(1):45–65.

Ebster-Grosz, D. and Pugh, D.S. (1996) *Anglo-German Business Co-operations*, Basingstoke: MacMillan.

Ellis, J. and Williams, D. (1995) *International Business Strategy*, London: Pitman Publishing.

Emmott, B. (1991) *Japan's Global Reach*. London: Century.

Enderwick, P. (1989) *Multinational Service Firms*, London: Routledge.

Erramilli, M.K. (1990) 'Entry mode choice in service industries', *International Marketing Review* , 7(5):50–62.

Faulkner, D. (1995a) *International Strategic Alliances,* Maidenhead: McGraw-Hill.

Faulkner, D. (1995b) 'Strategic alliance evolution through learning: the Rover/Honda alliance', in H. Thomas, D. O'Neal and J. Kelly (eds) *Strategic Renaissance and Business Transformation*, Chichester: Wiley.

Forsgren, M., Holm, U. and Johanson, J. (1995) 'Division headquarters go abroad – a step in the internationalization of the multinational corporation', *Journal of Management Studies* 32(4):475–91.

Garrette, B. and Dussauge, P. (1995) 'Patterns of strategic alliances between rival firms', *Group Decision and Negotiation* 4:429–52.

Ghoshal, S. (1987) 'Global strategy: an organising framework', *Strategic Management Journal* , 8(5):425–40.

Ghoshal, S. and Nohria, N. (1993) 'Horses for courses: organizational forms for multinational corporations', *Sloan Management Review* Winter:23–35.

Grant, R. (1991) 'The resource-based theory of competitive advantage: implications for strategy formulation', *California Management Review*, Spring:114–35.

Grindley, P. (1995) 'Regulation and standards policy: setting standards by committees and markets', in M. Bishop, J. Kay and C. Mayer (eds) *The Regulatory Challenge*, Oxford, Oxford University Press.

Hamel, G. (1991) 'Competition for competence and inter–partner learning within international strategic alliances', *Strategic Management Journal* 12 Special Issue, Summer:83–103.

Hamel, G., Doz, Y.L. and Prahalad, C.K. (1989) 'Collaborate with your competitors and win', *Harvard Business Review* Jan/Feb:133–9.

Hamel, G. and Prahalad, C.K. (1985) 'Do you really have a global strategy?', *Harvard Business Review* July-August:139–48.

Hamel, G. and Prahalad, C.K. (1989) 'Strategic Intent', *Harvard Business Review*, May-June:63–76.

Hampden-Turner, C. (1990) *Corporate Culture: From Vicious to Virtuous Circles*, London: The Economist Books.

Hampden-Turner, C. and Trompenaars, F. (1993) *The Seven Cultures of Capitalism*, New York: Doubleday.

Harrigan, K.R. (1986) *Managing for joint venture success*. Boston, MA: Lexington Books.

Hedberg, B. (1981) How organizations learn and unlearn, in P. Nystrom and W.H. Starbuck (eds) *Handbook of Organizational Design* Vol 1:3–27. New York: Oxford University Press.

Hedlund, G. (1986) 'The hypermodern MNC – a heterarchy?', *Human Resource Management* 25:9–25.

Hedlund, G. (1994) 'A model of knowledge management and the N–Form corporation', *Strategic Management Journal* Special Issue, Summer:73–90.

Henderson, B.D. (1989) 'The origin of strategy', *Harvard Business Review* Nov-Dec:139–43.

Heskett, J.L. (1986) *Managing in the Service Economy*, Boston, MA: Harvard Business School Press.

Hill, C.W.L. (1997) *International Business: Competing in the Global Marketplace*. Boston, MA: McGraw-Hill.

Hofstede, G. (1980) *Culture's Consequences: International Differences in Work–Related Values*, Beverly Hills, CA: Sage.

Hofstede, G. (1991) *Cultures and Organizations: Software of the Mind*, Maidenhead: McGraw-Hill.

Hofstede, G. and Bond, M.H. (1988) 'The Confucious connection: from cultural roots to economic growth', *Organizational Dynamics* 16:4–21.

Hosmer, L.T. (1994) 'Strategic planning as if ethics mattered', *Strategic Management Journal*, 15:17–34.

Hunt, B., Baden-Fuller, C. and Calori, R. (1995) *Novotel Case Study*, City University Business School.

Inkpen, A. (1995a) *The Management of International Joint Ventures: An Organizational Learning Perspective*, London: Routledge.

Inkpen, A. (1995b) 'The management of knowledge in international alliances', Carnegie Bosch Institute Working Paper No. 95–1, Pittsburgh, PA: Carnegie Mellon University.

Inkpen, A. and Crossan, M.M. (1995) Believing is seeing: joint ventures and organizational learning., *Journal of Management Studies*, 32:595–618.

Johanson, J. and Vahlne, J. (1977) 'The internationalisation process of the firm: a model of knowledge development on increasing foreign commitments', *Journal of International Business Studies*, Spring-Summer:23–32.

Johnson, G. (1990) 'Managing strategic change: the role of symbolic action', *British Journal of Management*, 1:183–200.

Jonsson, S.A. and Lundin R.A. (1977) 'Myths and wishful thinking as management tools' in P.C. Nystrom and W.H. Starbuck (eds) *Prescriptive Models of Organizations*, Amsterdam: North–Holland.

Jorde, T. M. and Teece, D.J. (1989) 'Competition and co-operation: Striking the right balance', *California Management Review*, 31:25–37.

Kanter, R.M. (1989) *When Giants Learn to Dance*, London: Simon and Schuster.

Katrishen, F.A. and Scordis, N.A. (1998) 'Economies of scale in services: a study of multinational insurers', *Journal of International Business Studies*, 29(2):305–23.

Kay, J. (1993) *Foundations of Corporate Success*, Oxford: Oxford University Press.

Keesing, R.M. (1974) 'Theories of culture', *Annual Review of Anthropology*, 3:73–97.

Kobrin, S.J. (1991) 'An empirical investigation of the determinants of global integration', *Strategic Management Journal*, 12:17–31, Special Issue, Summer.

Kogut, B. (1985) 'Designing global strategies: comparative and competitive value added chains', *Sloan Management Review*, 26(4):15–28.

Kogut, B. (1989) 'A note on global strategies', *Strategic Management Journal*, 10(4):383–89.

Kogut, B. and Zander, U. (1993) 'Knowledge of the firm and the evolutionary theory of the multinational corporation', *Journal of International Business Studies*, 24(4):625–45.

Kotler, P. (1985) 'Global standardisation – courting danger?' Panel Discussion, 23rd American Marketing Association Conference, Washington, DC.

Kotter, J.P. (1979) 'Managing external dependence', *Academy of Management Review*, 4(1):87–92.

Krugman, P. (1995) *Development, Geography, and Economic Theory*, Cambridge, MA:MIT Press.

Larsson, R., Bengtsson, L., Henriksson, K. and Sparks, J. (1998) 'The interorganizational learning dilemma: collective knowledge development in strategic alliances', *Organization Science*, 9(3):285–305.

Levinthal, D.A. and March, J.G. (1993) 'The myopia of learning', *Strategic Management Journal*, 14:95–112 Special Issue, Winter.

Levitt, T. (1983) 'The globalisation of markets', *Harvard Business Review*, May-June:92–102.

Levitt, T. (1986) *The Marketing Imagination*, New York: The Free Press.

Levitt, B. and March, J.G. (1988) 'Organisational learning', *Annual Review of Sociology*, 14:319–40.

Liebeskind, J.P. (1996) 'Knowledge, strategy, and the theory of the firm', *Strategic Management Journal*, 17:93–107 Special Issue, Winter.

Lorange, P. and Probst, G.J.B. (1987) 'Joint ventures as self-organising systems: a key to successful joint venture design and implementation', *Columbia Journal of World Business*, Summer:71–7.

Lovelock, C.H. and Yip, G.S. (1996) 'Developing global strategies for service businesses', *California Management Review*, 38(2):64–86.

Lynch, R.P. (1990) 'Building alliances to penetrate European markets', *Journal of Business Strategy*, March-April:4–8.

Makhija, M.V., Kim, K. and Williamson, S.D. (1997) 'Measuring globalisation of industries using a national industry approach: empirical evidence across 5 countries over time', *Journal of International Business Studies*, 28(4):679–709

Malnight, T.W. (1996) 'The transition from decentralized to network-based MNC structures; an evolutionary perspective', *Journal of International Business Studies*, 27(1): 43–65.

Marglin, S.A. and Schor, J.B. (1990) *The Golden Age of Capitalism*, Oxford: Clarendon Press.

Mariti, P. and Smiley, R.H. (1983) 'Co–operative agreements and the organization of industry', *Journal of Industrial Economics*, 31:437–51.

Markoczy, L. and Child, J. (1995) 'International mixed management organizations and economic liberalization in Hungary: from state bureaucracy to new paternalism' In H. Thomas, D. O'Neal and J. Kelly (eds) *Strategic Renaissance and Business Transformation*, Chichester: Wiley.

McGee, J. and Segal-Horn, S. (1990) 'Strategic space and industry dynamics: the implications for international marketing strategy', *Journal of Marketing Management*, 6(3):175–93.

McGee, J. and Segal-Horn, S. (1992) 'Will there be a European food processing industry?' in S. Young and J. Hamill (eds.) *Europe and the Multinationals*, London: Edward Elgar.

McGee, J. and Thomas, H. (1986) 'Strategic group analysis and strategic management', in J. McGee and H. Thomas (eds) *Strategic Management Research*, Chichester: Wiley.

McGee, J. and Thomas, H. (1989) 'Strategic groups: a further comment', *Strategic Management Journal*, 10(1):105–7.

Melin, L. (1992) 'Internationalization as a strategy process', *Strategic Management Journal*, 13:99–118 Special Issue, Winter.

Mohr, J. and Spekman, R. (1994) 'Characteristics of partnership success', *Strategic Management Journal*, 15:135–52.

Nayyar, P.R. (1990) 'Information asymmetries: a source of competitive advantage for diversified service firms', *Strategic Management Journal*, 11:513–19.

Newman, W.H. (1992a) *Birth of a Successful Joint Venture*, Lanham, MD: University Press of America.

Newman, W.H. (1992b) 'Launching a viable joint venture', *California Management Review*, 35:68–80.

Niederkofler, M. (1991) 'The evolution of strategic alliances: opportunities for managerial influence', *Journal of Business Venturing*, 6:237–57.

Nonaka, I. (1989) 'Managing globalisation as a self-renewing process: experience of Japanese multinationals', Paper presented to Oxford colloquium, Templeton College, May.

Nonaka, I. and Takeuchi, H. (1995) *The Knowledge-Creating Company,* Oxford, Oxford University Press.

Normann, R. (1984) *Service Management: Strategy and Leadership in Service Businesses*, Chichester: Wiley.

Ohmae, K. (1985) *Triad power: the coming shape of global competition,* New York: The Free Press.

Ohmae, K. (1989) 'Managing in a borderless world', *Harvard Business Review,* May-June:152–61.

Perlmutter, H.V. (1969) 'The tortuous evolution of the MNC', *Columbia Journal of World Business*, 4:9–18.

Pfeffer, J. and Salancik, G. (1978) *The External Control of Organisations*, New York: Harper.

Polanyi, M. (1966) *The Tacit Dimension*, London: Routledge & Kegan Paul.

Porter, M.E. (1980) *Competitive Strategy*, New York: The Free Press.

Porter, M.E. (1985) *Competitive Advantage*, New York: Free Press.

Porter, M.E. (ed.) (1986) *Competition in Global Industries,* Boston, MA: Harvard Business School Press.

Porter, M.E. (1987) 'From competitive advantage to corporate strategy', *Harvard Business Review*, May/June: 43–59.

Porter, M.E. (1990) *The Competitive Advantage of Nations*, London: Macmillan.

Porter, M.E. (1998) 'Clusters and the new economics of competition', *Harvard Business Review*, Nov-Dec:77–90.

Porter, M.E. and Fuller, M.B. (1986) 'Coalitions and global strategy', in M. E. Porter, (ed.) *Competition in Global Industries*, Cambridge, MA: Harvard University Press.

Prahalad, C.K.and Doz, Y. (1987) *The Multinational Mission,* New York: Free Press.

Prahalad, C.K. and Hamel, G. (1990) 'The Core Competences of the Corporation', *Harvard Business Review*, May/June:79–91.

Quelch, J.A. and Hoff, E.J. (1986) 'Customising global marketing', *Harvard Business Review*, May/June:59–68.

Quinn, J.B. (1992) *Intelligent Enterprise,* New York: Free Press.

Rangan, S. (1998) 'Do multinationals operate flexibly? Theories and evidence', *Journal of International Business Studies*, 29(2):217–37.

Reisenbeck, H. and Freeling, A. (1991) 'How global are global brands? *The McKinsey Quarterly*, Winter(4):1–14.

Richardson, G.B. (1972) The organization of industry. *Economic Journal*, 82:883–96.

Ricardo, D. (1817) *On the Principles of Political Economy and Taxation*, London: (reprinted Harmondsworth, 1971).

Riddle, D.L. (1986) *Service–Led Growth*, New York: Praeger.

Ridley, M. (1994) *The Red Queen*, Harmondsworth: Penguin.

Ring, P.S. (1996) 'Patterns of process in cooperative interorganizational relationships?', 'Global perspectives on cooperative strategies' Conference, London: Ontario, March.

Rugman, A. and D'Cruz, R.D. (1993) 'The double diamond model of international competitiveness: the Canadian experience', *Management International Review*, 2:17–39.

Rugman, A.M. and D'Cruz, J.R. (1997) 'The Theory of the Flagship Firm', paper presented at the 5th International Conference on Competetive Strategy, Oxford.

Rugman, A.M., Lecraw, D.J. and Booth, L.D. (1985) *International Business: Firm and Environment*, New York: McGraw-Hill.

Rumelt, R.P. (1991) 'How Much Does Industry Matter?' *Strategic Management Journal*, 12:167–85.

Sasser, W.E., Wycoff, D.D. and Olsen, M. (1978) *The Management of Service Operations*, London: Allyn and Bacon.

Schein, E.H. (1985) *Organizational Culture and Leadership*, San Francisco, CA: Jossey-Bass.

Segal-Horn, S. (1992) 'Looking for opportunities: the idea of strategic space' in D. Faulkner and G. Johnson (eds.) *The Challenge of Strategic Management*, London: Kogan Page.

Segal-Horn, S. (1993) 'The Internationalisation of service firms' *Advances in Strategic Management*, 9:31–61.

Segal-Horn, S. (1995) 'Core competence and international strategy in service multinationals', in R. Teare and C. Armistead (eds) *Services Management: New Directions, New Perspectives,* London: Cassell.

Senge, P.M.(1992) *The Fifth Discipline*, London: Century Business.

Shane, S. (1994) 'The effect of national culture on the choice between licensing and direct foreign investment', *Strategic Management Journal*, 15:627–42.

Shenkar, O. and Zeira, Y. (1992) 'Role conflict and role ambiguity of chief executive officers in international joint ventures', *Journal of International Business Studies*, 23:55–75.

Sheth, J. (1983) 'Marketing megatrends', *Journal of Consumer Marketing*, 1, Summer:5–13.

Smith, A. (1776) *An Enquiry Into the Nature and Causes of the Wealth of Nations,* London, (reprinted in E. Cannon (ed.) New York, 1937).

Stopford, J. and Strange, S. (1991) *Rival States, Rival Firms,* Cambridge, Cambridge University Press.

Stopford, J.M. and Wells, L. (1972) *Managing the Multinational Enterprise,* London: Longman.

Szulanski, G. (1996) 'Exploring internal stickiness: impediments to the transfer of best practice within the firm', *Strategic Management Journal,* 17:27–43 Special Issue, Winter.

Tajfel, H. (ed.) (1982) *Social Identity and Intergroup Relations*, Cambridge: Cambridge University Press.

Tallman, S.B. and Shenkar, O. (1994) 'A managerial decision model of international cooperative venture formation' *Journal of International Business Studies*, 25:91–113.

Taucher, G. (1988) *Beyond Alliances,* IMD Perspectives for Managers No. 1.

Teece, D. (1980) 'Economies of scope and the scope of the Enterprise', *Journal of Economic Behaviour and Organisation*, 1(3):223–47.

Teece, D. (1997) 'Dynamic Capabilities and Strategic Management', *Strategic Management Journal*, 18:509–33.

Teece, D., Pisano G. and Shuen A. (1990) 'Firm capabilities, resources and the concept of strategy', Working paper EAP–38, University of California.

Trompenaars, F. (1993) *Riding the Waves of Culture: Understanding Cultural Diversity in Business*, London: The Economist Books.

Tung, R.L. (1993) 'Managing cross-national and intra-national diversity', *Human Resource Management*, 32:461–77.

Vandermerwe, S. (1993) *From Tin Soldiers to Russian Dolls: Creating Added Value Through Services,* Oxford, Butterworth-Heinemann.

Vernon, R. (1966) 'International investment and international trade in the product cycle', *Quarterly Journal of Economics*, May:190–207.

Whittington, R. (1993) *What Is Strategy – and Does It Matter?* London, Routledge.

Williamson, O.E. (1975) *Markets and Hierarchies*, New York: The Free Press.

Yetton, P., Davis J. and Craig J. (1994) 'Redefining the multi-domestic: a new ideal type MNC', Working paper 95–016, Australian Graduate School of Management, Sydney NSW.

Yip, G. (1991) 'Global strategy ... in a world of nations', in H. Mintzberg and J.B. Quinn (eds) *The Strategy Process,* Englewood-Cliffs, NJ: Prentice-Hall.

Yip, G. (1992) *Total Global Strategy,* Englewood Cliffs, NJ, Prentice-Hall.

Yip, G.S. and Madsen, T.L. (1996) 'Global account management: the new frontier in relationship marketing', *International Marketing Review*, 13(3):24–42.

Yoshino, M.Y. and Rangan, U.S. (1995) *Strategic Alliances: An Entrepreneurial Approach to Globalization*, Boston, MA: Harvard Business School Press.

Index

ABB (Asea Brown Boveri) 4, 161, 166–7
Access 64
acquisitions 216
adaptation/standardization debate 60–2, 121
advanced factors 37–9
advertising 62, 193
Africa 54–5
Aiken, M. and Hage, J. 210
Alden, V.R. 59
alliance motivation, eclectic theory 211–12
alliances *see* strategic alliance
American Express 193, 195–6, 200–1, 266
Amit, R. and Schoemaker, P.J.H. 7, 39, 201
Anand, J. and Delios, A. 124, 214
Anderson, J. and Narus, J. 233
Andersson, T. and Fredriksson, T. 152, 154, 155
Andreu, R. and Ciborra, C. 239
Ansoff, I. 126
APEC 51
arbitrage opportunities 18
Argyris, C. and Schon, D. 237, 246
ASEAN 51, 52
Axelrod, R. 223

back-office/front-office difference 189–90
Banco Santander 218–20
Barnett, W.P. and Hansen, M.T. 260, 261
barriers to trade 3, 17, 38–9, 118–19, 136
Bartlett, C.A. 113, 119, 132, 140; and Ghoshal, S. 9–10, 59, 113, 114, 121–2, 125, 131–2, 142, 149, 159, 160, 165, 166–9, 171, 183, 264
Barwise, P. and Robertson, T. 115
Baumol, W.J. *et al* 47n
Begg, D. *et al* 42
Benetton 60, 258
Benetton diamond 40–1
Bertelsmann 162–3
Bhagwati, J. 55
Birkinshaw, J. 141, 145, 147; *et al* 110
Bjorkman, I. 112
Black, J.S. and Mendenhall, M. 103
borderless world 258–9
boundary spanning 104
Bowen, D.E. *et al* 185
Bowman, C. and Faulkner, D. 115, 119, 210, 240
branded products 30, 39, 42, 64–5, 198
Brown, A. 90, 99
Buckley, P.J. and Casson, M.C. 110, 111, 140, 142, 152, 171, 257, 265
Burns, T. and Stalker, G.M. 180

Campbell, A. and Verbeke, A. 185
Cap Gemini Sogeti (CGS) 172–4
capital resources 6
Carlzon, J. 185
Carman, J. and Langeard, E. 185

Casson, M. 95; *et al* 152
Caterpillar 33–5, 257
Caves, R.E. 164, 198; and Porter, M.E. 83
center/periphery link *see* headquarters/subsidiary link
centralization/decentralization 73, 167–9, 198
Chamberlain, E. 44
Chandler, A.D. 4, 63, 112, 122, 154, 191–4, 200, 205
Child, J., and David, P. 240; *et al* 97; and Faulkner, D. 91, 93, 227, 239, 240–1, 242, 245, 255; and Markoczy, L. 242; and Rodrigues, S. 232, 250
China 66, 245, 265
Choi, J.J. and Rajan, M. 18
cleaning industry 186–8
co-operation 205–6, 220–1; choice of alliance form 218–20; external stimuli 212–14; internal stimuli 214–16; partner selection 216–17; reasons 209–12; success 222–3; types 206–9; *see also* strategic alliance; strategicalliance management
co-ordination 110, 120, 125, 191; *see also* configuration/co-ordination matrix
Cohen, W.M. and Levinthal, D.A. 246
Collins, T. and Doorley, T. 231
Common Agricultural Plicy (CAP) 44
communication 253–5; global 146; multidomestic 133–4
comparative advantage 5–7, 150; country-specific 257–60; internal 257;
short-lived 257; vs competitive advantage 33–5
comparative costs 30
competition 11–14, 146; ability 87–8; approaches 15–16; defensibility of home market 15; degree of rivalry 15; food industry 76–82; international dynamics 70–6; investment timing 16; knowledge 260–6; level of risk 16; oligopolistic 199–200; perfect 43–4; resource endowment of firm 15–16; technology/differentiation advantage 16
competitive advantage 116, 117, 139, 150, 211, 213, 257–60; sustainable
266–7; vs comparative advantage 33–5
competitive leverage 148
competiton, monopolistic 44–6
computer reservation systems (CRS) 193
configuration/co-ordination matrix 61, 109–11, 118, 120, 153–4, 189, 201; *see*
also coordination
consortium 220, 230
consumers 60–1, 81
contingency theory 159–60
Contractor, F.J. and Lorange, P. 126
convenience stores 2
copyright 265
corporate culture 135
corporate structure *see* industry structure; international corporate structure
model
cost-push 81–2
costs 62; advantage 191, 194; reduction 148; transport 119
country-specific advantage (CSA) 109, 152, 153, 201, 257–60
cross-border policies 58, 118, 184, 205; managing intangibles 185–8
cultural barrier 93–5
cultural diversity 99–102, 232
cultural fit 99, 217; achieving 102–5; communication 104; personal 103–4; teams 105
culture 66–7, 105–6; benefits 98–9; corporate 135; management practices 95–7; national/organizational 89–95; problems 97–8; relevance 92–3
customer matrix 119
De Geus, A. 237

De Koning, A. *et al* 68
De la Torre, J. and Neckar, D.H. 19
Deal, T.E. and Kennedy, A.A. 99
decentralization *see* centralization/decentralization
decision-making 1, 2, 93–4, 119; global 146; multidomestic 133–4
DeFillippi, R. and Reed, R. 212
demand-pull 81–2
deregulation 69–70
Diageo 87
diamond framework 39–41, 257, 260
differentiated markets 134, 136–7
Digital Equipment Co 166
distributor/supplier relationship 206–7
Douglas, S. and Wind, Y. 59, 61, 134, 148
Dunning, J.H. 30–1, 109, 119, 189, 201, 203, 257

East India Company 29
eclectic theory 30–2, 129, 201–2; internalization (I) 31, 193–4, 201; localization (L) 31, 201; ownership (O) factors 31, 201
eclectic theory of alliance motivation 211–12
economic models 41–3; monopolistic competition 44–6; oligopoly 46–7; perfect competition 43–4
economies of scale/scope 7–8, 45–6, 63–4, 68, 116, 117, 121, 205, 266, 267;
potential 196–201; service industry 188–91, 192–3, 196–201, 202–3; strategic alliances 212, 213
Ellis, J. and Williams, D. 135, 139, 149
Emmott, B. 149
Enderwick, P. 183, 201, 203, 257
Enichem 229–30
entrepreneurial firms 205
Erramilli, M.K. 185
ethics 18–22
European Union (EU) 51–2, 53, 54, 69; framework directives 58
Eurovynil Chloride Corporation (EVC) 229–30
export firms *see* international exporter firms
external drivers, strategic alliances 211–12, 214

family of companies 126
Faulkner, D. 207, 232, 235, 246, 247, 251, 264
financial markets 18
firm-specific advantage (FSA) 109, 153, 201, 214
first-mover advantage (FMA) 267
five forces model 36–7
flexibility 16–22, 140–1, 172–8, 267
food industry (European) 76–7; background/developments 77–80; changes 77–82; strategies 81–2
foreign direct investment (FDI) 3–4, 30, 53, 97, 111, 214, 265
Forsgren, M. *et al* 68, 92
Free Trade Area of the Americas (FTAA) 52
Free Trade Association (FTA) 52, 55
front-office/back-office difference 189–90
frontal assault strategy 16
Fujitsu 126
fuzzy boundaries 202

General Agreement on Tariffs and Trade (GATT) 51, 55, 144
Ghoshal, S. 116, 129, 183, 190; and Nohria, N. 120, 142
Gillette 7–8, 145–6, 161
global: co-ordination 18; competition 13–14
global firms 9, 10, 120, 122–3, 144–8; modern 150–4; traditional 148–50
global/local dilemma 163–7, 259
globalization 205, 213; advantages 62–4; brands 64–5; emergence 59–60; vs regionalization 55–6
glocalization 63, 75–6, 110
Goodyear 13–14
government: policies 17–18, 260; role 10–11

Grant, R. 180, 193, 201
Greenpeace 21
Grindley, P. 6, 11

Hamel, G. 239, 244, 245, 249, 264; *et al* 209, 264; and Prahalad, C.K. 13–14, 15–16, 35, 70
Hampden-Turner, C. 99; and Trompenaars, F. 94
Harrigan, K.R. 222
headquarters/subsidiary link 258–9; global 146–7; multidomestic 133–4, 137–43; transnational 167–9
Hedberg, B. 245
Hedlund, G. 178–9, 253
Henderson, B.D. 10, 266
Heskett, J.L. 185, 186
Hewlett-Packard (HP) 169–71, 261
hierarchies 206, 207
Hill, C.W.L. 134, 135, 137, 149
Hofstede, G. 89, 91, 92, 97; and Bond, M.H. 89, 91
Honda 105, 209, 210, 212, 218, 234, 235, 246–7
Hosmer, L.T. 18–19
Hudson Bay Company 29
human resource management (HRM) 6, 98
Hunt, B., Baden-Fuller, C. and Calori, R. 177

ICI 229–30
Inchcape Plc 29
industrialization of services 198–200
industry attractiveness 37
industry dynamics: deregulation 69–70; food industry 76–82; international 70–6; living with 256–7; and strategic groups 82–6; and strategic space 86–7
industry structure 35–7; branded products 39; mobile factors of production 37–8; mobility barriers 38–9; monopoly power 38; technology 38
information 142, 193
information redundancy 253–4
information technology (IT) 189, 253–4
infrastructure 6
Inkpen, A. 240, 251; and Crossan, M.M. 233, 252
insurance industry 56, 198
integration/responsiveness framework 113–14, 119; *see also* responsiveness
internal drivers, strategic alliances 211–12, 214–16
internalization (I) *see* eclectic theory
international corporate structure model 120–2; global company 122–3;
international exporter 123; multidomestic 123–4; transnational organization form 125–8
international exporter firms 9, 120, 123, 155–7; learning in 242
investment 53; inward 17; timing 16
ISS 186–8, 261

Johanson, J. and Vahlne, J. 111
Johnson, G. 102
Johnson Wax 59–60, 164
joint ventures 210–11, 226, 229–30, 231, 245, 252
Jonsson, S.A. and Lundin, R.A. 250
Jorde, T.M. and Teece, D.J. 205

Kanter, R.M. 231, 233
Katrishen, F.A. and Scordis, N.A. 198
Kay, J. 223
Keesing, R.M. 89
Kentucky Fried Chicken (KFC) 62, 63
knowledge 247–8; combination 248; competition 260–6; creation *see* organizational learning; externalization 248; internalization 248; management 186–8; myopias 262; protection 264–6; resources 6, 172, 193; socialization 248; stickiness 262–4; tacit/explicit 238, 248, 265; transfer 249–50

Kobrin, S.J. 202
Kogut, B. 17, 18, 32, 69, 115, 119, 150, 264; and Zander, U. 142
Komatsu 33–5, 257
Koning, *et al* 110
Kotler, P. 59
Kotter, J.P. 224
Krugman, P. 30
Kwik-Fit Euro 198

labour: child 22; mobility 37–8
Larsson, R. *et al* 264
learning *see* organizational learning
Levinthal, D.A. and March, J.G. 262
Levitt, B. and March, J.G. 261, 262
Levitt, T. 59, 61, 115, 118, 144, 188, 198, 213
Liebeskind, J.P. 265
link alliance 218
local firms 1–2, 3, 30
localization (L) *see* eclectic theory
location-specific advantages 201, 259
Lorange, P. and Probst, G.J.B. 231
Lovelock, C.H. 202
Lynch, R.P. 233

M-form (multidivisional) 167, 169, 178–9, 205, 259
McDonald's 66–7
McGee, J., and Segal-Horn, S. 77, 84, 85, 86; and Thomas, H. 38, 82, 83
McKinsey 127–8
make/acquire/ally matrix 209–10
Makhija, M.V. *et al* 59, 116
Malnight, T.W. 128
management 4–5, 125–6, 223–4; accordion 126; administrative 225; clear organizational arrangements 234; committing 225; communication 232; compressive 126; congruent long-term goals 235; critical tasks 233; general 224–31; information dissemination 231; knowledge barriers 263–4; learning 234–5, 252–3; national differences 95–7; negotiational 224; positive partner attitude 232–3; role conflict/ambiguity 226, 228–30; role requirements 171, 225–6, 227; senior 259; skill requirements 226; strategic awareness 231; success factors 231–5; transactional 224–5; trust/flexibility 233, 235; understanding 225
Marglin, S.A. and Schor, J.B. 140
Mariti, P. and Smiley, R.H. 215
markets 206
Markoczy, L. and Child, J. 241
MasterCard 64
matrix structures 164–6
Matsushita 73, 74–6, 137, 161, 166
Melin, L. 9, 111
Mercosur 52–3
Ministry of International Trade and Investment (MITI) 11
mobility barriers 83, 84
modern global corporation 150–3; configuration issues 153–4; coordination issues 154
modern multidomestic company 124, 137–43
Mohr, J. and Spekman, R. 234
monopolies 44–6; power 38
multidomestic firms 9–10, 120, 123–4, 131–2, 143; learning in 242–3; modern 124, 137–43; pure 132–7
multinational corporations (MNCs) 1, 47–8; ability to compete 87–8; Australian 139; comparative vs competitive advantage 33–5; cultural diversity 92–3, 97–102; domestic/international expansion 2–3; flexibility, risk, ethics 16–22; global/local dilemma 163–7; growth 3–4, 194–5; learning in 242–3, 255; rise 30–2; structures 120–6, 130; transitional pathways 128–9; truly 160–2; as war game 11–14; *see also* exporter firms; global firms; multidomestic firms

N-form (network) 169, 171, 178–9, 179, 206, 259
national culture 90–92; implications 93–5
Nayyar, P.R. 193, 198
Nestlé 138–9
Newman, W.H. 104
Niederkofler, M. 222, 231
Nike 56
Nonaka, I. 125–6; and Takeuchi, H. 193, 237, 247–8, 249, 252, 253, 261, 264
Normann, R. 185
North American Free Trade Association (NAFTA) 51, 52, 54
Novotel 174–8, 188, 256–7

Ohmae, K. 38, 49–50, 70, 76, 91, 115, 125, 160, 183, 213, 259
OLI theory *see* eclectic theory oligopolies 46–7
Organization for Economic Cooperation and Development (OECD) 51
Organization of Petroleum Exporting Countries (OPEC) 12–13
organizational: culture 89–90; framework 117–18
organizational learning 174, 207–8, 212, 234–5, 242–3, 255, 260–1; absorptive competence 246; barriers 248–50; blocked 241; categories 238–40; cognitive barriers 250–1; emotional barriers 251; facilitation 252; forced 241; forms 240–2; imitative 241; integrated 242; learning capacity 245–6; learning intent 244–5; management 250–4; nature 237–8; non-learning 242; open communication/information circulation 253–4; organizational barriers 251–3; received 241–2; receptivity 245–6; requirements 243–8; segmented 242; strategic 240; systemic 239–40; technical 239
organizational types: culture clash 100, 101–2; ethnocentric 100, 101; geocentric 100, 101; polycentric 100, 101 ownership (O) *see* eclectic theory partnership: selection 216–17; structures 164

patents 265
PepsiCo 56, 87, 254–5
perfect competition 43–4
Perlmutter, H.V. 100, 111, 150, 156
Pfeffer, J. and Salancik, G. 211, 215
pharmaceutical industry 36–7, 121
Philip Morris 12
Philips 64, 71–3, 136, 137, 166
physical resources 6
pincer strategy 16
Polanyi, M. 238
Porter, M.E. 6, 9, 29, 36, 37, 38–9, 41, 109, 110, 119, 123, 129, 132, 133, 150, 153, 159, 183, 222, 257, 258, 259, 263, 266; and Fuller, M.B. 206, 215
Prahalad, C.K., and Doz, Y. 14, 113, 165, 183; and Hamel, G. 180, 193
Prisoners' Dilemma 223
Procter & Gamble 12, 63, 163–4
product lifecycle 111, 212, 213
production, internationally mobile factors 37–8; matrix 119; mobile vs immobile 5–7; resourcing 118–20; shifting 17–18
professional service firms (PSFs) 196–7
protectionism 70, 213
Proton 156–7
push-pull strategies 81–2

quality 148
Quelch, J.A. and Hoff, E.J. 59
Quinn, J.B. 261

Rangan, S. 152, 164
Red Queen 260, 267–8
regional strategy 49, 67–8;

developments 56–8; growth 51–5; political/economic impact 51–5; standardization/adaptation debate 60–2; the Triad 49–51; vs globalization 55–6, 65–7
regulation 10–11, 17
relational contracting 206
Rentokil 187
resource deficiency 214, 215–16
resource dependency theory 211
responsiveness 172–8, 267; *see also* integration/responsiveness framework retail industry 197–8
Ricardo, D. 5
Richardson, G.B. 206
Riddle, D.L. 183
Ridley, M. 267
Riesenbeck, H. and Freeling, A. 154
Ring, P.S. 224, 234, 264
risk 16, 216; management 117; political/ethical 18–19
Rover 105, 209, 210, 212, 218, 234, 235, 246–7
Royal Bank of Scotland 218–20
Royal Dutch/Shell 162
Rugman, A.M. 30, 109; and D'Cruz, R.D. 41, 260; *et al* 31, 119, 152, 257
Rumelt, R.P. 88, 201, 203

Sasser, W.E. *et al* 185
scale alliance 218
scale/scope economies *see* economies of scale/scope
Schein, E.H. 90
Segal-Horn, S. 177, 190, 192
service triangle 185–6
ServiceMaster 187
services 183, 203–4; Chandler's model 191–4; changed potential 194–6; characteristics 202, 203–4; future 202–3; growth 183–5, 202; hard/soft 185, 189; industrialization 198–200; managing intangibles across borders 185–8; rethinking 201–2; scale/scope 188–91, 192–3, 196–201, 202–3; specialization/standardization 184–5; standardization/customization 190; structure 191–2, 202
Shane, S. 97
Shenkar, O. and Zeira, Y. 228
Sheth, J. 59, 115
skill: acquisition 214–15; substitution 207
Smith, A. 5
sprinkler model 111
stage models 111
standardization 198; adaptation debate 60–2; global benefits 148; services
184–5, 190
STAR TV 65–6
Stopford, J.M. and Wells, L. 9, 112, 164
strategic alliance management 222–4, 235–6; nature 224–31; success factors 231–5
strategic alliances 206–9; boundary spanning 231; conditions 212–13; consortiums 220, 230; failure 222; internal/external drivers 211–12, 214; link 218; reasons 209–12; scale 218; *see also* co-operation
strategic change 77–80; impact 80–1; implications 81–2
strategic fit 217
strategic group map 83–4
strategic groups 82–5, 87
strategic issues 114–16; controlling corporation 120; resourcing global production 118–20; where to compete 116–18
strategic market 115–16
strategic objectives: efficiency 117; innovation learning/adaptation 117; risk management 117
strategic space 86–7, 88
strategy: competitive approaches 15–16; as different 2–3; economies of scope 7–8; effect of 1–2; flexibility, risk, ethics 16–20, 22;

government role/regulation 10–11; history 29–30; management 3–5; sustainability 266–7; types 9–10
strategy/structure link 112–13
subsidiaries *see* headquarters/subsidiary link
supplier/distributor relationship 206–7
Szulanski, G. 263, 264

Tajfel, H. 249
Tallman, S.B. and Shenkar, O. 211, 264
Taucher, G. 231
tax 17–18
teams, multicultural 105
technology 6, 16, 50–1, 189–91, 213, 215, 267; specific/fast changing 38
Teece, D. 192, 265; *et al* 46, 180
Toni and Guy 198
training 103–4
transaction cost theory 211, 216, 265
transitions 128–9
transnationals 9, 10, 120, 125–8, 159–60; flexibility/responsiveness 172–8; learning in 243; as truly multinational 160–2
transport 62, 257; costs 119
Triad trading bloc 49–54
Trompenaar, F. 91–2, 93
Tung, R.L. 101
turbulence 266

Unilever 12
Uppsala model 111

value chains 32, 218
Vandermerwe, S. 193, 204
Vernon, R. 111
VISA international 56

walled city strategy 16
war games 11–13
waterfall model 111
Whittington, R. 11–12
Williamson, O.E. 206, 207, 211, 265
World Trade Organization (WTO) 51, 55, 183

Yetton, P. *et al* 123, 124, 139, 140
Yip, G. 110, 137, 148, 151, 159; and Madsen, T.L. 171
Yoshino, M.Y. and Rangan, U.S. 231, 233